Martial masculinities

MANCHESTER
1824

Manchester University Press

Cultural History of Modern War
Series editors

Ana Carden-Coyne, Peter Gatrell, Max Jones, Penny Summerfield and
Bertrand Taithe

Already published

Carol Acton and Jane Potter   *Working in a world of hurt: trauma and
resilience in the narratives of medical personnel in warzones*

Julie Anderson   *War, disability and rehabilitation in Britain: soul of a nation*

Quintin Colville and James Davey (eds)   *A new naval history*

James E. Connolly   *The experience of occupation in the Nord, 1914–18: living
with the enemy in First-World-War France*

Lindsey Dodd   *French children under the Allied bombs, 1940–45: an oral history*

Rachel Duffett   *The stomach for fighting: food and the soldiers of the First World War*

Peter Gatrell and Lyubov Zhvanko (eds)   *Europe on the move: refugees in the
era of the Great War*

Christine E. Hallett   *Containing trauma: nursing work in the First World War*

Grace Huxford   *The Korean War in Britain: citizenship, selfhood and forgetting*

Jo Laycock   *Imagining Armenia: orientalism, ambiguity and intervention*

Chris Millington   *From victory to Vichy: veterans in inter-war France*

Juliette Pattinson   *Behind enemy lines: gender, passing and the Special
Operations Executive in the Second World War*

Chris Pearson   *Mobilizing nature: the environmental history of war and
militarization in Modern France*

Jeffrey S. Reznick   *Healing the nation: soldiers and the culture of caregiving in
Britain during the Great War*

Jeffrey S. Reznick   *John Galsworthy and disabled soldiers of the Great War:
with an illustrated selection of his writings*

Michael Roper   *The secret battle: emotional survival in the Great War*

Penny Summerfield and Corinna Peniston-Bird   *Contesting home defence:
men, women and the Home Guard in the Second World War*

Trudi Tate and Kate Kennedy (eds)   *The silent morning: culture and memory
after the Armistice*

Spiros Tsoutsoumpis   *The People's Armies: a history of the Greek resistance*

Laura Ugolini   *Civvies: middle-class men on the English Home Front, 1914–18*

Wendy Ugolini   *Experiencing war as the 'enemy other': Italian Scottish experience in
World War II*

Colette Wilson   *Paris and the Commune, 1871–78: the politics of forgetting*

Centre for the
Cultural History
of War

https://www.alc.manchester.ac.uk/history/research/centres/cultural-history-of-war//

Martial masculinities

Experiencing and imagining the military
in the long nineteenth century

~

EDITED BY MICHAEL BROWN, ANNA MARIA
BARRY AND JOANNE BEGIATO

Manchester University Press

Published by Manchester University Press
Oxford Road, Manchester M13 9PL
www.manchesteruniversitypress.co.uk

British Library Cataloguing-in-Publication Data
A catalogue record for this book is available from the British Library

ISBN 978 1 5261 3562 9 hardback
ISBN 978 1 526 6044 7 paperback

First published 2019
Paperback published 2020

Typeset by Deanta Global Publishing Services

Contents

Contents

Figures

Contributors

Julia Banister is Senior Lecturer in English Literature at Leeds Beckett University. She works on masculinity and militarism in the long eighteenth century, and her publications include *Masculinity, Militarism and Eighteenth-Century Culture, 1689–1815* (Cambridge University Press, 2018).

Anna Maria Barry is a researcher at the Royal College of Music Museum in London. She recently completed her PhD at Oxford Brookes University, where she also worked as a lecturer. Her thesis examines the figure of the male opera singer in nineteenth-century British culture. Anna's research focuses on singers and explores their relationships with literature, visual culture and celebrity culture. She has published on a range of these topics and writes regularly for a number of popular magazines. Anna has curated several exhibitions based on her research.

Joanne Begiato (Bailey) is Professor of History and Head of History, Philosophy and Culture at Oxford Brookes University. She specialises in the history of masculinities, family and marriage. She has published many articles and chapters on subjects as diverse as wife-beating, fatherhood, pregnancy, married women's status under the law and tearful sailors. Her books include *Unquiet Lives: Marriage and Marriage Breakdown in England 1660–1800* (Cambridge University Press, 2003), *Parenting in England 1760–1830: Emotions, Identity and Generation* (Oxford University Press, 2012) and *Sex and the Church in the Long Eighteenth Century: Religion, Enlightenment and the Sexual Revolution* (I B Tauris, 2017) with William Gibson. Her most recent monograph is *Manliness in Britain, 1760–1900: Bodies, Emotion and Material Culture* (Manchester University Press, forthcoming). She is also the editor of *Law, Lawyers and Litigants in Early Modern English Society: Essays in Memory of*

Christopher W. Brooks (Cambridge University Press, 2019) with Michael Lobban and Adrian Green, and *Negotiating Masculinities and Modernity in the Maritime World 1815–1940: A Sailor's Progress?* (Palgrave, forthcoming) with Karen Downing and Johnathan Thayer.

Michael Brown is Reader in history in the Department of Humanities at the University of Roehampton. He works on the cultural history of medicine and surgery in the long nineteenth century, as well as the histories of gender, war and emotion. He is the author of *Performing Medicine: Medical Culture and Identity in Provincial England, c. 1760–1850* (Manchester University Press, 2011) as well as numerous articles and book chapters. He is currently a Wellcome Trust Investigator in Medical Humanities and Social Sciences, leading a team investigating the relationships between surgery and emotion in Britain from 1800 to the present.

Louise Carter is Lecturer in history at the University of Suffolk. She gained her PhD from the University of Cambridge researching British women and the Revolutionary and Napoleonic Wars. She has published work on cultural aspects of warfare in the eighteenth and nineteenth centuries and is currently working on a monograph.

Helen Goodman is a postdoctoral research assistant at Bath Spa University, specialising in nineteenth-century literature, gender, psychology, health and emotions. In her PhD (Royal Holloway, University of London, 2015), she investigated representations of madness and masculinity in Victorian literature, the popular press, medical journals and lunatic asylum records. Dr Goodman has taught at Royal Holloway, New York University (London campus) and Regent's Park College, Oxford, and has published on subjects including male asylum patients, monomania and jealousy, domestic abuse, and masculinity and travel.

Isaac Land is Professor of History at Indiana State University. His most recent publication is '"Each Song Was Just Like a Little Sermon": Dibdin's Victorian Afterlives', in *Charles Dibdin and Late Georgian Culture* (Oxford University Press, 2018). Since the publication of his book *War, Nationalism, and the British Sailor, 1750–1850* (Palgrave Macmillan, 2009), he has become deeply involved in developing the new subfield of Coastal History, publishing a series of short thought-pieces: 'Humours of Sailortown', 'Doing Urban History in the Coastal Zone',

'Antagonistic Tolerance and Other Port Town Paradoxes', 'Port Towns and the Paramaritime' and 'The Urban Amphibious'. The first Coastal History conference was held in Dornoch, Scotland in 2016, and there are plans for an interdisciplinary academic journal.

Barbara Leonardi earned her Arts and Humanities Research Council (AHRC)-funded PhD in English Studies from the University of Stirling, for which she was awarded the Professor G. Ross Roy Medal for the top PhD thesis submitted in 2013. Her AHRC-funded postdoctorate focused on 'James Hogg's Contribution to International Periodicals'. She has published extensively on James Hogg, Walter Scott and pragmatics linguistics for literature. She is a reviewer for *The Year's Work in English Studies* (Oxford University Press) from volume 96 for the section on the Romantic novel and has sole edited the volume *Intersections of Gender, Class, and Race in the Long Nineteenth Century and Beyond* (Palgrave, 2018).

Elly McCausland is Senior Lecturer at the University of Oslo, where she teaches British and American literature. She researches, and has published on, children's literature, medievalism, Victorian adventure fiction and adaptation. Her first monograph is *Malory's Magic Book: King Arthur and the Child, 1862–1980* (Boydell & Brewer, 2019) and she is currently working on a second book about adventure in children's literature.

Helen Metcalfe was awarded her AHRC-funded doctorate by the University of Manchester in 2017, and is currently a Teaching Fellow at the University of York. Helen's doctoral research examined the social experience of bachelorhood in England, c. 1760–1830. She is a social, gender and family historian of Late-Georgian Britain specialising in the history of masculinities, the home and material culture, and has recently completed a case study exploring Charles Lamb's experiences of domestic comfort (forthcoming with Bloomsbury). Helen continues to develop her research interests in the history of emotions and sensory history, and in her next research project seeks to evaluate the relationship between physical and emotional responses to, and experiences of, grief, loss and resilience in Georgian society.

Lorenzo Servitje is Assistant Professor of Literature and Medicine at Lehigh University. His current book project, 'Medicine is War: The Martial Metaphor in Victorian Literature and Culture', traces the metaphorical militarisation of medicine in the nineteenth century. His articles have appeared in journals including *Literature and Medicine, Journal of Medical Humanities* and *Science Fiction Studies*. He is co-editor of *The Walking Med: Zombies and the Medical Image* (Pennsylvania State University Press, 2016); *Endemic: Essays in Contagion Theory* (Palgrave, 2016); and *Syphilis and Subjectivity: From the Victorians to the Present* (Palgrave, 2017).

Karen Turner's PhD research examined notions of masculinity and morality in women's nineteenth-century fiction, with particular focus on male goodness, clergymen in fiction and military masculinity. She has taught a wide range of specialist courses, including the Victorian novel, English poetry and children's fiction, as well as publishing several short stories. Dr Turner currently works at the University of Hull's Graduate School, supporting postgraduate development.

Susan Walton is an honorary research associate in the Centre for Nineteenth-Century Studies at the University of Hull. Graduating from the University of St Andrews with a degree in medieval and modern history, she later studied for an interdisciplinary MA at the University of York, and then gained a PhD in the Department of English at the University of Hull. Her book *Imagining Soldiers and Fathers in the Mid-Victorian Era* was published in 2010, and she has published articles on various aspects of Victorian history and literature. Her main research focuses on nineteenth-century conservative women writers and scholars.

Acknowledgements

This collection originated in a conference entitled 'Military Masculinities in the Long Nineteenth Century', which was organised by Dr Anna Maria Barry and Dr Emma Butcher and held at the University of Hull on 20 and 21 May 2015, to mark the 200th anniversary of the Battle of Waterloo. The conference was generously supported by the Royal Historical Society, the British Association for Romantic Studies and the British Association for Victorian Studies. The organisers are grateful to all who participated in this event. In time, the editorial duties for this collection were taken up by Professor Joanne Begiato and Dr Michael Brown along with Dr Anna Maria Barry and, together, they would like to thank the contributors for their good-natured, timely and professional assistance. It has been a pleasure and privilege to read their work. The editors are also grateful to the staff at Manchester University Press for their guidance and support throughout this project. Professor Begiato and Dr Brown have a particular investment in this project, for it was at this conference that they first met, and they were married a year later. It is, for them, quite literally a labour of love.

Introduction

Michael Brown and Joanne Begiato

On 18 June 1915, as the Anglo-French offensive in the Artois sector petered out amidst accusations of British 'inaction' from the French commander Joseph Joffre (1852–1931), British newspapers contemplated a time when Anglo-French relations had been even less cordial.[1] That day marked the centenary of the Battle of Waterloo, and many newspapers commemorated the event by reflecting on the connections between these two historical moments. According to the *Huddersfield Daily Examiner*,

> There is a similarity between 1815 and 1915 which goes deeper than accidental or superficial differences. Once more, as a hundred years ago, our country and the best of Europe are ranged against a cruel and autocratic despotism which threatens the liberties of the world. Once more we are fighting a tyrant whose success means the ruin of all fair hopes of liberty, and a crushing defeat to civilization. And it is this feature, above all, which makes us look back to Waterloo Day with a strong and inspiring consciousness that as we fought with and conquered the Corsican despot, so we will fight with and conquer Teutonic militarism and the hateful rule of Kaiserdom.

Allies and antagonists had been transposed since 1815, making it difficult to speak in anything other than generalities, and perhaps necessitating an emphasis on Napoleon's Corsican heritage rather than his title as Emperor of France. Yet if friends and foe had changed, the peril facing Britain, and the moral imperative to confront it, seemingly had not. Nor, according to the paper, had Britain's essential character:

> The odds were against us before; perhaps they are against us still. But there is no lack in Great Britain of that stern and steadfast resolve which,

undeterred by perils and fearless in the face of danger, accepts each difficulty as it comes as a fresh incentive to manliness and bravery. On Waterloo Day, at all events, we are proud to take up our burden and face what fortune may have in store for us. Under its auspicious star our flag will triumph, as it did in the days of yore.[2]

For those looking back across the expanse of the nineteenth century, from one momentous conflict to another, the stalwart qualities of British military masculinity served as a linking thread, shaping a mythology of British national identity. In that intervening period, Britain had come to global prominence as an imperial power and had fought numerous wars, ranging from small-scale colonial affairs to larger conflicts such as the Crimean War (1853–56), Indian Rebellion (1857–58) and Second Anglo-Boer War (1899–1902). Even so, the reality was rather more complex than the rhetoric implied. British military masculinity had never been without its anxieties and discontents. Far from it; towards the end of the century in particular, all manner of commentators expressed profound concerns about the state of British manhood and its capacity to ensure national and imperial security in an increasingly competitive and complex geopolitical environment.[3] And yet, it could be argued, it was precisely because of these underlying anxieties that the narrative of British masculine prowess was so frequently deployed and rehearsed.

Martial Masculinities: Experiencing and Imagining the Military in the Long Nineteenth Century has its origins in an equivalent moment of historical reflection, some 100 years later still; this was a conference held at the University of Hull in May 2015 to mark the bicentenary of Waterloo.[4] Though certainly more considered in its analysis than the *Huddersfield Daily Examiner* of 1915, this conference also took place against the backdrop of conflict, notably the end of a more-than-a-decade-long intervention by British troops in Afghanistan, and at a time which saw the resurgence of an equally politically charged valorisation of British military masculinities, epitomised by the growth of such organisations as Help for Heroes and by increasingly fraught debates over the meanings of Remembrance Day.[5] However, if this conference was timed to coincide with a major anniversary, and facilitated reflection on the social and cultural continuities of nineteenth-century British militarism, then it also provided a most opportune moment to take stock of a growing body of interdisciplinary scholarship which has developed over the preceding decade and a half, and which explores the issue of military masculinities – their realities, representations and ramifications.

Although the study of military masculinities has shaped the scholarship on various chronological periods, nations and cultural contexts, the British long nineteenth century (defined here as 1789–1914) has yielded particularly rich intellectual pickings. To be sure, the lion's share of scholarly attention has been directed at either end of this period, namely the French wars (1793–1815) and the First World War (1914–18). Even so, there is a substantial body of material exploring the place of masculinity in relation to Britain's 'small wars' of empire and, as we shall see, a marked degree of recent interest, particularly among literary scholars, in the Crimean War. This volume seeks to explore the richness of the long nineteenth century as a site for the interdisciplinary study of martial masculinities. Of course, any chronological framing is, to an extent, arbitrary, but to do justice to the particularities of the nineteenth century, this volume sets its endpoint at the opening of the First World War. This is not to say that certain chapters do not anticipate or consider the First World War, nor does it suggest that the editors and contributors are blind to the continuities between masculinity and militarism in the later nineteenth and early twentieth centuries; as this introduction hopefully suggests, we are not. Nonetheless, we believe that the conflictual watersheds of the French wars and First World War serve as important cultural markers, the former being arguably the first war of the modern world and the latter the first major war of technological modernity.[6] By setting our limits thus, we can consider the development of military masculinities in a vital transitional period; one before the advent of mass military participation (in Britain at least), but one that nevertheless saw the rise of mass society, culture and consumption, as well as a transformation in the relations between the military, the state and the public at large.

In the introduction to their edited collection on soldiering in the age of revolution, Catriona Kennedy and Matthew McCormack acknowledge the persistent perception of military history as a conservative, even reactionary, field of study, 'a bastion of Rankean empiricism, grand narrative and Whiggish teleology', concerned, for the most part, with 'technical details, generals and battles' as well as 'operational effectiveness and the factors which determine victory or defeat'.[7] Certainly, academic military historians have often been wary of, if not downright hostile to, the theoretical and methodological approaches of cultural and gender history. Nonetheless, even before the explosion of research into the cultural history of war that has taken place since the millennium, there were historians who eschewed the conventional focus on strategy and organisation to consider the social and cultural dimensions of conflict. One of the most remarkable early examples of this tendency was Olive Anderson, whose work on the economic, social and religious dimensions of the Crimean War, and of mid-Victorian militarism more generally, was notable for its analytical inclusivity and imagination.[8] Though somewhat outside our period, Arthur Marwick's contemporaneous work on the First World War, *The Deluge* (1965), was similarly striking for the ways in which it considered the social and cultural effects of war. By the 1970s, even some avowedly military historians were demonstrating the interesting new directions that the discipline might take. Thus, John Keegan's *The Face of Battle* (1976) was critical of traditionally instrumentalist conceptions of military history and sought to apply a more historicist sensibility to the study of battle, including a sensitivity to the experience of the rank-and-file soldier. Equally, by the 1980s, historians from other disciplines, such as Joan Hichberger, a historian of art, were beginning to consider the ways in which war was represented and its values communicated to, and disseminated throughout, Victorian society.[9]

However, it was really in the late 1980s and 1990s, with the advent of the 'cultural turn', that the history of war was brought increasingly into line with the concerns of mainstream academic history. Works such as Daniel Pick's *War Machine* (1993) sought to understand war not as a universal phenomenon with its own higher logic, but rather as a cultural product, shaped, in the case of the nineteenth and early twentieth centuries, by medical, scientific and philosophical currents. Likewise, in his *British Military Spectacle* (1996), Scott Hughes Myerly opened up the study of army uniforms, conventionally the esoteric concern of militaria specialists, allowing historians to appreciate how they shaped the cultures, identities and popular perceptions of the army in early nineteenth-century Britain.

One of the most important strands of scholarship to emerge from the social and cultural history of war since the 1980s has been that focused on gender and masculinity. Alongside scholars like Peter Stearns, whose pioneering *Be a Man!* (1979) did much to encourage the emergent historical study of masculinities, imperial historians J. A. Mangan and John M. Mackenzie used masculinity as a prism through which to understand how such activities as sport and hunting shaped notions of national character and identity, as well as how those activities served as potent metaphors for war and its supposed virtues.[10] The notion that war and empire might function both as arenas for the shaping and testing of masculine identities, as well as fantastical spaces wherein such identities might be imaginatively constructed and/or projected, was brought to the fore by Graham Dawson's *Soldier Heroes* (1994). Dawson's specifically Kleinian psychoanalytic approach may not have spawned many imitators (although Pick's near contemporary use of psychoanalysis in *War Machine* suggests a trend in the early to mid-1990s), but his sensitivity to the psychology of war was more influential. Indeed, the voluminous literature on 'shell shock' in the First World War has demonstrated the importance of ideas about masculinity and appropriately masculine behaviours in shaping clinical categories and diagnoses, while Michael Roper's *The Secret Battle* (2009) highlights the wider implications of psychology and emotion for men's 'survival'.[11] In his highly influential account of 'modern war culture', Yuval Noah Harari has likewise drawn attention to the psychological impact of war and the notion of war as a form of personal revelation that emerged in the early nineteenth century.[12] However, perhaps because of the huge toll it took on men's minds and bodies, and because, in Britain at least, it marked the first time that the experience of war became more generally diffused among the nation's population, especially its men, it is the First World War that has generated a particularly rich cultural historiography in this regard. Indeed, the First World War is often represented as the culmination of nineteenth-century trends. Especially notable for its focus on embodiment and masculinity is Joanna Bourke's seminal *Dismembering the Male* (1996). Nevertheless, studies on martial embodiment in an earlier period now exist, such as Philip Shaw's work on wounded soldiers and Matthew McCormack's *Embodying the Militia in Georgian England* (2015).[13]

Although the focus of this volume is on soldiers, with only two chapters exploring the cultural power of naval masculinities, it is essential to recognise the enormous power of the navy in contributing to and disseminating constructions of military masculinities. Far more men were employed in the navy during this period, and Britain's role as a sea power meant that naval officers and ratings were significant types of military manliness, held up for celebration and, occasionally, criticism. Scholarly trends in naval history have followed a similar trajectory to those of the army, though with something of a time lag. Accounts of British naval might published in the 1990s and 2000s focus on control of the seas and navies as projections of power.[14] Like early military histories, they analyse national policy and finance, military strategy and logistics. Alongside these sweeping grand narratives are social histories of life below decks.[15] As the 2005 bicentenary of the Battle of

Trafalgar hove into view, however, a number of publications emerged which marked a cultural turn in naval studies. Margarette Lincoln's *Representing the Royal Navy: British Sea Power, 1750–1815* (2002), for instance, used visual and some material culture to investigate the impact of the navy on British society. The cult of Nelson was also mined for its insights into the cultural significance of naval officers, battles and heroism.[16] For instance, the collection edited by David Cannadine, *Admiral Lord Nelson: Context and Legacy* (2005), surveys Nelson's appeal in his own time and long after, exploring Nelson as a historical subject and enduring professional inspiration, but also as an alluring symbol of patriotic military manliness, reaching mythical status.

More recently, the ordinary seaman in the eighteenth and nineteenth centuries has come under closer investigation. Isaac Land's *War, Nationalism, and the British Sailor, 1750–1850* (2009) is a cultural history of the many intersections between masculinity and nationalism which exposes the ambiguous national, political, occupational and gender identities of those serving in the navy in an age of revolution. Mary Conley explores depictions of 'Jack Tar' in the age of empire, during which time the image of the navy in society shifted. The navy's function was to protect imperial trade routes, and thus 'naval manhood came to be aligned with imperial manliness' by the First World War.[17] By the end of the nineteenth century, uniformed sailors were 'a central part of national and imperial pageantry, of state funerals and other occasions, suitably drilled and disciplined for their ceremonial roles'.[18] In the last decade, studies of the figure of the Tar have revealed his ambiguities: at any one time depicted as comical, bawdy, sentimental, heroic, pathetic and virile.[19] These studies, and others like them, expose the multivalent and complex nature of military masculinities.

Collectively, what much of this work on martial masculinities suggests is that military and naval identities were not shaped solely by the act of fighting. Indeed, active combat was a relatively infrequent part of the soldier or sailor's daily life, even on the Western Front of the First World War, let alone on campaign or at sea in the nineteenth century. Bourke's work has demonstrated the importance of homosociality in allowing men to cope with both the strains of battle and the tedium of trench life. Other work, meanwhile, has shown how these affective relationships were often shaped by domestic models and how familial relations structured military life, both directly (in terms of continued contact with home) and indirectly (in terms of substitute families formed in service). Recent work on life on board ships of the Royal Navy shows the ways in which the spaces were configured to create a domestic environment for the men.[20] Meanwhile, Roper's work and Holly Furneaux's *Military Men of Feeling* (2016) have shown how 'family feeling' was integral to unit cohesion in the First World War and Crimea, respectively. Furthermore, Furneaux and Sue Pritchard have drawn attention to the ways in which soldiers, during extended periods of inaction, would often indulge in craft activities such as quilting, now generally associated with feminine domesticity.[21] Likewise, Jeannine Hurl-Eamon's *Marriage and the British Army in the Long Eighteenth Century* (2014) has demonstrated how such domestic ties bound men to home, even when far away from it. Indeed, popular depictions of the soldier's and sailor's 'Farewell' and 'Return' shaped sensible and sentimental modes of patriotic military masculinities throughout the long nineteenth century.

Such concerns with domesticity are symptomatic of an ever-widening analytical frame for scholars interested in martial masculinities across the nineteenth century. While the navy may have been the largest single employer in industrial Britain, with the most powerful fleet in the world, the army was, up until the First World War at least, comparatively tiny, positively dwarfed by its rivals' standing armies. As such, relatively few men in Britain had direct experience of army service, with far more having served at sea. Even so, as the scholarship has demonstrated, the importance of martial masculinities extended far beyond the confines of personal experience. In this respect, the work of scholars such as Dawson and Michael Paris has been particularly influential in fostering the concept of a 'pleasure-culture of war' in which the values of militarism and military masculinities were elaborated, communicated and disseminated through literature, poetry, art and song, as well as through play, education and socialisation at home, in school or in organisations such as the Boys' Brigade.[22] This interest in the wider cultures of martial masculinity has been taken forward by scholars such as Catriona Kennedy and Neil Ramsey, who consider the broader resonances and reception of war narratives in early nineteenth-century Britain, as well as by historians of naval masculinities like Land, Joanne Begiato and James Davey, who consider the ways in which the profusion of naval-themed song, balladry, imagery and material culture during the nineteenth century shaped ideas not simply about naval masculinities but also about national identity more broadly.[23] Meanwhile, Michael Brown has shown how civilians might draw on a metaphoric language of war, empire and martial masculinity to buttress their own claims to public recognition and professional respectability.[24]

This volume is intended to reflect this outward turn in the scholarship from personal experience to the cultural imaginary and its impact on individual subjectivities and national identities. But as well as this, it is also intended to reflect the methodological and disciplinary breadth of recent work in the field. In particular, the study of war, and of military masculinities, is no longer the sole preserve of historians, but has also been embraced by literary scholars. Romanticists such as Shaw led the way with their interdisciplinary studies of war and its cultural power, and Victorianists have followed suit. Indeed, according to one recent account, 'Victorianists have rediscovered war'.[25] The Crimean conflict, in particular, has been subject to a great deal of literary analysis, including Stephanie Markovits' *The Crimean War in the British Imagination* (2009), Furneaux's *Military Men of Feeling* and a 2015 issue of *19: Interdisciplinary Studies in the Long Nineteenth Century* on 'Charting the Crimean War: Contexts, Nationhood, Afterlives'. What all of this research has shown is the extent to which militarism, military values and martial masculinities permeated British culture, thought and social practice, not simply in the heady years of New Imperialism, but across the century as a whole.

This volume constitutes an interdisciplinary intervention into the study of martial masculinities. It draws on a variety of disciplines; historical, art historical, literary, material and musical. The contributions are divided into two parts, one on 'experiencing', the other on 'imagining' martial masculinities. We recognise that experience and imagination are not distinct categories of analysis, that they are intimately intertwined and mutually constitutive. We do not seek to establish an artificial distinction between the kinds of sources studied. After all, it is evident that soldiers' letters are as much textual forms as H. Rider Haggard's novels, while Lord Uxbridge's body was as 'representational' as any poem. Neither do we wish to separate out historical and literary methodologies, or to align experience with the former and imagination with the latter. While the historians in this volume can indeed be found in the former part, the use of historicist approaches by literary scholars and textually sensitive readings by historians render such disciplinary distinctions largely moot. Rather, what we do hope to achieve through this structure is to emphasise the ways in which martial masculinities travelled through culture and through time, working their way into diverse aspects of thought, practice and representation. The first half is thus rooted in military men's experience of battle, and their life after service, but draws outwards from the individual and the intimate to the representational and the public. It begins with Julia Banister's exploration of Lord Uxbridge's amputated leg, and the contested reception of the hero's (dismembered) body. It then moves through Louise Carter and Helen Metcalfe's discussion of military service and of the kinds of emotional relationships that soldiers formed with each other, and with those back home. Next, Anna Maria Barry concerns herself with the case of Charles Incledon, a man who used his experience as a sailor to shape his public identity as singer of patriotic and sentimental songs. Michael Brown and Joanne Begiato conclude the first half with their study of the representation of the aged veteran, and of the ways in which lived experiences might be transmuted into varied cultural forms to serve a shifting range of social, cultural and political agendas.

The second half widens the lens further, exploring the ways in which martial masculinities served as meditation and metaphor for writers and readers alike. Barbara Leonardi examines the work of the 'Ettrick Shepherd', James Hogg, its representation of the horrors of war and its oblique reflection on Waterloo and Scottish martial masculinity. Susan Walton considers Charlotte Yonge and the ways in which martial values and regimental pride could be passed through generations and across genders. Next, Lorenzo Servitje explores Alfred Tennyson's poem 'Locksley Hall' (1842) and its frustrated protagonist's sublimation of his identity into a collective military masculinity. Karen Turner, meanwhile, considers Charlotte Brontë's obsession with military history and her extensive use of martial metaphors in *Jane Eyre* (1847) to describe acts of love and courtship. And in the final two chapters, Elly McCausland and Helen Goodman explore the realm of late nineteenth-century and early twentieth-century children's and adolescents' fiction, using Arthurian tales and H. Rider Haggard's novels, respectively, to point up the varied and complex ways in which both writers and readers imagined the relationship between masculinity, maturity and adventure.

A number of key themes emerge from this collection. First, the interplay between military and civil worlds is striking. The language and metaphors of martial masculinities permeated people's ways of thinking and expressing themselves. Walton's analysis of Yonge's life-writing and fiction shows that military characteristics could be aspired to by both sexes, and by children as well as adults. As Isaac Land indicates in his Epilogue, women have fought in battle on land and sea, and, as we shall see in this volume, many more reproduced martial values in their lives and work. Thus, Charlotte Brontë deployed a military vocabulary and martial strategy to construct elements of her fiction. Moreover, her construction of the 'metaphorical soldier', as Turner describes Brontë's warrior-priest characters, represents courtship as a battle. Crucially, for our purposes, as in the case of *Jane Eyre*, this was a style of combat from which the woman could emerge victor, because she too knew the rules of engagement. By the end of the century, as McCausland and Goodman show, adventure literature for children and adolescents was saturated with exemplary protagonists, from youths to old men, who embodied inspirational martial qualities. Military masculinity was thus a performance, whether personal, like Charles Incledon, who, as Barry argues, deployed his early career as a sailor to enhance his reputation as a singer, or collective, such as indicated by the photographs, processions and theatrical spectacles of Crimean and Indian Mutiny veterans in their regimental uniforms.

The performance of military masculinities was, however, by no means simple or straightforward, and a second theme that marks out this volume is the multiplicity of martial identities and their inherent ambiguities. There is no doubt that there were certain qualities associated with military manliness, yet these were constantly in tension. Servitje, for example, proposes that Tennyson's 'Locksley Hall' exposes the underlying complexities of military masculinities. The poem conveys the ways in which the individual soldier is sublimated into the whole, manipulated into serving the empire and nation. Similarly, Leonardi shows how military masculinity could be positioned as tainted because it opened the individual to exploitation. Her examination of Hogg's writing argues that he denounced the human loss of the Napoleonic Wars and, in so doing, undermined the myth of the Highland Warrior. For him, the soldier risked being a 'mere machine' because patriotism and military values led him to blindly fight and needlessly die for his 'feudal' overlords. On the one hand, Hogg used medievalism to critique war. McCausland's examination of Arthuriana in late nineteenth-century boys' fiction, on the other hand, shows that medieval chivalry could be co-opted to shore up traditionally ascribed warrior values in the face of modern and de-individualised conflict. Here, the moral rather than physical virtues of the soldier hero were given prominence. Indeed, throughout the long nineteenth century, the very materiality of military masculinity could simultaneously promote and undermine it.

Thirdly, the body was central to military masculinity but also, therefore, a means by which it was vulnerable. As Banister demonstrates, accounts of martial heroism were put under strain when the hero was physically damaged. Lord Uxbridge emerged from battle a hero, but his loss of a limb, even if stoically borne, undermined the ideals of a military masculinity forged through whole, strong male bodies. Cultural restoration work was required to maintain Uxbridge in the role of military hero. Charles Incledon discovered that his own body became a liability in his attempt to transform his martial past into popular fame. A former Jack Tar, he could benefit from the sailor's appealing persona while his body fitted the public stereotype of naval manhood, although he was less well-served by the accompanying stereotypes of the Tar as man of appetite when his own reputation for womanising could not be offset by the risks and glamour of actual naval service. Moreover, once he grew fat, his donning of a uniform simply served to highlight the potential discrepancies between sinewy military and soft, civilian bodies. For veterans, on the one hand, bodies were markers of military valour and prompts for others to respect their service and sacrifice. On the other hand, infirmity exposed aged veterans to poverty, and while it could be used to remind the state of its responsibilities to its soldiers and sailors, it produced, at best, sympathy, and, at worst, neglect.

The veteran was often depicted in the act of returning to domesticity through this period. Yet the military was never a domain that was isolated from the domestic or familial. Thus, our fourth theme explores the interconnectedness of the military and the domestic. Metcalfe uses bachelor soldiers' correspondence to reveal how they recreated domestic, homely spaces while on active service. This was not merely a material practice designed to produce temporary comfort. It was a form of nostalgia that helped manage the medical condition's symptoms. Moreover, their discussions and evocations of these homes in letters exchanged with family members offered emotional comfort and demonstrated the critical links between civilian and military spheres. There is still some degree of debate about how far domestic and military masculinities were antithetical modes. For Servitje, on the one hand, Tennyson's 'Locksley Hall' reveals the opposition of domestic and military forms of masculinity. The poem's narrator is subjected to a military life because he is unsuccessful in marrying and setting up home. Carter, on the other hand, uses soldiers' life-writings to reveal the continuity and similarity between them. While soldiering could undermine family life, since men were required to leave home to serve and often discouraged from combining marriage and family with a profession in arms, military men's masculine identity was still rooted in the domestic. They cultivated links with family members as best they could, and they constructed surrogate family relationships within their regiments, just as sailors did on board ship. Here, commanding officers were paternal figures, while fellow soldiers were brothers in arms. It is thus unsurprising that when military men returned home and set up families, they cultivated martial values across the generations, characteristics which, as we see from both Charlotte Yonge's family life and the cultural motif of the aged veteran, their wives and daughters, as well as their sons, were encouraged to uphold.

In such ways, this volume highlights the complexities and ambiguities of martial masculinities in nineteenth-century Britain. At a time when the trope of the noble, self-sacrificing and wounded soldier continues to be deployed to serve a variety of interests and agendas, such sensitivity to history, meaning and representation is not simply an intellectual exercise but a social and political responsibility. We hope that what follows will serve to facilitate an ongoing interdisciplinary conversation about these themes and will stimulate further research into what is both a flourishing and timely field of scholarship.

Notes

1   Robert A. Doughty, *Pyrrhic Victory: French Strategy and Operations in the Great War* (Cambridge, MA: Belknap Press, 2005), pp. 161–2.

2   *Huddersfield Daily Examiner*, 18 June 1915, p. 2, col. D. Some of this material is credited to the *Daily Telegraph*, although exactly how much is unclear.

3   For example, see Michael Brown, 'Cold Steel Weak Flesh: Mechanism, Masculinity and the Anxieties of Late Victorian Empire', *Cultural and Social History* 14:2 (2017), 155–81.

4   The conference, 'Military Masculinities in the Long Nineteenth Century', 20–21 May 2015, was organised by Anna Maria Barry and Emma Butcher and was affiliated with Waterloo200, the official body recognised by the UK government to commemorate the bicentenary. For more details on the conference, see https://militarymasculinities.wordpress.com/ (accessed 23 July 2018).

5   The year 2015 also saw the announcement by the British government that women would be able to serve in combat roles in the British army, something which was formally introduced in 2016. Nonetheless, the culture of the military and its representation remains overwhelmingly masculinist.

6   David Bell, *The First Total War: Napoleon's Europe and the Birth of Modern Warfare as We Know It* (Boston, MA: Houghton Mifflin, 2007); Daniel Pick, *War Machine: The Rationalisation of Slaughter in the Modern Age* (New Haven, CT: Yale University Press, 1993).

7   Catriona Kennedy and Matthew McCormack (eds), *Soldiering in Britain and Ireland, 1750–1850: Men of Arms* (Basingstoke: Palgrave Macmillan, 2013), pp. 3–4.

8   Olive Anderson, *A Liberal State at War: English Politics and Economics during the Crimean War* (London: Macmillan, 1967); Olive Anderson, 'The Growth of Christian Militarism in mid-Victorian Britain', *English Historical Review* 86 (1971), 46–72.

9   J. W. M. Hichberger, *Images of the Army: The Military in British Art, 1815–1914* (Manchester: Manchester University Press, 1988).

10 Both have published widely but, for example, see J. A. Mangan, *The Games Ethic and Imperialism: Aspects of the Diffusion of an Ideal* (Harmondsworth: Penguin, 1986); J. A. Mangan, '"Muscular, Militaristic and Manly": The British Middle-Class Hero as Moral Messenger', *International Journal for the History of Sport* 13:1 (1996), 28–47; J. A. Mangan and Callum McKenzie, *Militarism, Hunting, Imperialism: 'Blooding' the Martial Male* (London: Routledge, 2010); John M. Mackenzie, 'The Imperial Pioneer and Hunter and the British Masculine Stereotype in Late Victorian and Edwardian Times', in J. A. Mangan and James Walvin (eds), *Manliness and Morality: Middle-Class Masculinity in Britain and America, 1800–1940* (Manchester: Manchester University Press, 1991), pp. 176–98.

11 The literature on 'shell shock' and war neuroses in the First World War is vast, but, for a recent account, see Tracey Loughran, *Shell-Shock and Medical Culture in First World War Britain* (Cambridge: Cambridge University Press, 2017). For a more general account of masculinity in the First World War, see Jessica Meyer, *Men of War: Masculinity and the First World War in Britain* (Basingstoke: Palgrave Macmillan, 2009).

12 Yuval Noah Harari, *The Ultimate Experience: Battlefield Revelations and the Making of Modern War Culture, 1450–2000* (Basingstoke: Palgrave Macmillan, 2008).

13 Philip Shaw, *Waterloo and the Romantic Imagination* (Basingstoke: Palgrave Macmillan, 2002); Philip Shaw, *Suffering and Sentiment in Romantic Military Art* (Aldershot: Ashgate, 2013).

14 Jeremy Black, *Naval Power: A History of Warfare and the Sea from 1500 Onwards* (Basingstoke: Palgrave Macmillan, 2009); N. A. M. Rodgers, *The Safeguard of the Sea: A Naval History of Britain, 660–1649* (London: Penguin, 1997); N. A. M. Rodgers, *The Command of the Ocean: A Naval History of Britain, 1649–1815* (London: Penguin, 2004); Brian Lavery, *Nelson's Navy: The Ships, Men and Organisation 1793–1815* (London: Conway, 1989).

15 N. A. M. Rodgers, *The Wooden World: An Anatomy of the Georgian Navy* (Glasgow: William Collins, 1986).

16 Nelson is the subject of a sizeable number of publications.

17 Mary Conley, *From Jack Tar to Union Jack: Representing Naval Manhood in the British Empire, 1870–1918* (Manchester: Manchester University Press, 2009), p. 1.

18 James MacKenzie, 'Preface', in Mary Conley (ed.), *From Jack Tar to Union Jack: Representing Naval Manhood in the British Empire, 1870–1918* (Manchester: Manchester University Press, 2009), p. ix.

19 A remarkably early example of interest in the cultural representation of the sailor is Charles Napier Robinson's *The British Tar in Fact and Fiction: The Poetry, Pathos, and Humour of the Sailor's Life* (1911), which gathered textual and visual images of the Tar from the sixteenth century onwards. Recent analysis building on Land and Conley includes Joanne Begiato (Bailey), 'Tears and the Manly Sailor in England, c. 1760–1860', *Journal for Maritime Research* 17:2 (2015), 117–33 and Beverly Lemire, 'A Question of Trousers: Seafarers, Masculinity and Empire in the Shaping of British Male Dress, c. 1600–1800', *Cultural and Social History* 13:1 (2016), 1–22.

20 Elin Jones, 'Masculinity, Materiality and Space Onboard the Royal Naval Ship, 1756–1815' (Unpublished PhD thesis, Queen Mary University of London, 2016), chapter 2.

21 Holly Furneaux and Sue Pritchard, 'Contested Objects: Curating Soldier Art', *Museum and Society* 13:4 (2015), 447–61.

22 Graham Dawson, *Soldier Heroes: British Adventure, Empire and the Imagining of Masculinities* (Abingdon: Routledge, 1994); Michael Paris, *Warrior Nation: Images of War in British Popular Culture, 1850–2000* (London: Reaktion, 2000). The literature on masculinity, empire and socialisation is too vast to list here, but, for an early example, see J. A. Mangan (ed.), *Making Imperial Mentalities: Socialisation and British Imperialism* (Manchester: Manchester University Press, 1990), and for more recent work, see Joseph A. Kestner, *Masculinities in British Adventure Fiction, 1880–1915* (Aldershot: Ashgate, 2010) and Stephanie Olsen, *Juvenile Nation: Youth, Emotions and the Making of the Modern British Citizen, 1880–1914* (London: Bloomsbury, 2014).

23 Neil Ramsey, *The Military Memoir and Romantic Literary Culture, 1780–1835* (Aldershot: Ashgate, 2011); Catriona Kennedy, *Narratives of the Revolutionary and Napoleonic Wars: Military and Civilian Experience in Britain and Ireland* (Basingstoke: Palgrave Macmillan, 2013); Isaac Land, *War, Nationalism, and the British Sailor, 1750–1850* (Basingstoke: Palgrave Macmillan, 2009); Begiato (Bailey), 'Tears and the Manly Sailor'; James Davey, 'Singing for the Nation: Balladry, Naval Recruitment and the Language of Patriotism in Eighteenth-century Britain', *The Mariner's Mirror* 103:1 (2017), 43–66.

24 Michael Brown, '"Like a Devoted Army": Medicine, Heroic Masculinity, and the Military Paradigm in Victorian Britain', *Journal of British Studies* 43:9 (2010), 592–622.

25 Michelle Tusan, 'War and the Victorians: Response', *Victorian Studies* 58:2 (2016), 324–31.

Part I

Experiencing martial masculinities

1

Burying Lord Uxbridge's leg: the body of the hero in the early nineteenth century

Julia Banister

A year after the Battle of Waterloo (1815), the battle that brought to a close the French Revolutionary and Napoleonic Wars, a marble column paid for by public subscription was erected on the Welsh island of Anglesey to celebrate the commander of the allied cavalry, Henry William Paget, Earl of Uxbridge and Marquess of Anglesey.[1] William Thomas Fitzgerald, a clerk in the navy pay office and minor poet of patriotic verse, had predicted that the soldiers whose deaths had secured Britain's 'high renown! And EUROPE her repose!' would be commemorated by the grateful nation with everlasting monuments: on 'lofty COLUMNS of eternal Fame / Shall BRITISH GRATITUDE record each name'.[2] Given that the two most conspicuous British heroes of the wars, Admiral Lord Nelson and Arthur Wellesley, Duke of Wellington, only one of whom died in action, were honoured in this way, the fact that Paget was also celebrated in this manner attests to his standing as a hero figure in the early nineteenth century. That said, a comparison between the figures atop Nelson's column in Trafalgar Square, completed in 1843, and Paget's column, completed in 1860, reveals a difference in the representation of the body of the hero. Whereas Nelson's column is topped by a statue of the naval hero wearing the empty left sleeve of his jacket pinned across his chest, the figure atop Paget's column gives no indication that, as a result of an injury sustained during the battle, his right leg had been amputated above the knee.[3]

Teresa Michals has argued that eighteenth-century artists struggled to combine heroism and amputation, and often resorted to eliding physical disability – what she terms 'invisible amputation' – so as to create an 'ideal form' of 'heroic masculinity'.[4] However, the fact that Paget had lost his leg at Waterloo was widely known in the nineteenth century, not least because the leg had been buried in a marked grave near the battlefield and the site of the burial visited by innumerable tourists.[5] Such attention to (part of) a military body was unusual. True, Nelson's corpse had been immersed in a barrel of brandy in the aftermath of the Battle of Trafalgar (1805), but only so that it might be transported to England; the hero was honoured with a grand state funeral two months after his death.[6] It might be thought that the burial of Paget's leg served likewise to mark a noble corporeal sacrifice, albeit on a smaller scale. In fact, it proved to be controversial for reasons that, I argue, reveal the complexity of the hero's body as an 'ideal form'. The military services of the eighteenth and nineteenth centuries required intense physical activity – whether marching or engaging with the enemy, hauling sails or loading cannon – and this, coupled with the requirement that those involved pledge their lives and limbs to the service, made the military life appear to be one that required essentially, in the sense of physically, 'masculine' attributes and capacities. In other words, military heroes could serve as models of and for masculinity because they seemed to have excelled at being, in a bodily sense, 'men'. Of course, this works only if the cultural construction of the physical relationship between gender ideals and the matter of the body is artfully obscured. As this chapter will show, responses to the burial of Paget's leg suggest that, rather than solemnising his heroism, the burial of the body part exposed the artificiality of the connection between 'masculinity' and the matter of the 'male' body. Much as the burial of the amputated leg courted those inclined to hero-worship, elevating a limb in such a way also reduced it to the level of common corporeal matter and thereby undermined the military hero as a model of and for essential masculinity.

Henry Paget had embarked on a military career soon after the outbreak of war with Revolutionary France.[7] His first position was commander of the 80th Regiment of Foot, a volunteer regiment with whom he saw active service in France. He moved through the ranks of army command with paper promotions, and by 1801 had become full colonel of the 7th Light Dragoons. In 1808, Paget joined General Sir John Moore as commander of the cavalry for the Peninsular War. Paget was instrumental in Moore's attempts to harry French forces in the northwest of Spain, and he cemented his reputation for bravery by covering Moore's retreat, at one point staving off thirteen regiments of French cavalry with only five of British.[8] This period of military success was soon to be overshadowed by incidents in his private life, however. Paget had married Lady Caroline Villiers in 1795, but shortly before leaving to join Moore he became involved romantically with Lady Charlotte Wellesley (née Cardogan), the Duke of Wellington's sister-in-law. The affair became a scandal when, on Paget's return from Spain, Charlotte eloped to be with him. As a result, Charlotte's brother challenged Paget to a duel, and her husband sued him for criminal conversation. Paget's lawyer, Mr Dallas, attempted to defend his client by stressing that Paget had sought to extricate himself from the affair by throwing himself into military action with Moore: 'careless of his safety, prodigal of his life, he seemed to search for danger wheresoever it was to be found; and to hunt after death in whatever shape it might appear'. Following Dallas's argument, Paget's good fortune not to be killed in battle became his misfortune at home. 'Fallen from a situation the most exalted, and the most enviable', Dallas argued, 'he has forfeited private esteem and public regard; and the hero who so lately glittered the brightest in the dazzling ranks of glory, and was the light and star of every professional scene in which he moved, is now reduced to have no other wish than that of complete solitude and seclusion'.[9]

Paget won the respite from heroism that he, apparently, so desired. After a brief reconciliation, he and Caroline divorced, and although he married Charlotte, the whole affair seems to have contributed to the stalling of his career. Paget participated in the Walcheren expedition in 1809, but did not see further active service in Wellington's wars until the summer of 1815. Wellington had not wanted Paget to join the Waterloo campaign, but the Prince Regent and Duke of York insisted. In the end, Wellington and Paget came to a working accord, and Paget acquitted himself so well that he secured his place in the pantheon of the nation's heroes. Paget's numerous contributions to the battle of Waterloo included marshalling and leading the cavalry into action to prevent Lieutenant-General Thomas Picton's infantry from being engulfed by three times the number of French soldiers at what was a crucial position for the allies, La Haye Sainte. Five days after the battle, *The Times* reported that Paget had been 'throughout the day foremost in danger and glory'.[10] According to a 'Memoir of the Most Noble Henry William Paget' printed in the *European Magazine, and London Review* (1821), 'next to the illustrious Commander-in-Chief, the Duke of Wellington, the success of the battle of Waterloo was, perhaps, more indebted to the "first Cavalry Officer in the world", as the gallant Marquess is justly entitled, than to any other of that band of heroes, who immortalized themselves on that eventful day'.[11] The *Gentleman's Magazine* (1854) repeated this sentiment in its obituary for Paget: 'next to the great leader of the host, the victory of Waterloo was more indebted to the Earl of Uxbridge than any other of the numerous warriors of that memorable day'. His 'gallantry' and 'dash' had inspired the men; his actions were 'prodigies of valour'.[12] Some fifteen years after the battle, the Scottish journalist and man of letters William Jerdan defended Paget's lieutenancy of Ireland on the basis that he had been 'one of the brightest military heroes of our age'.[13] In his life as a politician – a life that saw him come under attack for his sympathy for, among other things, Catholic emancipation – Paget acted, so the *Gentleman's Magazine* obituary asserts, 'with a moral courage not inferior to his brilliant physical bravery in the field'.[14]

Linda Colley has argued that the final battle of the Napoleonic Wars popularised 'a cult of military heroism and of a particular brand of "manliness"'.[15] According to Colley, this served the interests of the aristocracy by lending new glamour to old power, but I want to suggest that this was also a 'cult' that idealised the physicality of the male body. The dandy soldiers of the French Revolutionary and Napoleonic Wars, dressed in form-fitting breeches and high-waisted jackets, sought to create a masculine identity based on bodily brilliance, 'however inadequate [they and their bodies] might in fact be', as Colley puts it.[16] Though encouraged by the Prince Regent's love of military uniform, the dandy soldiers were ridiculed by the satirists of the age in images which imply that the cut of a well-made coat created an illusion of, rather than made manifest, an impressive physique.[17] In comparison to the dandily dressed military body, the injured or wounded body could be more easily represented as authentic and so admirable, as Philip Shaw has shown. In *Waterloo and the Romantic Imagination* and, more fully, in *Suffering and Sentiment in Romantic Military Art*, Shaw argues that literary and visual texts which acknowledged the human cost of war did not necessarily undermine attempts to celebrate victory, as bodily sacrifice could be co-opted so as to neutralise the 'felt contradiction between the waste and the wonder', that is the 'waste' of soldiers and the 'wonder' of the ideals to which they or their bodies had been sacrificed.[18] Just as Michals argues that Nelson could be represented as an amputee because his missing arm could be pinned in ways that echoed existing conventions for elite portraiture, so Shaw highlights a painting of Paget – Constantin Fidele Coene's *Imaginary Meeting of Sir Arthur Wellesley, Duke of Wellington and Sir Henry William Paget, 1st Marquess of Anglesey after the Amputation of his Leg* (1820) – that 'epitomizes the acceptable face of wounding', for the clean and bandaged stump in the centre of the painting 'provided ordinary men and women with a lesson in how to withstand the shock of death and injury', and at the same time ensured that 'the battle's material status as a history of violent death and injury is kept effectively under wraps'.[19]

If Coene found a visual language with which to wrap Paget's wound with glory, so written accounts of the battle were able to highlight the injury and amputation without exposing the redness and rawness of that which, under a surgeon's knife, is simply flesh and blood, bone and gristle. True, Paget had been wounded in the most pitiable of ways, and this contributed to the ease with which the injury could be narrated as a mark of heroism. Wellington's dispatch from the battle, as published in the newspapers, is economical in terms of its direct praise for Paget, but mentions that 'the Earl of Uxbridge, after having successfully got through this arduous day, received a wound by almost the last shot fired, which will, I am afraid, deprive his majesty for some time of his services'.[20] The 'almost' last shot damaged Paget's right knee and led to the amputation of his leg above the knee joint. In Nicholson Bain's *A Detailed Account of the Battles of Quatre Bras, Ligny and Waterloo* (1816), the injury and treatment are narrated in vivid colour:

> The enemy's fire had now almost completely ceased, but amongst the very last of their shot some of the most enterprising of our officers suffered. The gallant Earl of Uxbridge, who had escaped till this, although he exposed himself during the battle to every danger, which the cavalry under his command had encountered, [...] and directed every charge which has been made throughout the whole of the day, was now struck by a cannon ball, and in the farm-house of La Belle Alliance he endured the amputation of his leg, without one groan or contortion of his countenance; his noble exclamation is still remembered by those who were present: 'Who would not lose a leg for such a victory?'[21]

As unlikely as it is that this *bon mot* was Paget's only visible or audible response to the amputation of his leg, this claim can be found in a number of other historical surveys from the period.[22] John Booth's account of 'the gallant Earl's heroic sentiments at the moment of this severe trial' varies slightly from Bain's wording, but in fact emphasises the same points: in a footnote, added to the expanded editions of this history of the battle, the author mentions that '[Paget] was not seen to wince in the least, not even by contortion of his features, consoling those about him in saying: "Who would not lose a leg for such a victory? It is true, I have a limb less; but I have a higher name in the eyes of my country"'.[23] In repeating the phrase 'who would not lose a leg for such a victory', Bain,

Booth and their fellow panegyrists participate in celebrating the physicality of the hero, but also in preventing that physicality from being reduced to the level of mere bodily matter. In their narratives, the specifics of Paget's injury and the medical intervention to save his life are obscured by the emphasis on his courageously 'expos[ing] himself' in battle and on the stoic tranquillity of his countenance when exposed to the surgeon's knife. It is Paget's apparent disregard for his body in the moments when its bodiliness ought to be most pressing that ensures that the stringy, sinuous mundanity of human corporeality does not overpower the narrative of his heroism.

The euphemism 'lost' furthers the efforts made by Bain and Booth to carefully bandage over the material damage done to Paget by the slings and arrows of military misfortune. After all, the leg was not, in any sense, lost: penetrated by shot and then removed by a surgeon, it was deliberately buried in a marked grave. The unusual burial created a unique problem. The phrase 'who would not lose a leg' is able to celebrate the physicality of the hero's body and manage that physicality so as not to reduce the hero to the level of ordinary matter; a buried leg is much more viscerally physical, and that physicality is much less easy to wrap artfully. The first responses to the burial reveal that it was controversial from the start. One of the earliest accounts of the grave can be found in Robert Southey's laureate poem on the Battle of Waterloo: *The Poet's Pilgrimage to Waterloo* (1816). Southey had been one of the first tourists to visit Waterloo in the summer of 1815, and his poem narrates both his actual journey, which led to the battlefield, and his spiritual journey, which led him to patriotic and Christian fervour.[24] In the first part of the poem, Southey pauses to reflect on stone memorials to British soldiers placed in the church at Waterloo. In his explanatory notes, he lists the names of those soldiers and then comments on the more unusual memorial to Paget:

> Lord Uxbridge's leg is buried in a garden opposite to the inn, or rather public-house, at Waterloo. The owner of the house in which the amputation was performed considers it as a relic which has fallen to his share. He had deposited it at first behind the house, but as he intended to plant a tree upon the spot, he considered, that as the ground there was not his own property, the boys might injure or destroy the tree, and therefore he removed the leg into his own garden, where it lies in a proper sort of coffin, under a mound of earth about three or four feet in diameter. A tuft

of Michaelmas daisies was in blossom upon this mound when we were at Waterloo; but this was a temporary ornament: in November the owner meant to plant a weeping willow there. He was obliging enough to give me a copy of an epitaph which he had prepared, and which, he said, was then in the stone-cutter's hands.[25]

Here, Southey credits the French-speaking publican's desire to protect the memorial tree, but Southey's account of the businessman's interest in the leg as both a sacred 'relic' and his 'share' from the battle is redolent with Protestant suspicion of Catholic commerce. Southey's full footnote includes the French epitaph, the final line of which translates as 'His heroism in competing for the triumph of humankind in general, gloriously decided the brilliant victory of the day', but Southey does not include a translation.[26] The fact that the grave is not mentioned in the main body of the patriotic poem further implies ambivalence about whether or not it is a fit monument to a British hero.

There is evidence to suggest that Waterloo tourists were encouraged to visit the grave of the leg without any such scruples. After the end of the wars with France, Britons, including the middle classes, travelled to the continent in increasing numbers, and the literary marketplace saw a concurrent growth in the production and consumption of travel literature, whether in the form of first-hand narrative accounts or practical guides.[27] J. B. Romberg's *Brussels and its Environs* (1816) claims to be a guide to 'every object that can be interesting to strangers', including the grave of Paget's leg, which, he notes, 'strangers are permitted to visit'.[28] In *A New Picture of Brussels* (1820), Romberg phrases this slightly differently: he states that the grave is 'open to the inspection of visiters [sic]'.[29] With this, Romberg corrects the initial impression that the British tourist encounters the British hero's leg as though they were a 'stranger', that is, as if it was foreign to them. The change from 'strangers' to 'visiters' allows the British traveller to reclaim the publican's 'share' and symbolically repatriates the leg for the nation. One such visitor, the clergyman Daniel Wilson, takes such an approach when he mentions in his travel journal, *Letters from an Absent Brother* (1824), that in visiting the grave he was following in the king's footsteps, George IV having visited Waterloo in the early 1820s.[30]

That said, Southey's apparent suspicion about the grave can be likened to the outright criticism in Frances Trollope's travelogue, *Belgium and West Germany in 1833* (1834). Trollope's account of her travels in Belgium includes her visit to the village of Waterloo, the church and thence to other 'spots made memorable by having some connexion or other with the battle'.[31] Trollope is openly critical of 'the object, whose display was precluded with the most ceremony', the 'singular shrine' of Uxbridge's leg:

> There is something disagreeably approaching to the pathos, in passing from the graves of buried heroes to the repository of a severed limb. Had this brave and noble soldier left no other memorial of his presence at Waterloo than his leg, this strange devotion to it would be less annoying. Whoever they were who testified the fervour of their admiration by raising this singular mausoleum, they would have done better, had they trusted, for the recollection of the event, to the fame of the noble and well remembered firmness with which Lord Anglesey bore his loss: but as the leg itself was most assuredly the member to which the brave nobleman was the least likely to be indebted on the field of battle, some portion of the circumstance and ceremony respecting it might have been well spared.[32]

Like Southey's account of the leg as the publican's 'relic', Trollope's survey of the grave is coloured by her sense that it has been created by those predisposed to the excesses of 'strange devotion' and the 'fervour of admiration': Catholics.[33] This can also be read as a subtle attack on Paget for his sympathy for Catholic emancipation: Paget served in Wellington's government as Lord Lieutenant of Ireland in the late 1820s, until he was he was found to have been writing letters in support of the Catholics' cause. However, Trollope's broader point seems to be that the grave of a leg is too much for too little. She implies that a mausoleum for a single body part undermines the significance of the 'graves of buried heroes' in the little chapel at Waterloo and that it detracts from Paget's deserved fame. Trollope is complimentary to Paget – she commends him as a 'brave nobleman' – but, like Bain and Booth, she highlights his stoicism during the amputation rather than the subsequent burial of the amputated limb to celebrate Paget's 'firmness', a term that can be used for a physical substance that withstands pressure as well as moral rectitude.

Though Southey and Trollope address directly the burial of the leg, they both bury the burial – Southey in the footnotes to his lengthy poem, Trollope with her criticism of it as 'annoying'. Both writers are patriotic, and both are invested in the heroism of the men who fought at Waterloo. Given this, their reservations about the buried leg are, I suggest, an indication not of the weakness of that investment but of its strength, since in distancing the burial of the leg they distance the unremarkable materiality of the body to protect the exceptionality of (the body of) the hero, and thus his function as a model of essential masculinity. The art of distancing – or burying – the burial of the leg takes many forms. It is noticeable that Charlotte Waldie mentions the amputation, but not the burial, of Paget's leg in *Narrative of a Residence in Belgium during the Campaign of 1815* (1817). Waldie's *Narrative* is as unflinching in describing the loss of life at Waterloo as it is patriotic for the victory those lives secured. 'When I recalled all that the heroes of my country had done and dared and suffered for her honour and security and peace', Waldie writes, 'I blessed heaven that I was born an Englishwoman, and born in this, the proudest era of British glory.'[34] On their arrival at Waterloo, Waldie and her siblings Jane and John see first 'many a fresh-made, melancholy mound, which had served for the sol-dier's humble grave', and then the house where Uxbridge had 'remained after the amputation of his leg, until well enough to bear removal'.[35] As in Trollope's travelogue, this structure implicitly privileges soldiers' deaths above the removal of a leg, and this is reinforced when Waldie evaluates the significance of the names written in chalk on the doors of the houses in which the officers had stayed prior to the battle: the 'pompous names' of the officers who survived, albeit wounded, are jux-taposed with the 'lamented' names of those officers who 'sleep in the bed of honour'.[36]

The absence of any direct mention of the grave is equally revealing in Thomas Henry White's *Fragments of Italy and the Rhineland* (1841). White writes as an enthusiast for both the 'horrors' and the 'romance' of the Battle of Waterloo, both of which he conjures as though he were taking part.[37] In fact, White seems willing to embrace the mundane materiality of battles and bodies. White likens, albeit implicitly, the grave of Paget's leg to the internment of Major Frederick Howard's body in his family mausoleum in Castle Howard, Yorkshire. Having expressed regret that the 'kindly moss, the matted ivy and a thousand waving shrubs are already beginning to veil' the history of the battle, White reflects on the slim possibility that the 'remains now moulder-ing' in the Howard family tomb are actually Major Howard's.[38] White notes that the Howard family claimed to have recognised the body, but then borrows lines of poetry from Walter Scott to make the point that corpses on a battlefield are picked over by scavengers such that lord and vassal become indistinguishable. White's point seems to be that even heroes' bodily remains are really little more than mouldy matter. In other words, his lack of comment on the burial of the leg seems to be explained by his blunt scepticism about veiling the reality of battle by venerating the decomposing bones of battle casualties. However, his scepticism begins to waver when he observes that the French peasants sleeping in the sunshine have the same postures as the Waterloo dead: 'I had already uttered a conceit, and was checked by the simple terrors of the *truth*.'[39] Of course, with this the 'truth' of the Waterloo soldiers' deaths is only fleetingly acknowledged, for when sleeping bodies are likened to dead bodies, dead bodies are likened to sleeping bodies. White's desire to confront and expose the mundane matter of the military body comes to an end when he contemplates the Lion's Mound, an artificial hill that had been created on the battlefield after the battle: 'Waterloo scarcely needed any monument, and certainly ought not to have had one torn up from the bowels. It is hideous excrescence at the best.'[40] White's choice of the metaphor 'bowels' indicates that even he finds too much matter-of-fact bodiliness objectionable.

Though Waldie and White choose not to mention the grave of the leg directly, it would be misleading to suggests that all Waterloo tourists did likewise. One traveller, writing for *The Magazine of Domestic Economy* (1836) on the importance of continental travel as a 'necessary point of calculation' for families, contrasts his disappointment with the lack of a grand monument in the humble church at Waterloo with his deeper emotional response to the burial of the leg: 'our sentiments ... immediately sank to their proper level, on our being led to contemplate the spot rendered sacred as the grave of the Marquis of Anglesey's leg'.[41] And yet, even one of the most overtly celebratory responses to the burial distances the materiality of the leg with what I will term 'strategies of evasion'. Like Coene's painting of Paget's cleanly bandaged leg, Eliza Mary Hamilton's poem 'On Receiving a Leaf, Brought from the Weeping Willow that is Planted at Waterloo where the Marquis of Anglesey's Leg is Buried' (1828) both celebrates and obscures the body of the hero. Hamilton's poem admits that death and injury are inseparable from victory and glory: in the opening lines, the poet holds the leaf and imagines the 'glory, blood, and grief' of Waterloo.[42] The balance of these three elements tips towards the melancholy and she imagines 'the stillness deep, / The mournful plain where many sleep!' (ll. 17–18).

Just as Hamilton evades the finality of the 'sleep[ing]' soldiers' death, so she evades the corporeality of Paget's buried leg. That the injured Paget had been a hero is not in any doubt: 'The offering which to that small grave / He of the lion-spirit gave!' becomes, in the final lines of the poem, 'noble dust' that had once belonged to one 'whom 'mid that gallant mass / Of heroes, —none might dare surpass' (ll. 23–4, 41–2). The obscurity of the term 'offering' is compounded by the phrase 'noble dust', for although the latter alludes to decomposition, it seems also to deliberately conceal the original fleshy matter of the decade-dead limb. To refer to the leg as an 'offering' and as 'dust' is to suggests that it both is and is not present in the tomb, and with this the poem presents the physicality of the leg as less important than its symbolic status. After all, not only does the poem avoid addressing the bone and muscle of the leg directly, even its earthly resting place is obscured by the gracious 'green veil' (l.22) of the weeping willow. The poet claims to be in direct contact with a leaf from that willow, but the leaf replaces the grave and the leg within it as the focus for the poem. Ultimately, the poet's contact with the leaf leads her away from the leg in the grave, for although touching the leaf gives her a physical connection to the grave, the poem indicates that a physical thing is only really important as an aid to higher thought.

In focusing on a leaf rather than the grave, let alone the limb, Hamilton's poem exemplifies the way in which enthusiasts for heroism sought to evade the materiality made manifest by the burial of the leg. The legend of the burial of the leg grew in the telling, and while this might be thought to have reinforced its significance as a monument to heroism, the additions to the legend can also be seen as evasions of the muddy matter of the grave and the meaty matter of the leg within it. Romberg's first guide to Brussels mentions that tourists might see the chair in which Paget sat to have his leg removed as well as the grave, but by the mid-1830s the number of objects associated with the burial of the leg had expanded further, as Maria Frances Dickson's narrative of her 'pilgrimage to the little mound overhung by a willow-tree' illustrates:

> In the house they showed us the boot which was cut off the severed limb, and the table on which the operation was performed. [...] We were told that [Paget] visited the cottage about a year since with his family, and dined off the same table on which he was laid after the battle to have his leg amputated. Of all the heroes of Waterloo, Lord Anglesey seems to be the best remembered and most beloved by the people there, who dwell with great pleasure on any little circumstance connected with him. The way in which I heard him spoken of was particularly gratifying to my feelings, as I never can forget that to his kindness and personal exertions, I am indebted, under Providence for the preservation of my life.[43]

Here, Dickinson includes the apocryphal and much-repeated tale of Paget eating at the table on which his operation had been performed.[44] This echoes the early histories of the battle, in which Paget's heroism is associated with stoic firmness. However, as Dickson's account shows, the boot and the table are significant because of their connection with the leg, but the physicality of the leg is obscured by the association of the grave with other objects; the inanimate materiality of these objects is not the same as the materiality of the body, and their inclusion within the scene functions to ensure that the hero is mythologised rather than literalised by his buried limb. That even an enthusiast for the hero should participate in celebrating his heroism by multiplying the number of objects associated with his injury indicates how patriotic and pervasive such evasion was in the early nineteenth century.

My argument – that evasions of the materiality of Paget's buried leg sought to protect the cultural function of the hero as model of essential masculinity – encompasses a humorous poem which seems to have been the most widely circulated response to the burial of Paget's leg. The origins of the poem are obscure, though it was widely believed to have been written by the prominent politician George Canning.[45] Titled variously, its publication as 'An Epitaph over the Marquis of Anglesea's Leg' in *Poetic Flowers* (1815), a volume of poetry selected by Elizabeth Sandham, a minor author of children's tales, is among the earliest appearances of the seven-stanza poem, which was reprinted in whole and in part throughout the nineteenth century in a vast array of different texts. The 'Epitaph' addresses the materiality of the leg squarely, beginning in the first stanza: 'let no saucy knave, / Presume to sneer and laugh, / To learn that mould'ring in the grave, / Is laid a British calf'.[46] The bodily matter of the limb is made unambiguous by its 'mouldiness' and by the specificity of the word 'calf', to which the poem later adds 'sole' and 'toes' (ll. 8, 11). The humorist mines further the comic possibilities of the amputation, noting for example that Paget is able to move in London's social circles despite having 'one foot in the grave' (l. 24). So direct is the poem about the amputation that its comedy borders on callous. That said, where the poem is published in a shorter form it is usually reduced to the final stanzas, which end with a markedly different tone:

> But Fortune's pardon I must beg,
> She meant not to disarm,
> And when she lopp'd the hero's leg,
> She did not mean his h–*arm*;

And but indulged a harmless whim,
Since he could walk with one;
She saw two legs were lost on him
Who never meant to *run*. (ll. 29–36)

As in the previous examples, these lines laugh at the amputated and buried leg, but these closing stanzas also reveal that the poem is not intended to ridicule Paget's heroism, for the line he 'never meant to run' commends his bravery. Rather than mythologise the hero by concealing the fleshy matter of the buried leg, then, this poem protects the hero's capacity to function as a model for masculinity by laughing at those who would think the burial of a sole to be worthy of solemnity. The poem's wordplay evades the mundane materiality of the leg by presenting it as ludicrous.

The comic 'Epitaph' that became so prevalent in the early nineteenth century is not the only bluntly comic response to the burial of the leg. After Waterloo, Paget was associated with the parliamentary reform movement, and in 'An Authentic Report of a Dialogue Between his Excellency the Marquis of Anglesea and the Ghost of his Leg' (1831), printed in the Tory *Blackwood's Edinburgh Magazine*, the ghost of the amputated leg harangues Paget for supporting reform.[47] Here, the separation of leg and body is converted into comedy, and the common materiality of the leg is evaded by its absurd ghostliness. In his study of eighteenth-century attitudes to disability, David Turner has shown that physical impairment was all too often treated as a source of amusement by the non-disabled, much as the disabled person might seek to cooperate with or to subvert this 'comedy of impairment' so as to 'overcome the supposed horrors of affliction [and] (re)integrate themselves into non-disabled company'.[48] In Turner's view, such humour is twinned with fear and repression, and the laughter it elicits reveals both. With this in mind, comedic treatments of the burial of Paget's leg, as in John Roby's *Seven Weeks in Belgium, Switzerland, Lombardy, Piedmont* (1838), can be understood as attempts to repress and thereby evade the troubling vulnerability of the all-too-human body: Roby writes that 'in a cottage garden is a little monument to the celebrated "leg" of Lord Uxbridge, Marquis of Anglesea. While famous in arms, he cannot boast of legs; though he has a wider stride than the Colossus, seeing they are so far asunder'.[49] Although Roby seems to have no purpose other than that of making a joke, even this, I am arguing, works to defend the cultural function of the exceptionally physical hero as a model for masculinity by laughing at that which has the potential to undermine and expose investments in bodily exceptionality.

Much as the burial of Paget's leg invited pilgrim-tourists to pay homage to military heroism, as this chapter has shown, the various ways in which writers critique that burial reveal that too sharp a focus on what was only a severed, not a sleeping, limb threatened to demystify the necessarily hazy connection between masculinity and (men's) bodily matter. Like the texts that criticise devotion to relics, use euphemisms for death and decomposition or inflate the legend of the leg, comedic responses such as Roby's employ strategies of evasion, for in lampooning the burial of a leg they avoid acknowledging the weakness of the link between masculinity and the matter of the 'male' body. By way of a final comment, I want to suggest that those who laughed at the burial of the leg can also be said to have been repressing the fact that, after the amputation, Paget could 'stride' where he pleased, due to his adopting what was, at the time, a pioneering type of artificial leg.[50] This fact is exploited in one satirical response to the political disagreement between Paget and Wellington with regard to Catholic emancipation, which shows Paget hopping away from Wellington while carrying his artificial leg over his shoulder.[51] This satire is aimed at one who, far from accepting limitations, had overreached what his critics thought to be the bounds of his position; to picture him hopping is to figuratively reduce the mobility of one who had been, to his critics, overly 'mobile'. In other words, it is possible to see a connection between strategies for evading the burial of the leg and denials of Paget's ability. Vanessa Warne has argued that prosthetic limbs, like the one worn by Paget, troubled the boundary between the 'real' body and 'artefacts of culture' by equating flesh with other materials.[52] If the burial of Paget's leg threatened to undermine the hero as a model for essential masculinity by exposing the physicality of the hero's body, then the replacement of the leg with an artificial limb only further exposed the body of the hero as an assemblage of everyday materials.

Notes

1 *Black's Picturesque Guide to Wales, North and South and Monmouthshire* (Edinburgh: Adam and Charles Black; Chester: Catherall and Prichard, 1869), p. 67. Paget was given the marquisate as a token of thanks for his contribution to the battle.

2 William Thomas Fitzgerald, 'The Battle of Waterloo, or La Belle Alliance', in *The Gentleman's Magazine* (London: Nichols, Son and Bentley, 1815), vol. 85, p. 62. Also printed in *The New Monthly Magazine and Universal Register* (London: H. Coburn, 1815), vol. 4, pp. 34–5; *The European Magazine, and London Review* (London: James Asperne, 1815), vol. 68, pp. 55–6.

3 Nelson was frequently depicted with a pinned sleeve, most notably in a portrait by Lemuel Francis Abbot (1797).

4 Teresa Michals, 'Invisible Amputation and Heroic Masculinity', *Studies in Eighteenth-Century Culture* 44 (2015), pp. 17–39 (p. 27).

5 For the appeal of visiting Waterloo in the nineteenth century see Marysa Demoor, 'Waterloo as a Small "Realm of Memory": British Writers, Tourism, and the Periodical Press', *Victorian Periodicals Review* 48:4 (2015), pp. 453–68.

6 For the cultural significance of Nelson's funeral see Holger Hoock, 'Nelson Entombed: The Military and Naval Pantheon in St Paul's Cathedral', in David Cannadine (ed.), *Admiral Lord Nelson: Contexts and Legacy*, (Basingstoke: Palgrave Macmillan, 2005), pp. 115–43.

7 All biographical information is drawn from Marquess of Anglesey, *One-Leg: The Life and Letters of Henry William Paget, First Marquess of Anglesey* (London: Jonathan Cape, 1961).

8 James Moore, *A Narrative of the Campaign of the British Army in Spain*, 2nd ed. (London: Joseph Johnson, 1809), pp. 174–5.

9 *The Trial of the Right Honourable Lord Paget, for Criminal Conversation with Lady Charlotte Wellesley* (London: Sherwood, Neely and Jones; J. Stratford, 1809), pp. 25, 27.

10 *The Times*, Friday 23 June 1815.

11 'Memoir of the Most Noble Henry William Paget, Marquess of Anglesey', *The European Magazine, and London Review* (London: James Asperne, 1821), vol. 80, pp. 211–12 (p. 212).

12 'Obituary: The Marquess of Anglesey', *The Gentleman's Magazine and Historical Review* (London: John Bowyer Nichols, 1854), vol. 41, pp. 638–44 (p. 640).

13 William Jerdan, *National Portrait Gallery of Illustrious and Eminent Persons of the Nineteenth Century* (London: Fisher, Son and Jackson, 1831), vol. 2, pp. 177–82.

14 *The Gentleman's Magazine*, vol. 41, pp. 642–3.

15 Linda Colley, *Britons: Forging the Nation*, 3rd ed. (New Heaven, CT: Yale University Press, 2005), p. 193.

16 *Ibid.*, p. 185.

17 For the Prince Regent see Scott Hughes Myerly, *British Military Spectacle: From the Napoleonic Wars through the Crimea* (Cambridge, MA: Harvard University Press, 1996); John Mollo, *The Prince's Dolls: Scandals*,

Skirmishes and Splendours of the First British Hussars: 1793–1815 (London: Lee Cooper, 1997), pp. 33–43. For satire on dandy soldiers see, for example, *Military Dandies or Heroes of 1818* (1818), British Museum Satires no. 13059.

18   Shaw, *Suffering and Sentiment*, p. 34. See also *Waterloo and the Romantic Imagination*, esp. pp. 19–29. Simon Parkes makes a similar argument when he suggests that the '[physically] broken soldier' could function as a 'safe' figure in art and literature of the eighteenth century. See 'Wooden Legs and Tales of Sorrow Done: The Literary Broken Soldier of the Late Eighteenth Century', *Journal for Eighteenth-Century Studies* 36:2 (2013), pp. 191–206. For a survey of emotional responses to the victims of Waterloo see R. S. White, 'Victims of War: Battlefield Casualties and Literary Sensibility', in Neil Ramsey and Gillian Russell (eds), *Tracing War in British Enlightenment and Romantic Culture*, (Basingstoke: Palgrave Macmillan, 2015), pp. 61–76.

19   Shaw, *Suffering and Sentiment*, pp. 179, 180. For Michals see, 'Invisible Amputation', pp. 31–3.

20   *The London Gazette Extraordinary*, Thursday 22 June 1815, reprinted in *The Times*, Friday 23 June 1815.

21   Nicholson Bain, *A Detailed Account of the Battles of Quatre Bras, Ligny and Waterloo* (Edinburgh: John Thomson; Baldwin, Cradock and Joy; John Cumming, 1816), pp. 153–4.

22   Edmund Boyce, *The Second Usurpation of Buonaparte: Or, a History of the Causes, Progress and Termination of the Revolution in France in 1815* (London: Samuel Leigh, 1816), pp. 86–7; Hewson Clarke, *The History of the War from the Commencement of the French Revolution to the Present Time*, 3 vols (London: T. Kinnersley, 1816), vol. III, p. 239; Edward Baines, *History of the Wars of the French Revolution*, 2 vols (London: Longman, Hurst, Rees, Orme and Brown, 1818), vol. II, p. 468; John Parker, *A Concise Account of the Glorious Battle of Waterloo and Surrender of Paris* (Berwick: W. Lochhead, 1822), p. 114.

23   *The Battle of Waterloo*, 7th ed. (London: John Booth; T. Egerton; 1815), p. 123.

24   On Southey's Christian patriotism see Simon Bainbridge, *Napoleon and English Romanticism* (Cambridge: Cambridge University Press, 1995), pp. 160–9; Shaw, *Waterloo and the Romantic Imagination*, pp. 92–113.

25   Robert Southey, *The Poet's Pilgrimage to Waterloo* (London: Longman, Hurst, Rees, Orme and Brown, 1816), pp. 212–13.

26   *Ibid.*, p. 213.

27   Pieter François, 'If It's 1815, This Must Be Belgium: The Origins of the Modern Travel Guide', *Book History* 15 (2012), pp. 71–92.

28   J. B. Romberg, *Brussels and Its Environs* (London: Samuel Leigh, 1816), p. 112.

29   J. B. Romberg, *A New Picture of Brussels and Its Environs* (London: Samuel Leigh, 1820), p. 233.

30   Daniel Wilson, *Letters from an Absent Brother*, 2nd ed., 2 vols (London: George Wilson, 1824), vol. I, p. 31.

31   Frances Trollope, *Belgium and Western Germany in 1833*, 2 vols (Brussels: Ad. Wahlen, 1834), vol. I, p. 76.

32   *Ibid.*, pp. 77–8.

33   For the resurgence of Catholicism in Belgium in the 1830s see Pieter François, 'Belgium: Country of Liberals, Protestants and the Free: British Views on Belgium in the Mid Nineteenth Century', *Historical Research* 81 (2008), pp. 663–78. François notes that Trollope was notably hostile to Belgian Catholicism.

34   [Charlotte Waldie], *Narrative of a Residence in Belgium during the Campaign of 1815* (London: John Murray, 1817), p. 208.

35   *Ibid.*, pp. 257, 259.

36   *Ibid.*, pp. 259–60.

37   Thomas Henry White, *Fragments of Italy and the Rhineland* (London: William Pickering, 1841), p. 452.

38   *Ibid.*, pp. 453, 455.

39   *Ibid.*, p. 456.

40   *Ibid.*, p. 457.

41   'Tour on the Continent', *The Magazine of Domestic Economy* (London: Orr and Smith, 1836), vol. 1, pp. 363–7 (p. 366).

42   Eliza Mary Hamilton, *Poems* (Dublin: Hodges and Smith, 1838), pp. 84–6, l. 3. Subsequent references will be given as line numbers in the text.

43   Mary Francis Dickinson, *Souvenirs of a Summer in Germany in 1836*, 2 vols (London: Henry Colburn, 1837), vol. I, pp. 77–8. The nature of Dickson's personal connection to Paget is obscure.

44   Paget's biographer does not confirm whether or not this actually happened. See Anglesey, *One-Leg*, p. 151.

45   Perhaps because of his opposition to the Concert of Europe, a reactionary and conservative system developed by the leading nations in Europe in the aftermath of their defeat of Napoleon and intended to preserve their power. For Canning as author see, for example, John Styles, *Memoirs of the Life of the Right Hon. George Canning*, 2 vols (London: Thomas Tegg, 1828), vol. II, p. 262.

46   Elizabeth Sandham (ed.), *Poetic Flowers* (Southampton: T. Baker, 1815), pp. 58–9, ll. 1–4. Subsequent references will be given as line numbers in the text.

47   'An Authentic Report of a Dialogue Which Took Place Between his Excellency the Marquis of Anglesea and the Ghost of his Leg which was Amputated Upon the Plains of Waterloo', *Blackwood's Edinburgh Magazine* (Edinburgh: William Blackwood; London: T. Cadell, 1831), vol. 30, pp. 715–30.

48 David M. Turner, *Disability in the Eighteenth Century: Imagining Physical Impairment* (New York: Routledge, 2012), pp. 69, 70.

49 John Roby, *Seven Weeks in Belgium, Switzerland, Lombardy, Piedmont*, 2 vols (London: Longman, Orme, Brown, Green, and Longmans, 1838), vol. I, p. 137.

50 Alan J. Thurston, 'Paré and Prosthetics: The Early History of Artificial Limbs', *ANZ Journal of Surgery* 77 (2007), pp. 1114–19.

51 *Another X-ample of the Fatal Effects of Using* [sic] *too much Foolscap* (1828–30), British Museum Satires no. 15656.

52 Vanessa Warne, 'Artificial Leg', *Victorian Review* 34:1 (2008), pp. 29–33 (p. 33).

2

Brothers in arms? Martial masculinities and family feeling in old soldiers' memoirs, 1793–1815

Louise Carter

Farewell, my parents, loving, kind,
My friends dear to the feeling heart;
Farewell, sweet Nancy, lovely Maid,
Dearer than life, – oh we must part;
And part perhaps to meet no more,
My country calls and I must go,
To Egypt's hot and distant land,
To meet in battle our dread foe.[1]

The idea that martial duty necessitated the temporary cessation of family life can be found repeatedly in the cultural output of the Revolutionary and Napoleonic War era, for obvious reasons. From ballads such as 'The Girl I left Behind' to Gillray's print *John Bull's Progress* (1793), repeated images of sorrowful partings, lengthy absences and precarious futures brought home the personal impact of war on soldiers and sailors and their wives, children, parents and siblings.[2] This chapter will explore what more veterans' memoirs from this era might reveal about the interplay between family and martial life, and will suggest that far from uniformly necessitating the cessation of familial connection, military life frequently remained enmeshed with family in both literal and symbolic ways.

Images of soldiers or sailors taking leave of family, such as Cruikshank's *The Soldier's Farewell* (1803), in which a resolute red-coated officer departs from his tearful wife and children, understandably carried considerable resonance in the Revolutionary and Napoleonic period.[3] Margarette Lincoln argues that such imagery helped to normalise the ubiquity of such scenes being repeated across the country.[4] Joanne Begiato (Bailey), meanwhile, suggests that depictions of sailors' tearful farewells to family helped to reimagine and rehabilitate Jack Tar as 'an uxorious patriot' embodying 'all the admirable manly attributes of the age of sensibility'.[5] Yet, while tears might testify to a feeling character and the strength of family attachments, they could still be a trial to bear. As former soldier William Cobbett acknowledged, many a soldier embarked on foreign service with 'the remonstrances and lamentations of parents' weighing heavily on their conscience.[6] Yet conversely, as this 1804 call to arms none too subtly argued, it could be the very strength of domestic devotion that necessitated enlistment, since 'He is unworthy of the name of a man. He is unworthy of the name of a father, of a husband, of a brother, who does not at this important moment step forward to save his wife, his daughters, his sisters, his country and his King.'[7]

Indeed, a soldier's patriotic, self-sacrificing and stoic willingness to forego the pleasures of home and country to fight for their preservation was frequently cast as one of the most fundamental and creditable characteristic of martial masculinity. *The Soldier's Wife's Dream* went so far as to suggest that in leaving the familial fireside for war, a soldier became 'a man again'.[8] The interruption of family life was therefore represented as a necessary facet of military or naval service in time of war, and as a sacrifice wholly commensurate with the long-established correlation between masculinity and ideals of chivalry, patriotism, duty, honour and filial or uxorial devotion.[9] Meanwhile, for those governed by more rakish motivations, the prospect of familial separation could represent an entirely different inducement to enlist. Taking the King's shilling was seen by some as an opportunity to escape domestic responsibilities altogether, offering a chance to substitute 'Brown Bess sooner than bigg bell'd Betty', or to have 'in every town a different wife', according to a man's disposition.[10] Either way, whether defending or deserting family, popular culture repeatedly presented the idea that war required military and naval men to sacrifice familial identities, comforts and responsibilities for a season.[11]

The idea that soldiering was at odds with the pursuit of family life was further underscored by military regulation and custom. Prohibitions against rank-and-file soldiers marrying without the express permission of their commanding officer had existed since 1685.[12] For example, a 1796 regulation prohibited the enlistment of married men with more than two children.[13] Jennine Hurl-Eamon argues that matrimony was often considered 'more of a liability than an asset' for common soldiers by the eighteenth-century state and was actively discouraged, in much the same fashion as poor-relief officers attempted to curb marriage among the poorest.[14] A soldiering life involved lengthy absences, low pay, heightened intrinsic risk and the need to prioritise martial duty, none of which was easily compatible with patriarchal responsibility. This critically undermined the desirability of such unions in the eyes of many contemporary commentators. As one officer noted, 'It was a saying of Sir John Moore, that a soldier had nothing to do with a wife, and he frequently expressed a wish that no married man would select his regiment.'[15]

Neither were such concerns confined to the military hierarchy. William Cobbett was an enthusiastic advocate of an allowance for soldiers' parents, in recompense for the likely loss of their offspring's aid in later life, but opposed the idea of a similar allowance for wives and children, believing that such a scheme would serve as 'an encouragement to the breeding of beggars'.[16] Evidence to lend credence to such fears was not hard to find. Anti-impressment rioters frequently complained of the economic distress caused by the abduction of family breadwinners by the press gang.[17] Meanwhile, one the chief complaints of sailors involved in the naval mutinies at Spithead and the Nore in 1797 was that their pay was too low to keep their dependents from hardship.[18]

Officers faced no formal barriers to marriage, but were nevertheless expected to delay any nuptials until their careers were sufficiently advanced to be able to provide for dependents, should the worst occur. In Anglo-American novelist Susanna Rowson's cautionary tale *Charlotte: A Tale of Truth* (1791), a father impresses on his newly commissioned son that as a junior officer he has 'no business to think of a wife, till his rank is such as to place him above the fear of bringing into the world a train of helpless innocents, heirs only to penury and affliction'.[19] Unfortunately for the novel's titular heroine, officers could prove as capable of living up to the more scandalous stereotypes associated with soldiery as the lower ranks, and while the libertine son heeds his father's well-intentioned advice and remains unmarried, he commits even greater injury by seducing and abandoning Charlotte.

The views of parents arguably held even less consequence when it came to the issue of enlistment. Given that parental consent was a sufficiently prominent contemporary concern in the mid-eighteenth century to occasion a change in marriage law, it is noteworthy that minors making a contract with the British army were not required to secure formal parental approval. In contrast to the provisions of Hardwicke's Marriage Act 1753, David M. Rosen notes that English common law made no stipulation requiring parental consent for minors seeking to enlist, with the assumption that guardianship merely passed from the father to the army until the soldier came of age.[20] Indeed, while *The Parish Officer's Complete Guide* held that young people entering a wide variety of apprenticeships and forms of paid service should not be considered 'emancipated' from their parents until they reached majority, it noted that 'it has, however, been held, that if a son enlists himself as a soldier, he thereby emancipates himself from his father's family'.[21] Thus, while Georgian society upheld the primacy of parental authority in multiple arenas of civilian life, in law, the wishes of parents remained subordinate to the needs of the British army.

The potential tensions between army and family life were further exacerbated by the expectation that a soldier's loyalties to regiment and country should supplant all others, including family bonds. General Sir George T. Napier wrote to his sons on their entry into military life,

> Great as is my duty towards you, and bound as I am by every tie of nature to perform it; however great the personal and familial sacrifices I must make, still a soldier's first and paramount duty is to his country. All private benefit, all feelings, all affections, in short life itself, must yield to that.[22]

He warned them to be ever-mindful of the familial sacrifices that a military life required, since

> although bitter will be the pain of parting with the wife you love, your duty to your country is the primary object of a soldier, and to it all other feelings must give way. Neither wife, child or parent must stand in the way of duty if you wear a red coat, and during war you can wear no other.[23]

One commentator even offered the amnesiac suggestion that a soldier 'knows no country but the camp, acknowledges no family or friend but the armed associates who surround him'.[24] The notion that soldiers miraculously forgot friends and family as soon as they left British soil was clearly hyperbole. Yet the capacity of the soldier to 'abjure all family comfort and domestic society' was nevertheless repeatedly vaunted as one of the defining characteristics of military life by critics and advocates alike.[25]

At first glance then, all of this tends towards the idea that military and naval men's relationships to family differed from the norms associated with their civilian counterparts in quite a fundamental way. Fathers' legal guardianship of minors could be set aside when a son enlisted, aged parents could be left to shift for themselves, single men were discouraged from marriage and servicemen with children were expected to leave their dependants for significant periods of time, potentially with minimal provision for their welfare. This all stands in stark contrast to the work of John Tosh, Karen Harvey, Matthew McCormack and Joanne Begiato (Bailey), which has done so much to illuminate the central importance of family, home and domestic life to the construction and practice of civilian manhood in the late eighteenth and early nineteenth centuries.[26] Indeed, Tosh has argued that by the early nineteenth century, *the* key marker of adult male identity was establishing and maintaining a position as head of household.[27] Such conclusions appear to leave the figure of the soldier somewhat out in the cold – bivouacking in a distant clime and denied the comforts and status conferred on his civilian counterpart through familial connections. Held up in wartime propaganda as the epitome of manliness, in part because of his dutiful willingness to forego the pleasures and responsibilities of familial life, the soldier was thereby paradoxically excluded from fully partaking in one of the formative privileges and responsibilities most associated with Georgian adult manhood.

To assess the extent to which all this reflected soldiers' own experiences and understandings of soldiering, familial life and martial masculinities, the remainder of this chapter will turn to the evidence within veteran soldiers' memoirs. In the years following Waterloo, the public appetite for tales of the Great War was well supplied, with an outpouring of military and naval memoirs from across the ranks. As Catriona Kennedy has shown, these narratives drew on a wide variety of literary influences including epistolary writing, travel memoirs, the gothic novel, Romanticism, sensationalism, sensibility and religious texts. In the process, they forged their own genre of war writing, which whilst never constituting an unmediated and empirical take on reality, still affords the reader the opportunity to 'explore how [wartime] experiences are lived, constructed and interpreted through language'.[28] The varied mix of influences and interests informing these memoirs meant that not all dwelt on human details. Some were very dry affairs focused almost exclusively on military manoeuvres.[29] As Neil Ramsey has noted, while some memoirists pitched themselves with more than a nod to the Romantic tradition and the 'man of feeling', others served more as forerunners of the imperial adventure stories of the later nineteenth century that downplayed a soldier's private or inner life, forefronting politics, tactics or action.[30] Within those memoirs that did address the personal, however, discussions of family loomed large, both literally and symbolically, and they offer us much to explore.

In part, old soldiers' memoirs absolutely reiterate the classic view of military familial life already explored, namely that it was character- ised by lengthy separations from parents, siblings, wives and children. Descriptions of melancholy separations and emotional embarkations were a well-worn trope of the memoir genre. Thomas Pococke's account, for example, opens with an emotional departure scene and an admis- sion of enduring guilt over the anguish his enlistment had inflicted on his mother and father.[31] Yet despite the ubiquity of such accounts, vet- eran soldiers' memoirs also frequently unsettle the idea that soldiering automatically meant a denial of family life, and make plain its dogged persistence in a multitude of ways, from the wives and children who accompanied men on campaign to the family members serving within the same regiments, or the importance of maintaining a correspond- ence home.

Marriage was always a feature of many a Georgian soldier's expe- rience, irrespective of the impediments, as Jennine Hurl-Eamon has demonstrated.[32] The army's marital regulations could nevertheless pre- sent formidable obstacles to the course of true love. Memoirist Serjeant Butler recalled his disappointment when his first love mistakenly read his regiment's departure on campaign, while he was awaiting official leave to propose, as a sign of his disinterest and married someone else.[33] Once such barriers had been hurdled, though, a small number of mar- ried rank-and-file soldiers gained the opportunity to take their wives and children on foreign service, in return for the women fulfilling some of the support tasks required in camp.[34]

Memoirs illuminate the mixed fortunes that awaited families on campaign and the divided loyalties that could ensue. Sergeant Robertson recalled becoming separated from his wife and children in the course of one enemy attack on the regiment's camp, and the har- rowing seven days he spent before news of their safety reached him.[35] His colleague, Sergeant McGregor, was less fortunate. When his wife and three boys dropped behind on a march, he fell out of line in an unsuccessful bid to find them. Not only did he fail to find any trace of his family, but his actions led to his court-martial and demotion for neglect of duty. McGregor's experiences appear to have left him so broken that Robertson regarded it a blessing in disguise when the distraught man was subsequently killed in action and put out of his misery.[36] As such accounts indicate, the comfort and support of family on campaign could come at a heavy price.

Being witness to a succession of heart-wrenching separations between military spouses similarly left one officer in two minds over the relative costs and benefits of martial matrimony:

> The more I see of this interesting spectacle, the more do I become a convert to Sir John Moore's maxim – that a soldier should have nothing to do with a wife. And yet I think that some of these wives are too precious luxuries for us contentedly to give the monopoly of them to you non-military gentlemen.[37]

Conflicting sentiments also troubled Officer Moyle Sherer. Though on one hand he confessed to pangs of regret that he would leave no widow or child to weep over his grave should he fall, on the other hand he equally consoled himself that this spared him the additional burdens that family men carried when contemplating the prospect of their imminent death and its consequences.[38] Not everyone was so sympathetic or able to manage the emotions raised by the presence of women and children on campaign. A colleague of Rifleman Harris, irked by the personal discomfort he felt on encountering distraught wives seeking news of their husbands after battle, came to the conclusion that army wives were nothing but a nuisance and army husbands nothing but selfish.[39]

Such accounts testify to the stubborn endurance of civilian conceptions of masculinity in the psyches of serving soldiers, despite the best efforts of the army to inculcate its own values in recruits. Civilian life taught that family stewardship and protection were a man's most fundamental and sacred responsibilities, ordained by God and Nature, and memoirists' reflections tend to suggest a recognition that it did not come easy to override this precept to prioritise regiment. Indeed, some even took on additional domestic responsibilities while on campaign, as happened to Serjeant Butler who found himself standing *in loco parentis* to a fellow soldier's orphan daughter, admitting himself moved to take in the child by her plight and his wife's entreaties.[40]

Yet despite the evident potency of civilian conceptions of manhood prioritising domestic guardianship, it is worth noting the underlying significance of the army's attempt to propose an alternate model in which loyalty and duty to regiment trumped the claims of family, as General Napier had taught his sons.[41] The idea that patriarchal responsibilities were constructed and alterable, rather than set in stone in perpetuity by divine design, would take another century or more to germinate fully.[42] Yet the very idea that civilian masculine ideals *could* be altered, and *could* be set aside in the interests of military efficiency when national peril demanded such extraordinary measures, nevertheless hinted – however unwittingly and unintentionally – at the beginnings of the subversive idea that masculine identity was potentially pliable.

For those without wives and children on campaign with them, family crept into their lives in other ways. Those from military families often chose to join particular regiments because of longstanding familial or county connections and had fathers, uncles, brothers, cousins or friends in the service alongside them.[43] William Cobbett suggested that this practice enhanced the camaraderie of regiments and encouraged good behaviour from men aware that their exploits might well reach ears at home via regular networks of correspondence, or men returning home on furlough or discharge.[44] Such patterns were not simply about familial devotion or loyalty. Within higher ranks in particular, they also reflected networks of patronage, reminding us that the Georgian family was not merely a site of companionship but also one of connection.[45]

George Thomas Napier rose to the rank of general in the course of his long military career, but his memoirs acknowledge that in common with most officers, the starting point of his ascent had been his father's purchase of a commission for him. Aware that his son needed a steadying influence, Colonel Napier secured his son an initial posting in the 46th Regiment of Foot, where the commander was a close, trusted family friend, and where George's elder brother Charles was already aide-de-camp.[46] Such connections helped smooth Napier's adjustment to the service, and his memoirs recall the advantages he derived from this arrangement, including guidance, patronage, companionship and practical assistance.[47] George Napier and his brothers, William and Charles, were to cross paths many times during their various postings, not only in the performance of their military duties, but also to dine together and visit one another when sick or injured. For obvious reasons though, in wartime, human connections could represent a double-edged sword. On one particularly savage day in the Battle for Corunna 1809, Napier received news that his general, another close friend and his brother Charles had all been killed in action. He wrote,

You cannot my children conceive of the bitterness of my feelings at that moment. I had a few hours before seen the General I revered as a father carried off the field mortally wounded; I had met the bleeding, lifeless body of my friend Charles Stanhope; and now I learned that the brother I loved, who was my friend, my advisor, my constant companion, was amongst the slain, and that it was denied to me to close his dying eyes! And then the thought of my poor mother's misery! May the anguish I then suffered never be your lot.[48]

The fullness of time would reveal his brother Charles to have been taken a prisoner of war rather than killed, but the account nevertheless reveals the intense emotional highs and lows that the presence of close kin within the army could entail.[49] The filial regard for the general displayed here also hints at the way in which close regimental relationships could themselves take on a quasi-familial quality, as we will subsequently explore.

Family members and loved ones at a distance also played an important role in the lives of soldiers and sailors on foreign service. William Wheatley took solace in his separation from his beloved sweetheart, Eliza, by compiling a journal and sketchbook to share with her, and its pages movingly record his near-constant preoccupation with thoughts of her.[50] Among the many attributes praised in Major General Mackinnon's obituary, following his death in battle in 1812, was the observation that 'he seldom omitted writing to his mother at every opportunity; and has been known to pen a letter after being sixteen hours on horseback; and even under a hedge, during a march, to inform her of his welfare'.[51] Memoirs suggest that many servicemen put considerable effort into maintaining links with home, and testify to the comfort and support that could be gleaned from a regular correspondence with kin. A young officer in Lisbon in 1809, William Warre, noted his agitation whenever the mail was delayed, writing to his father,

I have been most truly vexed at not receiving your very affectionate letters of 5th July and 2nd August, annexed with my dear mother's of 10th July, till yesterday, late in the evening. The stupid clerks in the army post office sent them up to Lord Wellington's army. I have for some time been very fidgety at not hearing, and the last three packets do not bring me a line from anyone, or else they are gone to the English army while I am in Lisbon.[52]

His irritation underlines the importance he ascribed to maintaining these lines of communication, and it is clear that they represented a valuable source of comfort and an important emotional outlet. Warre used his letters to confide his fears and feelings to his family, sentiments that he confessed he was not comfortable sharing with anyone else. Meanwhile, his correspondence with his younger sister allowed him to set aside the propriety expected of an officer and indulge a more relaxed and playful side of his personality. He teased her in 1812:

> I am amused with your complaining of the noise the Parrot makes, which prevents your writing, when I am at this moment, and constantly since the siege began, serenaded by the roar of cannon and musketry of both sides. ... You must not quiz my spelling or writing, as please remember, I am writing in a tent on my bed, and that those varlets the French are making more noise than the Parrot. It really is quite impertinent of them, but they do not know that I am writing to you.[53]

Mike Roper has suggested that maintaining a connection with home was essential to the emotional survival of soldiers during the First World War, and in many cases, a similar argument can be made for the men of the earlier Great War.[54] As inconsequential as Warre's ribbing of his sister might appear, such correspondence allowed him to connect with home and maintain a sense of himself as a brother and son. In the process, it provided him with an opportunity for temporary release from the demands and pressures of his current situation, or at the very least, a safety valve to express his frustrations. The tone of his letter of May 1812 underscores this point, opening with the lines, 'I must begin in order to prepare you for the worst by telling you that this is a very stupid place, that I am very stupid, and that I have nothing to say, therefore you must receive a very stupid letter', followed by an account of his petty frustrations, boredom and an unsatisfactory hunt.[55] Family correspondence could therefore play a valuable role in maintaining a man's sense of his place in the world outside of war, and an indispensable channel for venting the pent-up aggravations of campaign life, away from the evaluating eyes of one's superiors or charges.

Although the greater wealth, leisure and literacy of the officer class more easily facilitated their regular correspondence home, the letters of men such as Private Wheeler make it plain that lower ranks also prized the maintenance of such links.[56] In Helen Watt and Anne Watkins' superb collection of letters from naval ratings, they argue that while letter writing was not universal among the lower ranks of the navy, sufficient epistles survive to demonstrate that maintaining links with family while on active service was not the sole preserve of the elite.[57]

William Cobbett noted that when an old soldier was discharged, he routinely 'took with him his knapsack full of letters into the county', along with undertakings to deliver messages on behalf of those unable to write.[58] Such accounts underline the importance ascribed to maintaining home attachments – something the government acknowledged and attempted to improve with the Postage Act of 1795, which granted soldiers and seamen concessionary postage rates.[59]

Though clearly never the primary focus of a wartime memoir, these narratives make it clear that thoughts of family and home continually intruded into military men's consciousness. Stories of parting from or reuniting with family bookend many memoirs, providing a symmetrical arc of departure, adventure and return to structure their tales. Meetings with family serve as a symbolic marker of the passage between martial and civilian worlds, and connect the narrators to the domestic realms more familiar to their readers. Return, in particular, offered authors an opportunity for reflection. In some cases, this entailed joyful musings on the pleasures of being reintegrated into the bosom of a loving family and the opportunity to enjoy the peacetime pleasures secured by war. Lieutenant Charles Crowe closed his narrative of martial service with an account of his joyful return to his parents in Lowestoft, and his speedy marriage to the sister of an old friend. He ended his tale of martial trials and travels with the words, 'we married 18 December 1818; midsummer 1822 we came to our present peaceful abode, where I trust we shall both come to a halt!!'[60] Crowe's deployment of the military 'halt' acts as a symbolic marker, signalling the end both of the book and of his migratory way of life, and setting the scene for the beginning of a more static, settled period of family life – his ultimate reward for his long, arduous march to secure peace. Closing his memoir with the embrace of familial responsibility signalled his restoration to the world of civilian masculine norms after the disruption of war, and his assumption of patriarchal headship as the apotheosis of all he had fought to defend.

Other accounts end with a more sombre reckoning with the fates of war. The relentless march of mortality continued apace while a soldier was absent following the drum, and families were not preserved in aspic. When Private Samuel Plummer returned home to share the journal he had kept of his time abroad with the 22nd Regiment of Foot, as his mother had encouraged him to do, he found both parents had died in his absence. Denied a joyful homecoming, his account ends with rather different reflections on a soldier's reintegration into civilian life and the sizeable familial cost that military service could entail. Plummer's mournful expressions of regret for the distress he had caused his parents by enlisting and leaving them alone in their old age serve as a salutary reminder of the price that had been paid to secure peace, and equally functions as advice literature, pointedly urging other restless young men to appreciate and support their parents before time ran out.[61]

Memoirs and letters also testify to men's desire to shield family from the full horrors of war and to minimise their worries. William Warre provided his mother with a jovial running commentary on his sunburn, exhaustion, accidents and sleepless nights, yet assured her that his motto remained 'Nil Desperandum'.[62] Injuries, close calls and proximity to death similarly brought family members, most especially mothers, often to mind. Warre commended himself to his parents on the eve of battle, thanking them for their love and affection and urging them not to grieve should he fall.[63] Even in extremity, fatally injured men often expended energy on urging comrades to spare their mothers the true details of their deaths and to assure them that the end had been quick and painless.[64] So, while military service clearly put some extreme challenges in the path of men's ability to perform the roles of son, husband, father and brother, the evidence of military memoirs suggests that it never entirely snuffed out the associations between familial and manly identities found in civilian life.

In addition to testifying to the stubborn endurance of literal family ties in wartime, old soldiers' memoirs also highlight the way in which the armed forces redirected and appropriated familial feeling to their own ends, presenting the regiment itself as a surrogate family. The standing orders of the 85th Light Infantry explicitly stated that 'every officer and soldier should consider his Regiment, in a great degree, as his home'.[65] The memoirs of Moyle Sherer similarly noted that, 'a regiment is ever, the best of homes to a single man'.[66]

The hierarchical structure of the military in some ways echoed that of the family. Commanding officers were depicted as paternal figures, combining authority over their men with a duty of care towards them.[67] An 1802 military dictionary advised that 'every officer should look upon himself as the father, the guardian and the protector of his men'.[68] Military guidebooks urged obedience and deference towards superior officers in a manner resonant of the advice issued to wives and children in civilian life, and with a corresponding promise of reciprocal reward, in that 'to such a soldier, every worthy officer will be a friend and a father'.[69] Memoirists echoed this language. Napier wrote of General Moore, 'it was impossible for any father to devote himself more to the welfare of his sons, than did Sir John to his officers, and no parent could be more revered and beloved than he was by us all'.[70] When Moore, the man Napier 'revered as a father', fell in battle, his grief was real and acute.[71] Meanwhile, Viscount Rowland Hill was similarly renowned for the particular devotion he showed to the welfare of those under his command, earning him the nickname 'Daddy Hill' in recognition of his 'feeling and humane disposition, and attention to their interests, that caused him to be so much beloved by the troops under his command, and gained for him the appellation of father'.[72] 'Sentiments of affection similar to those which unite the members of a family with their parent' were similarly cited as the inspiration for the funereal monument erected to honour Major General Ross by the 20th Regiment of Foot.[73] The idea that close relations with non-kin could be described in familial terms during the eighteenth century has been well documented by Naomi Tadmor.[74] What the evidence of these memoirists reveals is that such usage extended far beyond household, communal or political settings into military and naval arenas, too.

Despite frequently removing men from flesh and blood relations, then, military occupations also potentially offered men a proxy route to fulfilling the familial and patriarchal performance associated with civilian manhood.[75] The ubiquity of such paternal terminology is perhaps underscored by John Shipp's account of its rather comical usage among troops stationed at the Cape of Good Hope. In addition to referring to their own colonel as a 'father' in the standard manner, men of the 87th Regiment also christened a baboon who regularly raided their camp for food as 'Father Murphy', in recognition of his effective command over his fellow monkeys during these incursions.[76] This desire to replicate and forge surrogate familial connections is equally evident in the way some memoirists described their pleasure in being 'treated like a son of the family' when billeted in local households.[77]

Family offers the first model of community and connection that most people experience, and therefore lends itself to being used as a prism through which subsequent relationships can be mapped and understood.[78] The language of paternal authority was used within military circles as a readily understood shorthand, immediately conveying a wealth of information about the nature of relationships between commanding officers and subordinates and their reciprocal duties and responsibilities to each other. For the army, this had obvious benefits in helping to acclimatise new recruits to the hierarchical structure of the armed forces and potentially in assisting the recruitment of those eager to find a sense of belonging. This is not to suggest such bonds were in any way inauthentic or easily co-opted. William Cobbett, who was effusive about his own first-hand experiences of the familial attachments generated by regimental life, was nonetheless scornful when the government attempted to manufacture such 'family feeling' overnight between historic serving regiments and new militia units, scoffing that issuing 'scraps of dirty paper' would not achieve this end.[79]

Familial connections were further evoked in the terms 'brother soldier' and 'brother officer', which can be found repeatedly across multiple memoirs. A military dictionary defined the term 'brother soldier' as 'a term of affection which is commonly used in the British services for one who serves under the same banners and fights for the same cause with another. In more extensive signification it means any military man with respect to another'.[80] Memoirists wrote of the enduring brotherly bonds forged between soldiers through intimate acquaintance and mutual dependence, service and sacrifice.[81] As Pococke put it, 'mutual hardships made us all brothers'.[82] Such evocations drew on millennia-old ideas of military fraternal comradeship. Napier mourned a fellow officer with the admission that he had loved him 'with all a brother's affection', while Serjeant Butler was overcome by the kindness of a doctor who treated him without charge as a mark of his shared solidarity with 'an old fellow traveller and brother soldier'.[83] Naval men shared the same concept.[84] Nelson drew on Shakespearean fraternal imagery when commending his officers as 'Such a gallant set of fellows! Such a band of brothers! My heart swells at the thought of them!'[85]

As with the paternalistic language used for commanding officers, the language of fraternity harnessed and appropriated familial connection to convey the virtues and characteristics associated with the idealised family unit. The language of brotherhood conjured ideas of close kinship, loyalty and affection. The company of 'brother officers' was even suggested by one memoirist to be the best bulwark against forming more temporary, and potentially more morally and financially costly, liaisons with local women.[86] It was also used to license and render innocent experiences of intimacy and tenderness between men, dislocating them from any potential misgivings over such intense and prolonged homosocial fraternisation. Moyle Sherer drew on such imagery to draw a parallel between the intimate ministrations that soldiers might offer each other and those of blood relations. Though a soldier's sickbed might lack 'the anxious care and tender offices of a mother and the affectionate solicitude of a sister', still he argued,

> some warm-hearted friend will smooth the pillow for your feverish head; will speak to you in the manly yet feeling language of encouragement; will procure, and often prepare for you some delicacy; and, in the dark and silent hour of evening, will sit quietly by your side, consoling you by affectionate pressures of the hand, for pain and suffering, and watching anxiously that nothing may interrupt or scare your needful slumbers.[87]

Such fraternal language was a way of negotiating the potential dangers that haunted predominantly homosocial communities. Framing intimacies as an expression of familial love offered a means of legitimising and sanitising what Joanna Bourke has described as 'men's need to express the other side of masculinity, that is private and domestic'.[88] As Bourke has argued with respect to later conflicts, such encounters, though valued, were always seen as temporary and pragmatic and never posed a threat to the underlying assumption that peace would bring a return to the primacy of male/female domestic intimacies. It is probable, of course, that some of these intimacies between soldiers went beyond providing comradeship, as the work of Susan Gane indicates for an earlier period.[89] Whether out of delicacy, respect for privacy or regard for market appeal, however, this particular collection of memoirists went no further than detailing strong fraternal and platonic bonds. Rather, like Moyle Sherer, they presented a sanitised vision of brotherhood where 'no manner of life so effectually conceals from us the cheerlessness and the helplessness of celibacy, as the desultory life of a soldier'.[90]

Having literal or surrogate brothers in the service could bring cheer and comfort, but it could also bring heartache when death or reassignment intervened.[91] Equally, as in civilian familial life, proxy fraternal bonds carried the risk of turning sour. From 'incestuous criminal conversation' with a brother officer's wife while home on leave, to the actual murder of a brother Guardsman following a dispute in a public house, newspapers and pamphlets carried evidence that military fraternalism had not entirely escaped the troubled legacy of Cain and Abel.[92] Large numbers of soldiers from the 3rd Regiment of Guards attended John Hartley's execution following his conviction for killing a comrade, and he was reported to have bowed to them several times on his way to the gallows.[93] Whether he was acknowledging their solidarity in coming to witness his end or begging their pardon for his actions in slaying one of their own is unclear, but acknowledging their presence was clearly important to him, even moments away from death. The Guardsmen, in turn, equally appear to have been making a deliberate show of soldierly fellow-feeling by attending en masse, though whether for the condemned man or his victim, or both, is again hard to gauge.

For all the parallels with familial bonds though, conduct book author Thomas Gisborne was eager to remind officers not to forget the more delicate nature of *actual* civilian blood relations. He urged officers not to replicate military-style discipline at home, with the caution that

> He who has been long accustomed to the exercise of undisputed command, is in danger of expecting from his family and dependants a mechanical submission to his inclinations; and an unbounded deference to his opinions; or at least a tarnishing of the character of the master, the parent and the husband by the authoritative demeanour and peremptory tone of the officer.[94]

Rather than presenting the military man as exempt and adrift from the pivotal importance of family ascribed to civilian masculinities then, wartime memoirs are in fact testament to the stubborn persistence of family in constructions and experiences of martial masculinities. While affirming that familial separation and estrangement were not merely a trope of wartime propaganda, memoirs reveal a more multi-faceted relationship between military men, family and masculine identity. Tracing the contours of memoirists' accounts reveals soldiers variously taking wives and children on campaign, joining family members in the same regiment, deriving solace from a correspondence with home or forging proxy familial bonds with members of their regiment. That there were such different, and at times paradoxical, threads in the depiction and experience of military service, manhood and family should come as no surprise. Experiences varied enormously with age, rank, regiment, temperament, marital status and circumstance. Yet trends do emerge.

Military men undoubtedly faced bigger challenges than their civilian counterparts in performing the role of family man. Soldiers faced greater tensions in reconciling the competing calls of home and duty, greater dilemmas in balancing the desire for connection and the responsibility to shield loved ones from financial or emotional trauma, and greater vulnerabilities to the heartache of separation and loss. For some, the appropriate response to all this was to remain single; for others it was to attempt to juggle the competing claims of military and familial responsibility, or else to forge proxy relationships within the regiment; while as previously noted, some memoirists failed to mention or acknowledge family at all. Yet while multiple memoirs acknowledge the challenges that military service presented to family life, time and again they also reveal soldiers' deep investment in their status as sons, fathers, husbands, brothers and more.

All of this suggests that despite the obstacles and discouragements encountered, men's desire for attachment to real and surrogate families frequently remained too deeply ingrained to overcome. This echoes what Ferdinand Mount has called the family's status as 'the ultimate subversive organisation', i.e. one which has thwarted the state, the army, religion, ideology and all other challengers in their attempts to usurp the supremacy of familial ties and loyalties.[95] Familial identities mattered to men for a host of social, cultural, political, economic and emotional reasons, and despite the hurdles that army life put in the way of fulfilling and maintaining such identities, veterans' memoirs suggest that they remained pivotal to the soldiers' sense of self and emotional wellbeing. While wartime propaganda might have vaunted donning a red coat as *the* defining masculine trait, veterans' reminiscences and reflections suggest that soldiers nevertheless continued to regard wearing the mantle of son, father, husband and brother as equally vital and integral components of martial and manly identity.[96] The fact that the army also attempted to appropriate the lexicon of familial relationships for its own ends underscores the enduring significance and potency of the family unit within Georgian understandings of male identity, status, hierarchy and responsibility. Although soldiers' literal families could at times be a headache for the army, with order books full of injunctions against army wives hitching rides on baggage wagons or stealing food, family could also be one of the army's powerful resources and allies in terms of recruitment, morale, cohesion and order.[97] Perhaps in recognition of its limited success in attempting to supplant the primacy of familial ties, the army simultaneously sought to adopt, appropriate and re-work the language of kinship for its own ends. By casting commanders as fathers and comrades as brothers, military relationships could be constructed as deeply rooted, natural and familiar. Although such connections carried risks as well as rewards in wartime, at their best they could provide soldiers with the emotional support of a proxy home and the satisfaction of participating in a surrogate version of those familial duties so associated with manhood. Or, as Sherer so neatly put it, when he embraced his brother soldiers, he found himself 'at home'.[98]

Notes

1 'A Soldier's Departure', *Scots Magazine* 68 (September 1806), p. 695.

2 'Brighton Camp or The Girl I Left Behind', Bodleian Ballads, Harding B 11 (455); James Gillray, *John Bull's Progress* (London: 1793), BM Satires 8328. See also: John Raphael Samuel, 'The Soldier's Farewell on the Eve of Battle', Laurie and Whittle, London (1803) BM Reg No. 1872, 1109.470; 'The Soldier's Departure From His Sweetheart', Bodleian Ballads, Harding B 22 (270); Charles Dibdin, 'The Soldier's Adieu', Bodleian Ballads, Harding B 16 (252b); 'I'm Going for a Soldier, Jenny', Bodleian Ballads, Firth c. 14 (264); 'Soldier's Farewell to Manchester', Harding B 11 (2388); 'Dear Mary or Farewell to Old England', Harding B 25 (485); Jennine Hurl-Eamon, *Marriage and the British Army in the Long Eighteenth Century: 'The Girl I Left Behind Me'* (Oxford: Oxford University Press, 2014), pp. 161–8.

3 Isaac Cruikshank, after George Moutard Woodward, 'The Soldier's Farewell' (1803), BM Reg No. 1990,0303.18.

4 Margarette Lincoln, *Representing the Royal Navy: British Sea Power 1750–1815* (Aldershot: Ashgate, 2002), pp. 145–6.

5 Joanne Begiato (Bailey), 'Tears and the Manly Sailor in England, c. 1760–1860', *Journal for Maritime Research* 17:2 (2015), p. 124.

6 William Cobbett, *Cobbett's Political Register*, XVIII, July to December 1810 (London: T.C. Hansard, 1810), p. 56.

7 *The Anti Gallican or Standard of British Loyalty, Religion and Liberty* (London: Verner and Hood, Poultry and J. Asperne, 1804), p. 255.

8 'The Soldier's Wife's Dream', Bodleian Ballads, Harding B 11 (3585). See similar arguments regarding depictions of sailors' self-sacrifice in Begiato (Bailey), 'Tears and the Manly Sailor', p. 126.

9 Leo Braudy, *From Chivalry to Terrorism: War and the Changing Nature of Masculinity* (New York: Alfred A. Knopf, 2003), pp. xi, 246; Paul Higate, *Military Masculinities: Identity and the State* (London and Westport, CT: Praeger, 2003), p. xvii; Hurl-Eamon, *Marriage and the British Army*, pp. 161–8; Begiato (Bailey), 'Tears and the Manly Sailor', pp. 117–33. See also Matthew McCormack's discussion of the ways in which such ideals were used in the militia debates surrounding the Seven Years War, with the motivation of protecting family serving an even more prominent role for militia units confined to home soil – Matthew McCormack, 'The New Militia: War, Politics and Gender in 1750s Britain', *Gender & History* 19:3 (2007), p. 494.

10 Brown Bess was the nickname of the British army's standard flintlock musket. Samuel Collings, *The Recruiting Serjeant or Brown Bess sooner than Bigg Bell'd Betty* (London: John Smith, 1786), The Lewis Walpole Library, 786. 08.04.02; 'Rambling Soldier', Bodleian Ballads, Harding B 15 (252a). See also 'The Jolly Soldier', Bodleian Ballads, Harding B 17 (150a) which also celebrates the profligate life of a soldier while 'other fools keep wives'.

11 Begiato (Bailey), 'Tears and the Manly Sailor', p. 127.

12 Hurl-Eamon, *Marriage and the British Army*, p. 8.

13 *Ibid.*, p. 34.

14 *Ibid.*, pp. 59–60.

15 An Officer of the Eighty-First Regiment, *Letters from Flushing* (London: Richard Phillips, 1809), pp. 2–3. Sir John Moore was an influential General in the British army. He died in the Battle of Corunna, 1809.

16 Cobbett, *Cobbett's Political Register*, XVIII, p. 62.

17 John Stevenson, 'The London Crimp Riots of 1794', *International Review of Social History*, xvi (1971), p. 45, 57.

18 Family distress was cited by the 1797 mutineers as their chief grievance, see *The Scots Magazine* 59, May 1797 (Edinburgh: James Watson and Company, 1797), p. 357.

19 Mrs Rowson, *Charlotte Temple: A Tale of Truth* (New Haven, CT: I. Cook and Co, 1813), p. 41.

20 David M. Rosen, *Child Soldiers in the Western Imagination: From Patriots to Victims* (New Brunswick, NJ and London: Rutgers University Press, 2015), pp. 39–43. Rosen notes (p. 60) that by 1877, recruits to the British army under the age of sixteen required parental consent, while those between the ages of sixteen and twenty-one remained free to enlist without it. For debates about the motives behind the 1753 Marriage Act see Rebecca Probert, *Marriage Law and Practice in the Long Eighteenth Century: A Reassessment* (Cambridge: Cambridge University Press, 2009), pp. 210–11, 224–6.

21 John Paul Esq. Barrister at Law, *The Parish Officer's Complete Guide* (London: W. Richardson and G.G.J. and J. Robinson, 1793), p. 93.

22 W.C.E. Napier (ed.), *Passages in the Early Military Career of General Sir George T. Napier* (Cambridge: Cambridge University Press, 2011), [First published 1884], pp. 6–7. George Thomas Napier (1784–1855), brother of more famous commanders Charles and William, wrote his memoirs for his sons, who published them in 1884.

23 Napier (ed.), *Passages*, p. 234.

24 Charles James, *A New and Enlarged Military Dictionary* (London: T. Egerton, 1802), p. xlv.

25 Thomas Cooper, *A Reply to Mr Burke's Invective Against Mr Cooper and Mr Watt in the House of Commons* (London: J. Johnson, 1792), p. 59. By contrast, Matthew McCormack has shown that a man's ability to remain on hand to defend his home and family was one of the potential selling points of the militia service in the debates surrounding the Seven Years War. See McCormack, 'The New Militia', p. 494.

26 John Tosh, *A Man's Place: Masculinity and the Middle-Class Home in Victorian England* (New Haven, CT and London: Yale University Press, 1999); Karen Harvey, *The Little Republic: Masculinity and Domestic*

Authority in Eighteenth-Century Britain (Oxford: Oxford University Press, 2012); Matthew McCormack, *The Independent Man: Citizenship and Gender Politics in Georgian England* (Manchester: Manchester University Press, 2005); Joanne Bailey, *Parenting in England 1760–1830* (Oxford: Oxford University Press, 2012).

27 Tosh, *A Man's Place*, p. 1.

28 Kennedy, *Narratives of the Revolutionary and Napoleonic Wars*, pp. 17–23, p. 32.

29 Robert Brown, *An Impartial Journal of a Detachment from the Brigade of Foot Guards* (London: John Stockdale, 1795), for example, stuck strictly to political and military topics.

30 Ramsey, *The Military Memoir and Romantic Literary Culture, 1780–1835*, pp. 176–7.

31 See for example: Thomas Pococke, *Journal of a Soldier of the 71st or Glasgow Regiment from 1806 to 1815* (Edinburgh: William and Charles Tait, 1819), p. 132.

32 Hurl-Eamon, *Marriage and the British Army*, p. 217.

33 Robert Butler, *Narrative of the Life and Travels of Serjeant Butler* (Edinburgh: David Brown, 1823), pp. 31–3.

34 Lieut. Col. Gurwood, *The General Orders of Field Marshal The Duke of Wellington K.G. in Portugal, Spain and France 1809–1814* (London: W. Clowes and Son, 1832), p. 322.

35 Sergeant D. [David] Robertson, *The Journal of Sergeant D. Robertson, late 92nd Foot* (Perth: J. Fisher, 1842), p. 107.

36 *Ibid.*, p. 61.

37 An Officer, *Letters from Flushing*, p. 19.

38 Moyle Sherer, *Recollections of the Peninsula*, 4th ed. (London: Longman, Hurst, Rees, Orme, Brown and Green, 1825), p. 261. See also John Green, *The Vicissitudes of a Soldier's Life or a Series of Occurrences from 1806 to 1815* (Louth: J. and J. Jackson, 1827), p. 26.

39 Christopher Hibbert, *Reflections of Rifleman Harris as Told to Henry Curling* (London: L. Cooper, 1970), p. 20. See also George Farmer (ed. G. R. Gleig), *The Light Dragoon*, 2 vols (London: Henry Colburn, 1844), vol. I, chapter 3 on his discomfort encountering distressed wives.

40 Butler, *Narrative of the Life and Travels of Serjeant Butler*, p. 182.

41 Napier (ed.), *Passages*, pp. 6–7.

42 John Tosh, *Manliness and Masculinities in Nineteenth-Century Britain* (Harlow: Pearson Education, 2005), pp. 41–4.

43 Myerly, *British Military Spectacle*, p. 57.

44 William Cobbett, *Cobbett's Weekly Political Register*, XXXII (London: William Jackson, 1817), pp. 144–5.

45 J.E. Cookson, *The British Armed Nation 1793–1815* (Oxford: Clarendon Press, 1997), p. 131; Naomi Tadmor, *Family and Friends*

in *Eighteenth-Century England: Household, Kinship and Patronage* (Cambridge: Cambridge University Press, 2004), pp. 131–3.

46 Napier (ed.), *Passages*, p. 9. See also H. M. Chichester, 'Napier, Sir George Thomas (1784–1855), Army Officer and Colonial Governor', *Oxford Dictionary of National Biography*, 2004–09–23 (Oxford: Oxford University Press, 2018). Available at: http://www.oxforddnb.com.uos.idm.oclc.org/view/10.1093/ref:odnb/9780198614128.001.0001/odnb-9780198614128-e-19754 (accessed 28 October 2018).

47 Napier (ed.), *Passages*, pp. 107–8, 129, 196.

48 *Ibid.*, p. 73.

49 *Ibid.*, p. 93.

50 C. Hibbert (ed.), *The Wheatley Diary: A Journal and Sketchbook kept during the Peninsular War and Waterloo Campaign* (Moreton in Marsh: Windrush Press, 1997), p. 86.

51 *The Soldier's Companion or Martial Recorder* (London: Edward Cook, 1824), vol. I, p. 472.

52 William Warre, *Letters from the Peninsula, 1808–1812* (London: John Murray, 1909), pp. 81–2.

53 *Ibid.*, pp. 235–6.

54 Michael Roper, *The Secret Battle: Emotional Survival in the Great War* (Manchester: Manchester University Press, 2009), p. 72.

55 Warre, *Letters from the Peninsula 1808–1812*, p. 252.

56 Roper, *The Secret Battle*, p. 72.

57 Helen Watt and Anne Watkins (eds), *Letters of Seamen in the Wars with France, 1793–1815* (Woodbridge: Boydell Press, 2016), p. 9.

58 Cobbett, *Cobbett's Weekly Political Register*, XXXII, p. 1145.

59 Postage Act 1795, 35 Geo III, c. 53.

60 Gareth Glover (ed.), *An Eloquent Soldier: The Peninsular War Journals of Lieutenant Charles Crowe of the Inniskillings 1812–1814* (Barnsley: Frontline Books, Pen and Sword, 2011), p. 319.

61 Samuel Plummer (ed. John Rules), *The Journal of Samuel Plummer: A Private in the 22nd Regiment of Foot* (London: T. Cordeux, 1821), pp. 3, 83.

62 Warre, *Letters from the Peninsula 1808–1812*, p. 113.

63 *Ibid.*, p. 47.

64 Pococke, *Journal of a Soldier of the 71st or Glasgow Regiment from 1806 to 1815*, p. 132.

65 *Standing Orders and Regulations for the 85th Light Infantry* (London: T. Egerton, 1813), p. 99.

66 Sherer, *Recollections*, p. 261.

67 The same sentiments can be found during the Crimean War, see Holly Furneaux, *Military Men of Feeling: Emotion, Touch and Masculinity in the Crimean War* (Oxford: Oxford University Press, 2016), p. 121.

68 James, *A New and Enlarged Military Dictionary*, – FELLOW.

69 Richard Phillips, *Public Characters of 1799–1800* (London: J. Adlard, 1807), p. 299.

70 Napier (ed.), *Passages*, pp. 6–7.

71 *Ibid.*, p. 73.

72 Joseph Donaldson, *The Eventful Life of a Soldier during the Late War in Portugal, Spain and France by a Soldier of the Infantry* (Edinburgh: W. Tait, 1827), p. 331.

73 *The Soldier's Companion or Martial Recorder*, vol. I, p. 433.

74 Tadmor, *Family and Friends*, p. 272.

75 For a discussion of ways that childless men could fulfil the patriarchal role see Helen Berry and Elizabeth Foyster, 'Childless Men in Early Modern England', in Helen Berry and Elizabeth Foyster (eds), *The Family in Early Modern England* (Cambridge: Cambridge University Press, 2007), pp. 182–3.

76 John Shipp, *Memoirs of the Extraordinary Military Career of John Shipp, Late a Lieutenant in His Majesty's 87th Regiment, Written by Himself* (New York: J.J. Harper, 1829), vol. I, p. 66 and 47.

77 Pococke, *Journal*, p. 139.

78 There are multiple theories on the way the family operates as a site of primary socialisation, but few dispute the importance of the familial unit in primary social development, see Eleanor E. Maccoby, 'Historical Overview of Socialization Theory and Research', in Joan E. Grusec and Paul David Hastings (eds), *Handbook of Socialization: Theory and Research* (New York and London: The Guildford Press, 2015), pp. 3–27.

79 *Cobbett's Weekly Political Register*, vol. VII, January to June 1805, p. 251.

80 James, *A New and Enlarged Military Dictionary*, – SOLDIER BROTHER.

81 An Officer, *Letters from Flushing*, p. 2; William Cobbett, *Cobbett's Weekly Political Register*, XVIII, No. 2, July 1810, pp. 39–41.

82 Pococke, *Journal*, p. 186.

83 Napier (ed.), *Passages*, p. 107; Butler, *Narrative*, p. 298.

84 Isaac Land, *War, Nationalism and the British Sailor 1750–1850* (Basingstoke: Palgrave, 2009), p. 51.

85 Robert Southey, *The Life of Nelson*, 2nd ed. (London: John Murray, 1814), vol. II, pp. 211–12.

86 Shipp, *Memoirs*, p. 147.

87 Sherer, *Recollections*, pp. 103–4. Similar descriptions of soldiers tenderly nursing comrades can also found in other conflicts see e.g. Furneaux, *Military Men of Feeling*, pp. 188–9; Joanna Bourke, *Dismembering the Male: Men's Bodies, Britain and the Great War* (London: Reaktion Books, 1996), pp. 133–5; Roper, *The Secret Battle*, p. 284.

88 Bourke, *Dismembering the Male*, p. 126.

89 S. Gane, 'Common soldiers, Same-sex Love and Religion in the Early Eighteenth-Century British Army', *Gender & History*, Special Issue: Sex,

gender and the sacred: reconfiguring religion in gender history, 25:3 (November 2013), pp. 640–2.

90 Sherer, *Recollections*, p. 261.

91 Jonathan Leach, *Rough Sketches of the Life of an Old Soldier* (London: Longman, Rees, Orme, Brown and Green, 1831), p. 406.

92 Denniss vs Denniss, *Hampshire Telegraph and Sussex Chronicle*, 17 December 1804, p. 3; *The Trial of John Hartley (A Private in Third Regt of Guards) for the Wilful Murder of George Scott* (London: J. Davenport, 1800), p. 2.

93 *Hampshire Chronicle*, 3 March 1800, p. 2.

94 Thomas Gisborne, *An Enquiry into the Duties of Men* (London: T. Cadell and W. Davies, 1813), vol. I, p. 325.

95 Ferdinand Mount, *The Subversive Family: An Alternative History of Love and Marriage* (New York: Macmillan, 1982), p. 1.

96 For the potency of the red coat see Louise Carter, 'Scarlet Fever: Women's Enthusiasm for Men in Uniform 1780–1815', in Kevin Linch and Matthew McCormack (eds), *Britain's Soldiers: Rethinking War and Society, 1715–1815* (Liverpool: Liverpool University Press, 2014), p. 157.

97 Gurwood, *The General Orders*, p. 322.

98 Sherer, *Recollections*, p. 261.

3

Recalling the comforts of home: bachelor soldiers' narratives of nostalgia and the re-creation of the domestic interior

Helen Metcalfe

The domestic conditions that British bachelor soldiers encountered during the Napoleonic Wars presented at times a fragmentary and nomadic experience, creating something of a 'frontier of domesticity'.[1] Whilst on campaign, a combination of physical and emotional comforts were provided by soldiers' access to some semblance of shelter and domestic material goods, but such provisions often varied according to availability and social status. Billeting was a common practice in the towns and villages that the military passed through, with the quality of accommodation regularly determined by rank - which found commanding officers often quartered in the best house in the street. Army life could potentially disrupt traditional understandings of masculine ideals and provided an environment within which bachelors could invert conventional models of eighteenth-century masculinity: models that located domesticity firmly within the confines of marriage. The predominance of studies exploring normative masculinity has meant that men in their bachelorhood (in the military and civilian spheres) are frequently separated not only from histories of the home, but also from histories of the family and of the emotions. As this chapter will demonstrate, however, despite often inhospitable environments and lack of suitable housing, bachelor soldiers' life-writings show that they sought to remodel or classify the novel space of their temporary quarters in ways that achieved a sense of comfort from familiar domestic material objects and the rituals they associated with home.

The role of domestic material culture has come under close scrutiny recently. Important research by historians of the emotions, especially, has revealed that 'placing material culture at the centre of human emotional experience in the past offers new ways of exploring how objects have produced, regulated, symbolised, and represented human emotions through history'.[2] According to this research, emotions are embodied through interaction with material objects, but these objects can also embody something lost – whether the absence be a person, place or event. These 'transitional objects' serve as 'modes of communication, or memory cues', suggests Leora Auslander, through which identities can be imaginatively expressed and located in space and time.[3] Auslander's findings are of particular note here given that, as we shall see, military bachelors' access to, and interactions with, domestic material objects served several purposes whilst they were stationed abroad. During periods of separation and instability, the role of materiality, domesticity and comfort coalesced for several men discussed in this chapter, particularly when underpinned by feelings of nostalgia.

The main object of these men's nostalgia centred on the home, through which they derived their sense of comfort. Just as nostalgia can disrupt traditional understandings of temporal and spatial boundaries, memories and objects associated with the home, notes Auslander, have the capacity to 'connect the present with the past' because they provide the 'key to remembrance'.[4] Evaluating bachelors' response to these memories, and the objects these memories were tied to, reveals how feelings of nostalgia helped bridge the material, spatial and emotional experiences of men seeking comfort when displaced by war. Indeed, as Joanne Begiato maintains, as a 'repository of domestic objects', the home is 'often invoked in memories [and is] a particularly significant emotional object' in and of itself.[5] The benefits of domestic comforts were extolled by the officer John Mills (1789–1871) in a letter to his older sister, Charlotte, as he regretted the absence of them: 'the advice I would give anybody coming out to this country would be precisely the reverse of what was given me – I would say, bring out as many little comforts as you can'.[6] Mills's observations underscore how memories of familiar and comfortable domestic spaces were an important feature of some men's experiences of the physical separation from their homes and families, and enabled them to negotiate the barren landscapes and bleak living conditions of campaign life.[7] Moreover, as will be shown in this chapter, the achievement of comfort within the domestic environment was linked specifically to these men's assemblage of objects that evoked and provided a sense of not only physical but also emotional comfort.

As a result of changing practices in domestic material culture, ideas about what constituted comfort during the eighteenth century were increasingly associated with standards of satisfaction that were shaped by the redefinition of the value and subsequent role of domestic material goods.[8] John E. Crowley suggests that as the century progressed, contemporary commentators changed from using 'comfort' in a moral, emotional and spiritual sense to giving the term 'a new physical emphasis', attributable to a developing consumer-driven society.[9] This chapter explores the physical dimensions of comfort as expressions of bachelors' nostalgia for home, but it also examines how domestic material objects – and the memories, rituals and relationships associated with them – became 'mediators in emotional transactions' for men separated from their homes and families due to war.[10] By interrogating bachelors' interactions with, and their nostalgic recollections of, particular domestic material goods in their pursuit of emotional comfort, this chapter also seeks to recover the 'afterlife' of objects in their ability to construct what Begiato has defined as 'emotional landscapes'.[11] Eighteenth-century men have been reintroduced into the domestic realm through their engagement with domestic material culture in the respective works of Karen Harvey and Amanda Vickery. Harvey and Vickery have each demonstrated how household management and economy were crucial to manly independence and patriarchal authority, whilst newly married men's enthusiasm for soft furnishings, well-proportioned rooms and delicate tea-ware was indicative of their maturity.[12] Revealing that bachelor soldiers shared similar inclinations to married men about their living conditions and their commitment to domesticity suggests that martial and civilian masculine identities were not as disparate as is often supposed.

That the continuities between martial and civilian identities are an important feature of understanding the experience of soldiering is borne out by increasing numbers of scholarly works that turn to the individual narratives of men at war.[13] Catriona Kennedy has, for instance, demonstrated that the model of the polite gentleman 'still provided an element of continuity between military codes of conduct and the civilian world of polite society' for officers during the Napoleonic Wars.[14] In common with Kennedy, Kevin Linch and Matthew McCormack have assessed contemporary codes of politeness and gentlemanly honour to suggest that the hierarchical structures in the military reflected the more general 'widespread acceptance of communal values and hierarchical order in British society'.[15] The personal narratives of soldiers have been noted as a particularly rich source for 'revealing some of the tensions and continuities between civilian and martial gendered identities'.[16] It is precisely these tensions and continuities in the lives of military bachelors, as they rebuilt their domestic identities in unfamiliar settings, which make them invaluable historical subjects of analysis. This is because in the culture and confines of war, bachelor soldiers negotiated between different and often competing models of masculine conduct which up until now - like in the case of their civilian counterparts - have not been associated with the sphere of domesticity.

Considering the wealth of work on war, masculinity and national identity in this period, until recently there was a dearth of scholarship about how men's masculinity was 'formed and performed' in the military context, highlights Kennedy.[17] Traditional histories of campaign narratives, biographies of 'great men' and accounts of military strategy are now being replaced by social and cultural histories of soldiers' experiences of warfare throughout the ranks, all of which seek to overturn the narrative of a universal experience of soldiering.[18] However, it has also been claimed that as an organisation, the military 'values, promotes, and engages in practices that are the inverse of those valued, promoted, and practiced in the civilian sphere'.[19] But such a sweeping generalisation is highly problematic in that it fails to consider how the ideals shaping the social and cultural practices of wider society might come to be reflected within military culture itself.

Moreover, whilst several studies have turned their attention to the lived experiences of soldiers, historical assessments of bachelor soldiers have continued to reinforce the image of an immoral and unified bachelor soldier culture, thus overlooking the variables present in martial masculinities. Indeed, it is commonplace for scholars to reinforce contemporary characterisations of the British soldier by maintaining that young and single military men sought freedom from domestic constraints and commitment-free sexual gratification.[20] Jennine Hurl-Eamon's recent study on marriage in the British army, for instance, divides military masculinities between men that married and those that did not. Hurl-Eamon positions military masculinities on a 'spectrum' that finds bachelor soldiers 'eagerly embracing a licentious lifestyle', whilst men at the 'opposite end of the spectrum continued to desire a more monogamous domesticity'.[21] Hurl-Eamon's conclusions explicitly remove bachelor soldiers from narratives of domestic contentment simply because of their marital status. Yet, interrogating military bachelors' engagement with the rituals and atmosphere, values and attachments that they associated with the home reveals little evidence of a 'flight from domesticity' for these men, whose domesticity was not only achievable in a homosocial environment but was also not dependent on marriage.[22]

This chapter adds to the scholarship identifying continuities between martial and civilian masculinities, and argues that bachelor soldiers' memories of home centred on notions of physical and emotional comfort that were tied to the materiality of home, domesticity and familial attachments. The chapter examines military bachelors' interactions with this material culture and, in so doing, 'anchors' their emotions to the physical world around them.[23] It reveals how bachelors' achievement of domestic comfort through material and emotional means enabled these men to cope with the dislocations of war.[24] Through a close qualitative analysis of several bachelors' letters, journals and memoirs, this chapter examines how a common culture of nostalgia helped shape the ways in which bachelor soldiers shared and transferred notions of their emotional and physical domestic comfort between Britain and the continent, crossing not only geographical but also imagined boundaries. Moreover, it explores how bachelor soldiers 'returned' home by re-creating familiar domestic interiors that were underpinned by their nostalgic recollections of home comforts and loving familial relationships.

The focus of bachelors' nostalgia (home and family) combined traces of individual memories and imagination that recalled a 'past world that is the more potent for being absent or vanished'.[25] Nostalgia is often identified in either temporal or spatial terms, through which the longing for a distant lost past is seen as distinctive from a longing for home.[26] Yet, nostalgia has also been identified as a 'multi-layered structure' that has the capacity to 'meld time with space' due to an individual's desire to recapture not only memories of a lost time, but also the space within which these memories might be housed.[27] This overlap is emphasised in military bachelors' interactions with the emotional material objects that enabled them to 'return' home, as it was not only the location that generated their feelings of nostalgia, but also memories of past events and relationships, for example, and recollections of childhood or adolescence. In this way, bachelors expressed their feelings of nostalgia by accessing both temporal and spatial sources of emotional comfort, which they ameliorated through the memories they associated with home. According to Nadia Atia and Jeremy Davies, feelings of nostalgia during periods of unsettling change serve as a 'negotiation between continuity and discontinuity: it [nostalgia] insists on the bond between our present selves and a certain fragment of the past, but also on the force of our separation from what we have lost'.[28] Thus the concept of nostalgia offers a lens through which to recover and evaluate traces of bachelor soldiers' emotions which, when expressed through their recollections of home and family as well as their interactions with domestic material objects, sheds new light on single men's experiences of, and responses to, wartime separation and isolation during the Napoleonic Wars.[29]

The chapter is divided into three sections, starting with a brief discussion about the origins and changing use of 'nostalgia'. To bring bachelors' nostalgic recollections of home and their feelings of isolation into sharp relief, it then contextualises the privations of military life by introducing the bleak living conditions that bachelor soldiers faced on campaign in Portugal during the Peninsular War. The third section interrogates the lived experience of bachelor soldiers, whose nostalgic recollections of the comforts of home served as a vital emotional coping mechanism within a profession characterised by an unpredictable lifestyle and continuous domestic upheaval. Underpinning this section is a close qualitative analysis of these men's interactions with the material culture of home. Recent research by Stephanie Downes, Sally Holloway and Sarah Randles has shown how objects act as 'markers of emotional affiliation to a group, or a people, a family or an individual'.[30] It is within this context that this section explores the ways in which bachelors pursued domesticity and achieved comfort through their engagement with emotional material objects which, when combined with nostalgia, also helped communicate and consolidate familial bonds. Taking note of Begiato's call for a broad definition of materiality, one that 'equips us to explore the textual complexity of emotional material culture', this section extends the materiality of the home to recover traces of men's interactions with a variety of emotional objects that include the tangible, sensory, concealed and transitory.[31]

Nostalgia: a brief history

The potentially fatal repercussions of enforced separation informed the basis of Johannes Hofer's 1688 medical thesis on the pathology and prevention of *heimweh* (homesickness), a condition Hofer termed 'nostalgia'.[32] The first of its kind to identify homesickness as a clinical disease, Hofer's thesis established a new diagnosis – using a combination of the Greek words *nostos* (homecoming) and *algos* (pain or longing) – that resulted in widespread recognition in Western medicine of the status of nostalgia as both an emotional and medical disorder.[33] Emotional expressions of nostalgia were, and continue to be, heightened during periods of crisis and disruption, within which idealised notions of home and community provide a sense of stability and reassurance.[34]

The classification of nostalgia as a disease was twofold. As Thomas Dodman argues, Hofer's diagnosis did not proceed from a medical revolution but was, instead, informed by an increase in cases of nostalgia (underpinned by Hoffer's observation of patients' symptoms) which were seen to be a response to the instability and anxieties brought about by prolonged periods of social and political unrest, economic stagnation, population decline and warfare during the seventeenth century.[35]

In the centuries following Hofer's classification, discussions of nostalgia were not restricted to medical tracts, and included the reflections of novelists and artists, as well as the experiences of men in the military.[36] The clinical form of nostalgia is commonly associated with Napoleon's men, and is in part due to the particularly harsh conditions faced by French soldiers following the introduction of the *levée en masse* (mass national conscription) in 1793. Research by Lisa O'Sullivan and Dodman, for example, charts the changing meaning of nostalgia in France from the Revolutionary and Napoleonic Wars to the end of the nineteenth century. Recognised as a serious disease, cases of nostalgia were seen by French physicians as a reaction against displacement, alongside which, according to O'Sullivan, a diagnosis of nostalgia served 'as an avenue for medical practitioners to explore questions of patriotism, masculinity, citizenship and national identity'.[37] Nevertheless, attitudes towards nostalgia were evolving during this period, with medical diagnoses of nostalgia in the military becoming much less prevalent. Indeed, the concept of nostalgia has been explored by Tamara Wagner and Linda Austin, both of whom have shown that discussions of nostalgia were already well established in the novels of sensibility and Romantic literature of the eighteenth and early nineteenth centuries.[38]

Over the course of the nineteenth century, the medical definition of nostalgia coexisted alongside understandings of nostalgia that took shape in an increasingly wide variety of print culture, including not only novels but also autobiographies, memoirs and poetry. Thus, by the end of the nineteenth century, it was more common to consider feelings of nostalgia to be the result of an emotional experience and/or upheaval rather than a medical condition.[39] Whilst literary analyses of nostalgia have uncovered a variety of cultural responses to homesickness during the period under discussion, in historical assessments of nostalgia there remains an emphasis on the French military that has resulted in British military experiences being overlooked. By exploring the life-writings of British bachelor soldiers within this transitional period for what they reveal about single men's experiences of displacement and feelings of isolation, this chapter thus contributes to current historical assessments of the concept of nostalgia more broadly.

Seeking comfort

The lack of familiar home comforts prompted soldiers to give some thought to their living conditions whilst on campaign, and often led to a careful re-evaluation of ways to achieve comfort. Makeshift furniture, for example, was manufactured by soldiers in their pursuit of domestic comfort, as were extra clothing and personal items, all of which offered additional relief in the absence of soft furnishings. The commissioned officer Edward Charles Cocks (1786–1812), for instance, recounted to his sister that '[m]y table is rickety, one leg being too short ... The said table is covered by a blanket instead of green baize, which identical blanket, in the course of half an hour with the addition of a bear skin and a cloak will form my bed, bedstead and bedding'.[40] Yet for Cocks, shared material wants also instilled a sense of solidarity amongst the men:

> Privations are scarcely felt when experienced in common with so many others; your little comforts, and even absolute necessities, acquire a double relish from the consciousness that next day you may want them and perhaps a reflection that the day before you were without them.[41]

Thus, when driven by physical needs specifically, Cocks's particular circumstances show how the fulfilment and rewards of comfort could be realised through 'knowing what amenities one really needed, having them, and desiring no more'.[42] Crowley has documented the shifting meanings of comfort in eighteenth-century Anglo-American culture. According to Crowley, commentators 'reconceptualised values, redesigned material environments and urged the relearning of behaviour'. Early eighteenth-century political economists had made distinctions between luxury and necessity, but comfort increasingly became the middle ground, whether orientated around material culture or personal contentment in terms of the domestic arena.[43] As shown by Cocks's observations, soldiers' access to comfort was severely limited when on campaign, particularly in terms of fulfilling their basic physical needs. Thus men sought out creative solutions in the objects around them to resolve the shortage of resources.

Billets or tents furnished bachelor soldiers with some physical comfort, but it was also found in material objects and personal items that in some way improved their domestic surroundings. The desire for and, frequently, shortage of comfort for plebeian and elite military men alike was often acknowledged in their letters and journals. In a cold and snowy December in 1811, and in want of new clothing, Private William Wheeler (b. 1785) was quartered in a house in Portugal that was 'neither built for comfort or convenience', with no chimney: 'the place is so full of smoke you cannot see across the room, and as the fires are made of wood this is very disagreeable to the eyes'.[44] Little over a month later, however, having received 'new clothing and a supply of necessaries we were made comparatively comfortable', Wheeler recalled.[45] Wheeler went on to give a detailed account of how his material gains provided physical comfort back at his quarters:

> In one corner of the room I have collected a quantity of dry fern, this forms my bed ... every night the contents of my haversack is transferred to my knapsack. This forms my pillow ... the haversack is then converted into a night cap. Being stripped, my legs are thrust into the sleeves of an old watch coat, carefully tied at the cuffs to keep out the cold. The other part of the coat wrapped around my body ... for under blanket and sheet. Next my trousers are drawn on my legs over the sleeves of the coat, my red jacket has the distinguished place of covering my seat of honour and lastly my blankets cover all. In this manner I have slept as comfortable as a prince.[46]

So whilst camp life could be particularly harsh, with little or no shelter and poor access to basic provisions, Wheeler's testimony reveals how men's personal physical comfort could still be achieved – but that it greatly depended on items that facilitated comfort within the domestic space.

Domestic comforts played a vital role in the experience of some soldiers' physical and psychological separation from home and provided a welcome source of relief which, when combined with the social role of nostalgia, helped consolidate the bonds between men on campaign, but also between the men and their families at home.[47] The non-commissioned lieutenant Charles Crowe (1785–1855) took great pains to include in his journals the meticulous details of the billet he came to share with a fellow soldier and friend, Edward Close. Whilst quartered in a house in Lisbon, Crowe's inventory of the 'snug and comfortable' arrangements included the 'steps into a small garden behind the house, a stump bedstead and a straw palliasse ... a large chest, and a small round table'.[48] Two months before, this garden had been recorded in his journal as a space that 'we enjoyed the comfort of'; it was 'a regular retreat at the corner of the garden. The walk to it was planted on one side with orange trees, on the other with lemons each bearing half ripe fruit, and an abundance of blossoms'.[49] Mills offered a similar propensity to detail in his journal, alongside several letters to both his mother and his sister, through which he recorded a series of thoughts on the domestic comforts available to him in Portugal: 'Mildmay, Crofton and myself, are in a most excellent house', remarked Mills to his mother, 'I only hope we may remain here. We have each our separate bedroom, and one sitting room. To me it is a palace and the only comfortable house I have been in yet.' Mills's domestic arrangements at this point as a shared venture seemed to have suited him, and in a letter to his sister, Elizabeth, Mills observed, 'I assure you we live uncommonly well ... we have got our little flock of sheep, and get on famously.'[50] Drawing from experiences of home and family life, Mills's letters suggest that reflecting on material comforts also offered reassurance to his mother and sister by communicating shared notions of familiar domestic scenes. Yet, in recording the seemingly banal minutiae of domestic comforts the men here frequently return to, these bachelor soldiers were looking not only for mutual material comforts but for the familiar emotional, spatial and sociable qualities that they associated with their individual domestic lives at home.

Soldiers' changing fortunes and their subsequent level of comfort were also commented on by the memoirist and commissioned ensign Moyle Sherer (1789–1869) who, having found himself in a 'humble dwelling', noted that '[c]omfort is ever comparative; and, after all, if his wishes be moderate, how little does a man require. Sick, hungry, and exhausted, I wanted shelter, food, and repose'.[51] In common with Sherer, Crowe wrote reflectively on what campaign life offered in terms of domestic arrangements: 'However indifferent our quarters, we are all pleased to remain here, as the weather all night and this day has been most tremendous; rain, hail, snow, lightening, thunder and wind have made us fully enjoy the comforts of a house and good fire.'[52] Extracts such as these reinforce the reader's sense of the resilience, resourcefulness and fortitude of the soldier, and were a generic commonplace of the early nineteenth-century military memoirs that located soldiers as symbols of stoicism. They are, however, also indicative of how depictions of the soldier as a suffering traveller 'sought to bridge the imaginative distance between the British nation and its wars by establishing the reader's sympathies with the hardships of the nation's soldiers'.[53] The observations of Cocks and Wheeler, Sherer, Mills and Crowe also suggest that when faced with frequently stark conditions, the physical displacement brought about by war resulted in men's access to domestic comforts being viewed in a comparative light. The simple comforts came to be prized and, perhaps unsurprisingly, such deprivation and lack of domestic comforts engendered an appreciation for basic material needs that these men sought to overcome.

Experiencing comfort

Examining the life-writings of military men not only testifies to the various types of comfort that bachelor soldiers drew from whilst they were stationed abroad; they also often reveal the source of this comfort. In seeking to alleviate their feelings of isolations and loneliness, bachelor soldiers' nostalgic recollections emphasised the comforts of home. The following analysis of bachelor soldiers' letters and journals thus supplements the findings of Begiato and Harvey, each of whom has argued that to fully expose men's engagement with the domestic arena, the different dimensions of home need to be recognised. Begiato's research, for example, uncovers the 'emergence of the tender, protective, virtuous father'; a figure who came to be associated with a model of masculinity that 'secured future generations and a healthy society and nation'.[54] This model of masculinity, observes Begiato, originated in the culture of sensibility – where emotions, feelings and sensitivity were celebrated – and provided an 'ideological framework shaping manhood and fatherhood' that located men at the heart of the emotional dynamics of family life.[55] In common with Begiato, Harvey has identified how men were implicated in, even necessary to, the constitution of home 'whether constituted by authority, things, emotional or representational richness'.[56] The evidence presented here suggests the importance of these factors not only in the households of Britain but also for bachelor soldiers during their time on the continent.

Bachelor soldiers sought out the familiar features and ceremonies of the domestic environment to continually reaffirm their emotional attachments to the home and uphold prevailing notions of domesticity. In September 1809, having recently reached Europe for the ill-fated Walcheren campaign, William Thornton Keep (1791–1883) wrote in great detail to his mother on 'my present abode [to which] I have been removed from the lofty garret of a Chandler's Shop ... I have one neat little room, the bed very good, and floor covered with a fine Indian matting'. Thornton Keep reassured his mother thus: 'I live according to your prescription and as well as circumstances will permit, and on that subject I must let you know that I often wish you was my guest! for I could furnish you with a more delicate morning repast than you can get in London itself.'[57] Thornton Keep's assurances to his mother reflect the emotional functions of nostalgia for military men located far from home, and emphasise the ways in which the achievement of comfort served as a physical manifestation of feelings of nostalgia. Thornton Keep sought both solace and escape in his recollections of home, many of which were underpinned by his close relationship with his mother. Maintaining familial networks through the exchange of letters was far from unusual for men in the military and was a vital coping mechanism that underscores how men's 'tactile engagement' with their correspondence provided the means through which 'interpersonal emotions and networks' were both established and sustained.[58] Moreover, as Michael Roper also notes, soldiers' 'points of reference were domestic, concerning love and care, matters to which mothers, in particular, would be attuned'.[59] Such periods of separation saw increased feelings of anxiety between parents and their children, husbands and their wives. It was common for families to bolster their relationships through a language of domesticity, observes Begiato, that located the hearth and home at the centre of a 'shared value or familial culture'; thus correspondence between distant relatives often extended the 'warm glow' of the fireside by emphasising qualities associated with the home such as comfort, contentment, security and familial affection.[60] Indeed, Thornton Keep's letters demonstrate that his emotional and physical domestic comfort were intimately linked to the 'familiar material culture' of home, through which the social role of nostalgia consolidated familial bonds and provided a source of comfort for unmarried military men remote from their origins.[61]

Thornton Keep frequently returned to the domestic scene in his letters to his mother, using nostalgia as an expression of his longing for home, but also as a device by which to reduce the physical and emotional distance between himself and his family. Through nostalgic recollections of the rituals of home, Thornton Keep imagined his mother relocated before him when, as if in conversation, the letter continued:

My breakfast table is spread, [he noted] and if incredulous let me convince you of it. That bright polished brass urn contains a delicious cocoa, mixed with a milk as rich as cream. Those buns with plums are excellent in themselves, but the butter intended for them is an incomparable treat! … The china cups are of the finest fabrication and worthy to receive what may be so readily conveyed into them by turning that little spicket of the urn. Could you taste, you would confess how much my cocoa surpasses your best Bohea … Certain I am you would be proud to give your most fashionable friends such a treat. My dinners I cannot boast of … As we are over our cocoa I must gossip a little, and make you the confidante of our Regimental secrets, by touching on what we call parish news![62]

Thornton Keep's detailed description of the domestic scene, combined with the physical act of 'turning that little spicket of the urn', suggests that Thornton Keep's use of nostalgia was a way in which to re-orientate himself within a home setting to preserve a sense of belonging. This scene is also evidence of the materiality of the home and demonstrates Thornton Keep's interactions with domestic material objects of an ephemeral, sensory and tangible kind. Imbued with the sounds of hospitality, tempting flavours and the heady scent of chocolate, Thornton Keep used these objects to call the breakfast table to mind in a way that communicated his sense of absence from home. Yet, traces of interactions such as this also reveal the ways in which objects can produce and transmit feelings through a combination of handling, memory and description, even though the objects themselves do not emote.[63] Moreover, whilst the letter depicts the domestic scene in full, with the inclusion of Thornton Keep's desire to 'gossip a little', that his mother could not taste the contents of the urn serves here as an emotional reminder of the physical distance that remained between them.

By re-creating a familiar domestic scene, Thornton Keep's letter reveals how men invested their 'memories with a strong sense of the present'.[64] As Roper points out, confiding in those at home through the exchange of letters resulted in expressions of nostalgia that, whilst implicit, enabled soldiers to conduct their relationships from a distance.[65] The letters of this young soldier are filled with domestic particulars concerning 'snug fireplaces', 'tea parties' and 'pretty curtains for the bedstead'. By December 1813, Thornton Keep confided once more to his mother that 'I am in a most comfortable billet [and] I assure you we are very snug … and getting quite domestic.'[66] Thornton Keep's nostalgic re-creations of idealised social gatherings suggest that the rituals of home and memories of familial bonds could provide a significant source of comfort for men posted far from home. But Thornton Keep's various references to fashionable domestic material goods, soft furnishings and his access to a hearth are also evidence of this bachelor soldier's fulfilment of a subjective experience of home-making in that they offered the means for him to get 'quite domestic'.

Expressions of nostalgia and recollections of familial relationships often served to mitigate the loss of domestic comforts that men associated with home, with responses to spatial displacement reflecting what Dodman has described as the 'estrangement from one's self, from the time and place from one's former life'.[67] Written with the benefit of hindsight, perhaps, Sherer, for example, nostalgically lamented his loss of domestic comforts whilst on campaign:

> Oh! We hardly suspect, until the dreadful moment of separation arrives, how dear is the roof, be it of marble or of straw, which has, from infancy, been our home. Good God! How much does that one word convey! The chamber in which we have slept, the festive board round which we have so often assembled, the garden in which we have strayed, the many little holidays of the heart we have enjoyed there.[68]

Sherer's sentimental narrative draws from notions of home as a refuge, at the centre of which, in common with Thornton Keep's reflections, reside affective familial ties and sociable domestic scenes laden with sound and emotion. The same narrative of loss is evident in a letter from Mills to his sister when he reminded her that 'in this uncomfortable gipsy life it is pleasant to think of the scenes that are past, and our friends though at a distance, are associated with past events. The greatest luxury here is to have all your little comforts about you – any place is then tolerable and you are perfectly independent'.[69] A month later and we find Mills drinking a toast from the continent, after receiving some good news from his brother-in-law (although the cause of the celebrations remained undisclosed): 'I thought of you often in the course of yesterday and drank your health in bumper.'[70]

Bachelor soldiers' nostalgic recollections of home could be experienced in both visceral and tangible ways, and were often reinforced through the exchange of correspondence. Thornton Keep, for instance, found the trivial details of daily life at home a valuable source of comfort, reassurance and relief. Thornton Keep's letters continued to underscore the important role that correspondence played for bachelors in the maintenance of their family relationships during wartime separations. 'Pray let me know in your next how my Aunt is', he appealed to his mother:

and do not shorten your letters by omission of what you may mistake to be uninteresting to me. I have read those I am in possession of until I know them by heart. I husband them too well as I can, only allowing myself a perusal now and then.[71]

Due to the physical fragility of the letters, Thornton Keep chose to regulate how often they were read. The stories and sentiments enclosed within these letters held such meaning for Thornton Keep that he committed the lines to memory, lest the letters be lost or destroyed. That he disclosed this act of commemoration in response to his mother's words underlines the fact that, for Thornton Keep, these letters (whether in their material form or not) reinforced his emotional connection with his family back home. In concealing these 'emotional artefacts', Thornton Keep remained aware of them 'at the level of knowledge rather than handling or seeing them', demonstrating how nostalgia served as a bridge between memory, emotion and materiality.[72] Moreover, Thornton Keep's longing to be reminded of life at home also reflects how feelings of nostalgia exhibit 'ways of inhabiting many places at once', thus locating the concept of nostalgia within memory and imagination whilst 'giving shape and meaning to longing'.[73] The emotional value bachelor soldiers placed on exchanging letters with their family members was crucial to their ability to cope on campaign, but just as Thornton Keep treasured the words on the pages of his letters, bachelor soldiers also attached importance to the receipt and exchange of material objects.

Items that families sent to soldiers could be of a personal or useful kind and reminded them of home, whilst the presents sent from soldiers to their near relatives were often chosen as items to be remembered by. Hurl-Eamon has shown that couples separated by war in this period forged strong romantic bonds by means of exchanging letters, mementos and love tokens. Defined as 'emblems of affection', these items served as tender reflections of devotion between married couples and sweethearts.[74] But the exchange of material objects and affectionate letters at times of separation was not restricted to husbands and wives, and the items can be seen as 'instigators of nostalgia' in that they served to remind both sender and recipient of the world that was missed.[75] Major George Simmons (1785–1858), for instance, spent a great deal of time looking for 'baubles', 'trinkets' and 'curiosities' to send home, including a silver snuff box and topaz ring for his mother, and a 'parcel for Ann with my picture', alongside a gold chain, a topaz cross and a pair of earrings. The parcel for his sister Ann, in particular, was to 'occasionally serve as to remind her that her brother George, though far away, still loves and adores her'.[76] Simmons's sentiments reveal how objects such as these were also used to reinforce familial connections by locating recipient and sender within networks of relationships, because these objects (and the emotions associated with them) evoked or stood in for the absent person or place.[77] Simmons's use of terms such as 'baubles' and 'trinkets' is particularly telling, though, as they indicate that his selections were made on emotional and personal grounds rather than for monetary or practical reasons, and distinguishes these souvenirs from spoils or plunder.[78]

Bachelors' letters show that the receipt of material objects from home was an important coping mechanism, which preserved men's affective ties with their families and helped them maintain a physical connection to the domestic environment and family life they had left behind in England. In the same way that Simmons secured items to send to his family back home, letters from home were frequently supplemented with gifts, useful goods and keepsakes, all of which can be considered as an 'additional layer of communication' between family members.[79] Accordingly, objects included within letters and packages revealed the practical needs of the recipient but also allude to the affections, sincerity and concern of the sender. Thornton Keep, for instance, wrote to thank his mother following his receipt of a 'very affectionate letter with its valuable enclosures safe', confiding in her that he was 'deeply moved by the maternal love it assured me you feel for me'.[80] Despite Thornton Keep's letter not recording what these items were, the value he placed on these 'enclosures' – which he attributed to his mother's love – confirm that physical distance was often mediated through the receipt of material goods from home. Indeed, when separated from their loved ones, boxes from home, observes Roper, 'offered the most direct contact short of going on leave' and contributed to soldiers' emotional survival.[81]

A letter from Thornton Keep to his brother, Samuel, recounting his pleasure after having received a sketch of their familial home, further emphasises the importance of emotional comfort for bachelor soldiers. Indeed, this visual token offered Thornton Keep the means by which to better inform his nostalgic recollections of home: 'I imagine you are becoming impatient', Thornton Keep observed to Samuel, 'to get a few lines from me in acknowledgment of your long and entertaining letter [...] with the neat little drawing it contained, so precious an object for me to look at, when I think of home, and peruse its contents'. This neat little drawing and its accompanying letters, he assured his brother, remained 'in a breast pocket of my red jacket [...] where they be snug enough and next to my heart'.[82] In the same way that Thornton Keep preserved the letters from his mother by regulating how often they were read, he placed explicit emotional value on Samuel's sketch and letters by disclosing that these objects were kept next to his heart. Acknowledging this act suggests that Thornton Keep bound his memories of home to Samuel's sketch and letters, but also to his emotional and physical body.[83] By September of the same year, having survived the Battle of Maya (where the British were outnumbered by the French, with only 7,000 men to France's 21,000), Thornton Keep wrote to Samuel once more of the lasting comfort derived from his picture. 'The dear pretty cottage at home gives me pleasure to look at it, and fancy portrays all you have described to me in your last letter, and our little sisters running about in the garden there.'[84] Samuel's drawing reproduced a familiar and secure, if long lost, scene for Thornton Keep, from which he drew solace and contentment in what Furneaux describes as the creation of a 'visual familiarity' through 'shared scenes'.[85] Moreover, despite their physical separation, Thornton Keep's emotional response to Samuel's memento demonstrates that the sketch sustained Thornton Keep's nostalgic recollections of his domestic and familial life at home (at a time when he perhaps needed it most) by reinforcing his emotional memories through material means.

This chapter has looked beyond the traditional campaign narratives, biographical accounts and studies of troop mobilisation of the British military during the Napoleonic Wars to uncover how the experience of soldiering could at times mirror the domestic realms of home. Domestic martial masculinity helped bachelors validate their manhood and single status under terms other than marriage, and the home was a crucial site from which to create continuities between martial and civilian society. The presence of multiple martial masculinities has now been acknowledged by several scholars, despite the fact that some assessments of military men's experiences still take for granted that martial masculinity was underpinned by a rejection of all things domestic. The letters and journals of these men provided support and comfort during the wars, but they also reveal that in unfamiliar environments these bachelor soldiers sought out familiar material and domestic culture to regain a sense of place and belonging within the emotional landscape of the home. These soldiers' life-writings testify to the enthusiasm with which they pursued and re-assembled their physical and emotional domestic comforts whilst housed in derelict buildings or billets, despite the absence of basic provisions. In terms of types of comfort and individual material needs, the soldiers' testimony has also emphasised the importance of pursuing both emotional and physical comforts for men to attain stability, contentment and reassurance. Moreover, even when stripped of basic necessities, such as warmth and shelter, these bachelor soldiers shared in distinctive ways a common culture of comfort, centred on nostalgic recollections of home and the re-creation of the domestic interior in the houses they occupied and in the pages of their personal narratives.

Notes

1   Martin Francis, 'The Domestication of the Male? Recent Research on Nineteenth-and Twentieth-Century British Masculinity', *The Historical Journal* 45:3 (2002), pp. 637–52 (p. 643).

2   Stephanie Downes, Sally Holloway and Sarah Randles, 'A Feeling for Things, Past and Present', in Stephanie Downes *et al.* (eds), *Feeling Things: Objects and Emotions through History* (Oxford: Oxford University Press, 2018), pp. 8–26 (p. 8). See also, Alice Dolan and Sally Holloway, 'Emotional Textiles: An Introduction', *Textile* 14:2 (2016), pp. 152–9.

3   Leora Auslander, 'Beyond Words', *The American Historical Review* 110:4 (2005), pp. 1015–45 (pp. 1016, 1019).

4   *Ibid.*, pp. 1020–1.

5   Joanne Begiato, 'Moving Objects: Emotional Transformation, Tangibility, and Time Travel', in Downes *et al.* (eds), *Feeling Things: Objects and Emotions through History* (Oxford: Oxford University Press, 2018), pp. 229–42 (p. 241).

6   20 August 1811, John Mills to Charlotte Mills (ed. Ian Fletcher), *For King and Country: The Letters and Diaries of John Mills, Coldstream Guards, 1811–1814* (Staplehurst: Spellmount, 1995), p. 58.

7   Ramsey, *The Military Memoir and Romantic Literary Culture, 1780–1835*, p. 184.

8   John E. Crowley, *The Invention of Comfort: Sensibilities and Design in Early Modern Britain and Early America* (Baltimore, MD: Johns Hopkins University Press, 2010), pp. x, 142.

9   John E. Crowley, 'The Sensibility of Comfort', *The American Historical Review* 104:3 (1999), pp. 749–82 (p. 751). For assessments highlighting the continuing importance of spiritual comfort see Hannah Barker, 'Soul, Purse and Family: Middling and Lower-Class Masculinity in Eighteenth-Century Manchester', *Social History* 33:1 (2008), pp. 12–35; Jeremy Gregory, '*Homo Religiosus*: Masculinity and Religion in the Long Eighteenth Century', in Tim Hitchcock and Michèle Cohen (eds), *English Masculinities, 1660–1800* (London: Longman, 1999), pp. 85–110.

10   Downes, Holloway and Randles, 'A Feeling for Things', p. 9.
11   Begiato, 'Moving Objects', pp. 232, 238.
12   Harvey, *The Little Republic*, especially chapters 3, 4, 5; Amanda Vickery, *Behind Closed Doors: At Home in Georgian England* (London: Yale University Press, 2009), chapter 3.
13   See Linch and McCormack (eds), *Britain's Soldiers*; Kennedy and McCormack (eds), *Soldiering in Britain and Ireland, 1750–1850*; Kevin Linch and Matthew McCormack, 'Defining Soldiers: Britain's Military, c. 1740–1815', *War in History* 20:144 (2013), pp. 144–59.
14   Catriona Kennedy, 'John Bull into Battle: Military Masculinity and the British Army Officer during the Napoleonic Wars', in Karen Hagemann *et al.* (eds), *Gender, War and Politics: Transatlantic Perspectives, 1775–1830* (Houndmills: Palgrave Macmillan, 2010), pp. 127–47 (p. 139).
15   Linch and McCormack, 'Defining Soldiers', p. 147.
16   Kennedy, *Narratives of the Revolutionary and Napoleonic Wars*, p. 5. See also, Hurl-Eamon, *Marriage and the British Army in the Long Eighteenth Century*; Ramsey, *The Military Memoir*.
17   Kennedy, *Narratives of the Revolutionary and Napoleonic Wars*, p. 5. Notable exceptions are McCormack, *The Independent Man*; Kevin Linch, *Britain and Wellington's Army: Recruitment, Society and Tradition, 1807–1815* (Houndmills: Palgrave Macmillan, 2011).
18   See, Furneaux, *Military Men of Feeling*; Begiato (Bailey), 'Tears and the Manly Sailor', pp. 117–33; Alan Forrest *et al.* (eds), *Soldiers, Citizens and Civilians: Experiences and Perceptions of the Revolutionary and Napoleonic Wars 1790–1820* (Houndmills: Palgrave Macmillan, 2009); Erica Charters *et al.* (eds), *Civilians and War in Europe, 1618–1815* (Liverpool: Liverpool University Press, 2012); Stephanie Downes *et al.* (eds), *Emotions and War: Medieval to Romantic Literature* (Houndmills: Palgrave Macmillan, 2015); 'Passions of War: Gender, Sexuality and Conflict in the Long Eighteenth Century', special issue *Journal for Eighteenth-Century Studies*, December 2018.
19   Marcia Kovitz, 'The Roots of Military Masculinity', in Paul R. Higate (ed.), *Military Masculinities: Identity and the State* (Westport, CT: Praeger, 2003), pp. 1–25 (p. 9).
20   Stephen Conway, *War, State, and Society in Mid-Eighteenth Century Britain and Ireland* (Oxford: Oxford University Press, 2007), p. 117; John Tosh, 'Home and Away: The Flight from Domesticity in Late-Nineteenth-Century England Re-visited', *Gender & History* 27:3 (2015), pp. 561–75 (pp. 570, 571).
21   Hurl-Eamon, *Marriage and the British Army*, p. 217.
22   For the 'flight from domesticity' thesis see Tosh, *A Man's Place*; Tosh, 'Home and Away'.
23   Downes, Holloway and Randles, 'A Feeling for Things', p. 10.

24 Thomas Dodman's recent book on French soldiers' experiences makes a similar argument but focuses, instead, on examples of melancholy homesickness. See, Thomas Dodman, *What Nostalgia Was: War, Empire and the Time of a Deadly Emotion* (London: University of Chicago Press, 2018), pp. 10, 122. See also, Michael Roper, 'Nostalgia as an Emotional Experience in the Great War', *The Historical Journal* 54:2 (2011), pp. 421–51; Roper, *The Secret Battle*.

25 Edward S. Casey, 'The World of Nostalgia', *Man and World* 20:4 (1987), pp. 361–84 (pp. 378–9).

26 Christobal Silva, 'Nostalgia and the Good Life', *The Eighteenth Century* 55:1 (2014), pp. 123–8 (p. 124). Svetlana Boym breaks down these distinctions further by categorising the two types of nostalgia as either 'reflective' or 'restorative'. See Svetlana Boym, *The Future of Nostalgia* (New York: Basic Books, 2001), pp. xiii, 41, 44, 49; Dodman, *What Nostalgia Was*, pp. 122, 123.

27 Casey, 'The World of Nostalgia', pp. 361, 379; Susannah Radstone, 'Nostalgia, Home-Comings and Departures', *Memory Studies* 3:3 (2010), pp. 187–91 (p. 188). Dodman, *What Nostalgia Was*, p. 193.

28 Nadia Atia and Jeremy Davies, 'Nostalgia and the Shapes of History', *Memory Studies* 3:3 (2010), pp. 181–6 (p. 184).

29 For the complexities and challenges historians face retrieving emotions from the past, see Susan Matt and Peter Stearns (eds), *Doing Emotions History* (Urbana: University of Illinois Press, 2014); Rob Boddice, *The History of Emotions* (Manchester: Manchester University Press, 2018); Barbara Rosenwein, 'Problems and Methods in the History of Emotions', *Passions in Context* 1:1 (2010), pp. 1–32.

30 Downes, Holloway and Randles, 'A Feeling for Things', p. 16.

31 Begiato, 'Moving Objects', pp. 233, 235.

32 Johannes Hofer, *Dissertatio medica de nostalgia, oder Heimwehe* (Basel: Jacob Bertsch, 1688). Hofer observed how the condition affected soldiers, students, peasants and domestic servants, in particular.

33 Dodman, *What Nostalgia Was*, pp. 3, 17; Jean Starobinski, 'The Idea of Nostalgia', *Diogenes* 14:54 (1966), pp. 81–103 (p. 95); Kevin Goodman, '"Uncertain Diseases": Nostalgia, Pathologies of Motions, Practices of Reading', *Studies in Romanticism* 49:2 (2010), pp. 197–227 (p. 199). For an analysis of eighteenth-century British medical tracts on nostalgia see Philip Shaw, 'Longing for Home: Robert Hamilton, Nostalgia and the Emotional Life of the Eighteenth-Century Soldier', *Journal for Eighteenth-Century Studies* 39:1 (2016), pp. 25–40.

34 For assessments of emotional expressions of nostalgia in the twenty-first century, see Elena Oliete-Aldea, 'Fear and Nostalgia in Times of Crisis: The Paradoxes of Globalisation in Oliver Stone's *Money Never Sleeps* (2010)', *Culture Unbound: Journal of Current Cultural Research* 4:2

(2012), pp. 347–66; Janelle L. Wilson, *Nostalgia: Sanctuary of Meaning* (Lewisburg: Bucknell University Press, 2005), pp. 21–9; Stuart Elliott, 'Warm and Fuzzy Makes a Comeback', *New York Times* [online] 6 April 2009. Available at: www.nytimes.com/2009/04/07/business/media/07a dco.html (accessed 23 October 2017).

35 Dodman, *What Nostalgia Was*, pp. 30, 39; Goodman, '"Uncertain Diseases"', p. 206.

36 See Camilla Cassidy, 'Nostalgia or *das Heimweh*: Homesickness and the Press-Ganged Soldier in *Sylvia's Lovers* (1863)', *Journal of Victorian Culture* 22:4 (2017), pp. 482–502; Peter Mandler, 'Against "Englishness": English Culture and the Limits to Rural Nostalgia, 1850–1940', *Transactions of the Royal Historical Society* 7 (1997), pp. 155–75; Natasha Eaton, 'Nostalgia for the Exotic: Creating an Imperial Art in London, 1750–1793', *Eighteenth-Century Studies* 39:2 (2006), pp. 227–50; Ysanne Holt, 'Nature and Nostalgia: Philip Wilson Steer and Edwardian Landscapes', *Oxford Art Journal* 19:2 (1996), pp. 28–45; Roper, 'Nostalgia as an Emotional Experience'; Shaw, *Suffering and Sentiment*; Furneaux, *Military Men of Feeling*; Kelby Rose, 'Nostalgia and Imagination in Nineteenth-Century Sea Shanties', *The Mariner's Mirror* 98:2 (2013), pp. 147–60.

37 Lisa O'Sullivan, 'The Time and Place of Nostalgia: Re-Situating a French Disease', *Journal of the History of Medicine and Allied Sciences* 67:4 (2012), pp. 626–49 (pp. 629, 635); Dodman, *What Nostalgia Was*. See also, Michael Roth, 'Dying of the Past: Medical Studies of Nostalgia in Nineteenth-Century France', *History and Memory* 3:1 (1991), pp. 5–29; George Rosen, 'Nostalgia: A "Forgotten" Psychological Disorder', *Psychological Medicine* 5 (1975), pp. 340–54.

38 Tamara Wagner, *Longing: Narratives of Nostalgia in the British Novel, 1740–1890* (Lewisburg, PA: Bucknell University Press, 2004); Linda Austin, *Nostalgia in Transition, 1780–1917* (Charlottesville, VA: University of Virginia Press, 2007).

39 Dodman, *What Nostalgia Was*, pp. 125–8; Wagner, *Longing*; Austin, *Nostalgia in Transition*.

40 27 September 1812, Charles Edward Cocks to Margaret Maria Cocks (ed. Julia Page), *Intelligence Officer in the Peninsula War: Letters and Diaries of Major the Hon. Edward Charles Cocks, 1786–1812* (Tunbridge Wells: Spellmount, 1986), p. 198.

41 18 October 1809, Cocks to James, *Ibid.*, p. 40.

42 Crowley, 'The Sensibility of Comfort', p. 767.

43 *Ibid.*, pp. 751, 760.

44 28 December 1811, William Wheeler (ed. B. H. Liddell Hart), *The Letters of Private Wheeler, 1809–1828* (Moreton-in-Marsh, Gloucestershire: Windrush Press, 1997), p. 71.

45 30 January 1812, *Ibid.*, p. 74.

46 30 January 1812, *Ibid.*, p. 74.

47 Roper, 'Nostalgia as an Emotional Experience', p. 440.

48 4 January 1813, Charles Crowe (ed. Gareth Glover), *An Eloquent Soldier: The Peninsular War Journals of Lieutenant Charles Crowe of the Inniskillings 1812–1814* (Barnsley: Frontline, 2011), pp. 38, 39.

49 24 November 1812, *Ibid.*, p. 20.

50 2 October 1811, Mills to his mother; 8 October 1811, Mills to his sister Elizabeth, *For King and Country*, pp. 74, 77.

51 Moyle Sherer, *Recollections of the Peninsular* [London, 1823] (Staplehurst: Spellmount, 1996), p. 77.

52 3 March 1814, Crowe, *An Eloquent Soldier*, pp. 235, 236.

53 Ramsey, *The Military Memoir*, pp. 17, 26.

54 Joanne Begiato (Bailey), '"A Very Sensible Man": Imagining Fatherhood in England c, 1750–1830', *History* 95:319 (2010), pp. 267–92 (p. 287). See also, Joanne Begiato (Bailey), *Parenting in England, 1760–1830: Emotion, Identity, and Generation* (Oxford: Oxford University Press, 2015).

55 Begiato, '"A Very Sensible Man"', pp. 271, 275, 290.

56 Karen Harvey, 'Men Making Home: Masculinity and Domesticity in Eighteenth-Century Britain', *Gender and History* 21:3 (2009), pp. 520–40 (pp. 528–9).

57 18 September 1809, William Thornton Keep to his mother (ed. Ian Fletcher), *In the Service of the King: The Letters of William Thornton Keep at Home, at Walcheren, and in the Peninsular 1808–1814* (Staplehurst: Spellmount, 1997), pp. 62, 63.

58 Begiato, 'Moving Objects', p. 237.

59 Roper, 'Nostalgia as an Emotional Experience', pp. 445, 449. See also, Begiato (Bailey), *Parenting in England*, p. 223.

60 *Ibid.*, pp. 195, 196. As Begiato also notes, the trope of domesticity was part of a much longer tradition within which the family home was considered to be a safe haven, see *Parenting in England*, pp. 193–4.

61 Crowley, 'The Sensibility of Comfort', p. 760; Roper, 'Nostalgia as an Emotional Experience', p. 440; Casey, 'The World of Nostalgia', p. 363.

62 18 September 1809: Thornton Keep to his mother (from Flushing), *In the Service of the King*, p. 63.

63 Downes, Holloway and Randles, 'A Feeling for Things', p. 11; Begiato, 'Moving Objects', pp. 235, 263. See also, Mark M. Smith, *Sensory History* (Oxford: Berg, 2007); Carolyn Purnell, *The Sensational Past: How the Enlightenment Changed the Way We Used Our Senses* (London: W. W. Norton & Company, 2017).

64 Roper, 'Nostalgia as an Emotional Experience', p. 440.

65 *Ibid.*, p. 432.

66 18 September 1809: Thornton Keep to his mother, 12 August 1812: Thornton Keep to his brother Samuel Thornton Keep, 20 September

1812: Thornton Keep to Samuel, 28 December 1813: Thornton Keep to his mother, *In the Service of the King*, pp. 63, 84, 96, 190.

67   Dodman, *What Nostalgia Was*, p. 123.

68   Sherer, *Recollections of the Peninsular*, p. 119.

69   20 August 1811, Mills to Charlotte Mills, *For King and Country*, p. 58.

70   3 September 1811, Mills to Harry, *Ibid.*, p. 65.

71   18 September 1809, Thornton Keep to his mother, *In the Service of the King*, p. 64.

72   Begiato, 'Moving Objects', p. 235.

73   Boym, *The Future of Nostalgia*, pp. xviii, 41; Casey, 'The World of Nostalgia', p. 367; Starobinski, 'The Idea of Nostalgia', p. 89.

74   Hurl-Eamon, *Marriage and the British Army*, p. 175. See also, Sally Holloway, 'Love Objects', *The History of Emotions Blog* [online] 20 July 2011. Available at: https://emotionsblog.history.qmul.ac.uk/2011/07/lo ve-objects/ (accessed 23 October 2017).

75   Casey, 'The World of Nostalgia', p. 363.

76   16 January 1811; 12 December 1812, George Simmons to his parents (ed. Willoughby Verner), *A British Rifle Man* [London, 1899] (Uckfield: The Naval & Military Press, 2002), pp. 131, 132, 133, 266.

77   Downes, Holloway and Randles, 'A Feeling for Things', p. 16.

78   Furneaux, *Military Men of Feeling*, p. 167. For literature on emotional objects outside of military studies see, Juliet Ash, 'Memory and Objects', in Pat Kirkham (ed.), *The Gendered Object* (Manchester: Manchester University Press, 1996), pp. 219–24; Matt Houlbrook, 'Hidden Objects and Untold Histories', *Modern British Studies Birmingham Blog* [online] 12 May 2016. Available at: https://mbsbham.wordpress.com/2016/05/12/hidd en-objects/ (accessed 23 October 2017); John Styles, *Threads of Feeling: The London Foundling Hospital's Textile Tokens, 1740–1770* (London: The Foundling Museum, 2010); John Styles, 'Objects of Emotion: The London Foundling Hospital Tokens, 1741–60', in Anne Gerritsen and Georgio Riello (eds), *Writing Material Culture History* (London: Bloomsbury, 2015), pp. 165–71; Sarah Tarlow, 'The Archaeology of Emotion and Affect', *Annual Review of Anthropology* 41 (2012), pp. 169–85; Gerhard Jaritz (ed.), *Emotions and Material Culture* (Wien: Verlag, 2003); Anna Moran and Sorcha O'Brien (eds), *Love Objects: Emotions, Design and Material Culture* (London: Bloomsbury, 2014); https://emotionalobjects.wordpress.com/ (accessed 23 October 2017); Sally Holloway, 'Romantic Love in Words and Objects during Courtship and Adultery, c. 1730–1830' (Royal Holloway, University of London, Unpublished PhD Thesis, 2013).

79   Furneaux, *Military Men of Feeling*, p. 149.

80   30 August 1812, Thornton Keep to his mother, *In the Service of the King*, p. 89.

81   Roper, *The Secret Battle*, pp. 10, 11.

82   27 March 1813, Thornton Keep to Samuel, *In the Service of the King*, p. 131.
83   For the evolution of theories around the heart as an emotional, mechanical and/or symbolic organ see Fay Bound Alberti, *Matters of the Heart: History, Medicine and Emotion* (Oxford: Oxford University Press, 2010).
84   17 September 1813, Thornton Keep to Samuel, *In the Service of the King*, p. 171.
85   Furneaux, *Military Men of Feeling*, p. 149.

4

Charles Incledon: a singing sailor on the Georgian stage

Anna Maria Barry

Cornish tenor Charles Incledon (1763–1826) was a prominent figure in Britain during the Napoleonic Wars, entertaining patriotic crowds with popular naval ballads. Unlike other nationalistic singers of the period, however, he did not merely masquerade in a sailor's costume on stage – Incledon was an authentic sailor. He had served in the Royal Navy during the American Revolutionary Wars, and took every opportunity to make the public aware of his naval service. But despite his fame and popularity, Incledon was an especially problematic figure. His complex masculinity was the crux of this problem. Although he presented himself as a brave and respectable British Tar to enhance his performance of manliness in the civilian world, responses to the tenor reveal that this was not always straightforward. Many imagined Incledon in a manner that aligned with an alternative naval archetype – the rough and ready sailor with a penchant for women and grog. Incledon certainly lived up to this reputation too, as his rakish behaviour was widely reported in the press. The singer therefore embodied two different models of naval masculinity, and commentators were quick to point out the disjunction between them. Incledon's identity was complicated yet further by his status as a singer. In nineteenth-century Britain, music (and singing in particular) was seen as a feminine and foreign profession.[1] It was therefore at odds with the concept of respectable British masculinity. In Incledon's case, these prejudices were compounded by his love of ostentation - a trait more associated with frivolous Italian opera stars than manly English sailors. These ideas about music, gender and nationality coloured the tenor's reception, and he was frequently lampooned by those who found his complicated identity comedic. These responses reveal that the singer's personality, his profession and even his appearance fell far short of conforming to the ideal image of naval manliness that he sought to project. Incledon's masculinity was therefore intriguingly multi-faceted and contradictory. He was at once a brave British Tar and a ridiculous Regency rake – a patriotic ballad singer, but also an effeminate showman.

Linda Colley has argued that the wars against France in this period formed the context in which the concept of Britishness was forged. She contends that British identity was defined against the idea of the 'other': a Protestant, rational and masculine British identity formed in opposition to the French, who were imagined as Catholic, fickle and effeminate.[2] Scholars have subsequently challenged Colley's formation of 'the other', arguing that the picture was, in reality, far more nuanced.[3] Nevertheless, it remains true that this period was one of intense patriotism. Incledon's nationalistic musical performances, then, were both responding to and reflecting this political and social context. However, he was also helping to forge this context. In his work on popular Napoleonic song, Oskar Cox Jensen has argued that 'songs were employed actively to construct and contest identity and opinion, by writers, publishers, singers, and buyers'.[4] As a popular public figure whose musical performances and compositions reached substantial audiences, Incledon played a role in creating and disseminating the nationalistic British identity that Colley has identified in this period.

Scholars including Susan Valladares and Gillian Russell have demonstrated that the Georgian theatre was an intensely political space where the Revolutionary and Napoleonic Wars were represented, reflected and responded to.[5] However, the role of music in Britain during this era has received relatively little attention – though this is rapidly changing. In 2006, a co-authored section on music and politics in *Resisting Napoleon* considered the potential of this field, arguing that music 'played a crucial, but thus far little discussed role' in the 'struggle for the loyalty of the British public'.[6] Since then, much work has sought to fill this gap. Aside from the aforementioned work of Cox Jensen, Isaac Land has offered an illuminating consideration of the way in which popular ballads had an impact on perceptions of the navy.[7] Joanne Begiato has also examined a range of sea songs, exploring their representations of the sailor as a man of feeling.[8] The role of individual performers is being explored too; influential singer-songwriter Charles Dibdin, best remembered for his patriotic sea songs, is the subject of a recent edited collection.[9] I have written elsewhere about the important relationship that British opera singers forged with the navy during the nineteenth century.[10] The tenor John Braham, for example, turned himself into a 'poster boy' for patriotic naval pride during the Napoleonic Wars, thus mediating his problematic identity as a Jewish singer of continental opera. However, unlike Braham and other patriotic singers of the day, Charles Incledon had actually served in the navy. This adds a unique dimension to his career, as the tenor was widely seen as an authentic sailor rather than a singer who had just pulled on a pair of slops. Despite this existing work, scholarship that deals with the relationship between music and the navy more broadly is still lacking. In the introduction to their pioneering volume *Music and the British Military in the Long Nineteenth Century*, Trevor Herbert and Helen Barlow note that 'a book of this type about the music of the navy has yet to be written.'[11]

This chapter represents the first dedicated scholarly examination of Incledon's career.[12] Although it is essentially a case study of one quite atypical singer, it serves as a lens through which to interrogate the relationships between music, masculinity and the navy in late Georgian Britain. The chapter will begin by exploring Incledon's self-representation as a sailor-singer. We will see that this identity was constructed through a multimedia effort that incorporated song, performance, stage scenery, costume, iconography and life-writing. The chapter will then move on to consider the reception of this identity, exploring how audiences and critics responded to Incledon in a manner that revealed much about contemporary understandings of naval masculinity.

Incledon the sailor

One of the most important mediums through which Incledon constructed his identity as a sailor was biography. In the late Georgian period, performers were frequently profiled in newspapers, theatrical periodicals and biographical dictionaries. Charles Incledon was no exception, and versions of his biography were shared widely. It was through this medium that audiences became aware he was an authentic sailor. No contemporary account of Incledon's career was complete without reference to his time in the navy. Typically, profiles of the tenor began by describing his naval service, before explaining that his experiences at sea led him to the stage.[13] By far the most interesting is a lengthy biography of Incledon that appeared in the *Theatrical Inquisitor* in 1817.[14] This was 'detailed from a statement, in [Incledon's] own hand-writing, drawn up with all the rough energy of a vigorous mind, and meriting the most implicit reliance'.[15] It is unclear how much Incledon's own statement was edited or embellished; though it is recounted in the third person, it is possible that the singer wrote it in this way. Most suggestive of the authenticity of this profile, however, is the fact that it had originally been scheduled to appear in the October 1816 edition of the *Inquisitor*. Over the next ten months, the editor repeatedly apologised for the delay in producing this, reporting that there had been difficulties in acquiring reliable sources for the biography.[16] This suggests that its veracity was of utmost importance. Indeed, specific factual information contained within the profile is well supported by archival sources, as we shall see. Due to the combination of these factors, we might see Incledon's profile in the *Theatrical Inquisitor* as semi-autobiographical – it is the closest the tenor ever came to writing a memoir. Because of this, it is the source that offers us the best insight into how he wished to present himself.

Incledon's account of his life foregrounds his naval career in a heavily romanticised manner. His journey to sea, he suggests, was a preordained fate. To emphasise this, he shares an incident that occurred when he was a young singer at Exeter Cathedral. He explains that Commodore Walshingham of the *Thunderer* happened to overhear him singing in a church yard, and decided to take him back to his ship to entertain its officers. Incledon spent three days on board the *Thunderer*, docked at Torbay, so impressing his audience that Walshingham proposed to take the young singer to sea. Although the boy was keen to go, his mother forbade him. This, the singer explains, was fortunate, as 'Commodore Walshingham, and his whole crew, foundered soon after in the West Indies, when the *Thunderer* went down in a dreadful hurricane.'[17] This anecdote is related in both a sentimental and sensational manner; from the coincidence of Incledon being overheard singing 'a beautiful air' on a 'fine summer evening', to his narrow escape from shipwreck – he even employs quotations from *The Tempest* to further dramatise this latter event.[18] Whilst it may be tempting to view this anecdote as a factually precarious myth-making exercise, it is borne out by archival sources. The Master's logs of the *Thunderer* reveal that the ship was indeed docked in Torbay for several lengthy periods in 1779, mere months before it was wrecked in what has become known as the 'Great Hurricane of 1780'.[19]

Incledon goes on to explain that his experience on board the *Thunderer* inspired 'a fixed inclination for a nautical life'.[20] This wish was fulfilled several years later when he joined Captain Stanton of the *Formidable* (a man-of-war) for a period of two years, before being disabled by a wound and left at Portsmouth.[21] He then transferred to the *Raisonnable* under Lord Hervey, later the Earl of Bristol.[22] It was this second part of his naval career that Incledon presents as the most important. He again evokes themes of coincidence and fate, explaining that the chance events of one particular evening changed the course of his career. The occasion he describes took place on board his ship whilst it was stationed in St Lucia:

> [Incledon] agreed with his shipmates, upon that station, to club a week's grog, and drink '*Sweethearts and wives*', the very evening that Lord Hervey entertained the chief officers of the fleet at dinner. It was also settled that whosoever refused to sing when required, should undergo a severe punishment, to avoid which, Incledon complied with the general custom [...] Such was the vivid sensation these efforts had created, that a Lieutenant hurried to the cabin and acquainted Lord Hervey with the circumstance. His lordship proceeded to the quarter deck, heard Incledon in the fine old traditional song, '*Twas Thursday in the morn*', and after various questions upon his origin, tuition, &c. directed him to shift his apparel, and attend the cabin, where he sung, '*The Flight of the Monmouth and Foudroyant*', '*Rule Britannia*', &c. &c. and many of Jackson's most famous Canzonets. Here he was jocularly appointed singer to the British Fleet, released from the performance of manual duty, and set for the assist at every entertainment that succeeded. He rose highly in the favour of Admiral Pigot, the Commander-in-chief, and from the variety and latitude of his exertions, may be safely said to have sung our National Melodies even in the canon's mouth.[23]

Again, this tale is highly romanticised; the exotic location of St Lucia, the sensational performance, the happy coincidence of being overheard by Lord Hervey and the questionable suggestion that the singer performed patriotic anthems 'in the canon's mouth'. It is also notable that this account emphasises Incledon's transformation from regular Tar to something more important; he is relieved of his ordinary clothes and released from manual labour, instead being elevated to the well-heeled echelons of admirals and commanders. Although he would not have mixed with such men as their equal, he is nevertheless at pains to point out the distinctions that separated him from ordinary sailors.

It may be tempting to view Incledon's account of his naval career as exaggerated, or at least embellished, but once again naval records do support his claims. Benjamin Incledon (he adopted 'Charles' later) appears in muster lists of both the *Formidable* and *Raisonnable*.[24] These records also prove that he was indeed stationed in St Lucia on the latter ship during the period in which it was actively engaged in the American Revolutionary War. Furthermore, the records indicate that he was often moved around from ship to ship – a movement that appears to be atypical amongst his crewmates. This could be accounted for by Incledon's status as a singer, as he may have been sent to perform on different ships in the region – he later claimed that 'there is not a ship in the navy [...] that I have not sung in'.[25]

The *Inquisitor*'s biography ends its account of Incledon's time at sea by explaining that it was his naval career that led him to the stage. On his discharge, it explains, naval men such as Lord Hervey and Lord Mulgrave recommended Incledon to theatrical managers. Lord Hervey is described as a man 'to whose advice the public are indebted for Incledon's subsequent appearance in the theatre'.[26] In late Georgian Britain, it was particularly problematic for a British man to be a professional singer. This is because theatrical lifestyles were seen as suspect, and music was associated with effeminacy. As Deborah Rohr has argued, these assumptions 'automatically put male practitioners of the art on the defensive about their masculinity, their morality and respectability, and even their Britishness'.[27] By presenting his singing career as an extension of his naval career, Incledon was able to paint his musical ambitions with a veneer of patriotic respectability – it was surely more respectable for a naval man to take to the stage on the recommendation of revered naval commanders, than for an ordinary man to harbour a personal ambition to become a professional singer. His naval career, then, was in some ways remedial. It allowed him to bolster his compromised masculinity by presenting himself to the public as a brave and devoted sailor first – and a singer second.

Incledon the singer

Incledon left the navy in around 1783. He did not ascend to fame immediately, instead spending several years clawing his way up the professional ladder with a string of minor appearances in the provinces and at London's Vauxhall Gardens. One commentator has pointed out that Incledon 'began a more favourable career' around 1790.[28] This was no coincidence. Following the outbreak of the French Revolution in 1789, Britain became fearful that turmoil in France would make its way across the English Channel, threatening long-established British order and stability.[29] This fear was exacerbated during the Napoleonic Wars, when increasingly hysterical reports of Bonaparte's growing fleets in the English Channel were in wide circulation.[30] Unsurprisingly, British patriotism also ran high during this period and was manifested in popular support for the navy and 'almost unanimous loyalty to the crown'.[31] This climate offered fertile ground for Incledon to deploy his naval persona in the civilian world, and he was soon winning acclaim with his patriotic performances as a sailor-singer. During this period, Incledon's musical self-representation as a sailor had three strands: his appearances in naval-themed English operas, his participation in patriotic naval extravaganzas and his association with particular sea songs.

There were two distinct forms of opera in the late Georgian period. The first was continental opera, viewed by many as effeminate and dangerously foreign.[32] The second was English opera. This was not 'sung-through', instead employing spoken dialogue interspersed with songs and ballads. To British audiences this form of opera was 'decidedly preferable'.[33] It was this latter style of opera that Incledon performed. During the Napoleonic Wars, these English operas often reflected the patriotic sentiments of the day, frequently featuring sailors and naval themes. Incledon appeared in several such productions. Just one example was *The English Fleet in 1342*.[34] First performed in 1803, it starred Incledon in the role of a naval captain called Fitzwater. The plot of this opera, depicting a historic English naval victory over the French, was a thinly veiled attempt to appeal to the nationalistic feelings of an audience that lived in fear of attack from Napoleon's forces. The opera told the story of Jane of Flanders whose husband, the ruler of Brittany, had been held in captivity by French pretenders to his throne. Jane appealed to the British for help, before raising an army against the French intruders. This resulted in a long siege which almost compelled Jane to surrender, but at the last moment the British navy appeared and saved the day; Jane and the British navy are victorious, and the French are defeated.

It is quite obvious that this plot was a calculated appeal to nationalist fervour. This was noted by a critic at *The Times*, who said, 'Many of the situations are applicable to the present state of this country; and the sentiment, without any great straining, may not be deemed unappropriate to the ardent zeal and enthusiastic patriotism by which all ranks of people are animated in defence of their dearest rights.'[35] Incledon's key role within this patriotic production played on his status as an authentic sailor, which only added to the drama. We might draw a comparison with the role of his co-star John Braham, the aforementioned

Jewish tenor. Whilst Braham had not served in the navy and appeared in *The English Fleet* as a rank-and-file sailor, Incledon, the authentic Tar, starred as a captain. He stood before the public as an audible, visible symbol of the navy in a production that was designed to bolster patriotic sentiment. This, in turn, bolstered his own claim to masculinity.

Naval spectacles were the second type of performance through which Incledon presented himself to the public as a sailor. These multimedia celebrations of the navy were typically staged to mark a victory in the wars or to commemorate a fallen hero. At major London theatres, these short but elaborate productions were performed after an evening's main entertainment. Consisting of sea songs, dances, battle re-enactments and short dramas, they were big-budget affairs that often employed impressive stage technologies. Unsurprisingly, they were hugely popular. Incledon appeared in a great number of such productions. The year 1797 saw the British navy win a decisive victory at the battle of Camperdown, under the command of Admiral Duncan. Incledon was involved in a stage celebration of the battle at the Theatre Royal, entitled *England's Glory; Or, The Defeat of the Dutch Fleet by the Gallant Admiral Duncan*. This featured a re-enactment of the battle, complete with singing, dancing and an illuminated representation of Portsmouth.[36] Incledon featured several times, concluding the production with a performance of 'Rule, Britannia!' including 'two additional verses'.[37]

Incledon appeared in many similar productions during the Revolutionary and Napoleonic Wars, as is evidenced by the frequency with which his name pops up in Terence M. Freeman's important study of soldiers and sailors on the stage in this period.[38] As Freeman suggests, these productions did far more than merely celebrate important events – they functioned as a means of disseminating the news. He points to a production celebrating General Abercrombie's capture of Trinidad in 1797.[39] Performed at Covent Garden, *The Surrender of Trinidad* featured Incledon singing some of his best-known ballads. This production was advertised in the newspapers, which described the following scene: 'the Garrison march out with the Honours of War as mention'd in the Gazette'. Freeman argues, 'The reference to the *Gazette* makes very clear that Covent Garden means to be true to the facts reported in the newspaper, but to give shape and voice and dimension, as only a stage performance can, to the actions and emotions of the Redcoats and Tars involved.'[40] In other words, Incledon played a leading role in these productions that not only sought to disseminate accurate accounts of important naval events, but also functioned as a public place in which patriotic emotion could be vividly evoked and celebrated.

The final form of musical performance that fed into Incledon's persona as a sailor-singer was his association with particular sea songs. Although the tenor had many in his repertoire, there was one piece with which he was especially associated: a ballad entitled 'The Storm'. First performed in the 1790s, this ballad written by George Alexander Stevens became the cornerstone to Incledon's reputation – it was his greatest hit.[41] The song's lyrics are written in the voice of a sailor experiencing a dreadful storm from which he prays for salvation. They are full of references to nautical procedures and equipment, for example a 'preventer brace' and 'chain pump'. Even if these terms were alien to a London audience, the fact that Incledon was himself a former sailor who would understand them added to the air of authenticity that this piece produced. Incledon sang 'The Storm' without accompaniment and against a dramatic backdrop on which was painted a wild ocean scene. Surviving prints give us a good idea of what this would have looked like.[42] The tenor performed this ballad (as well as many others) in full sailor's dress. Frequent comments about his costume in the press indicate that this was an important element of Incledon's persona.

Other sea songs performed by Incledon more directly referenced the Napoleonic context of the period. In 1808, a volume was printed entitled *Fairburn's Incledonian and Vauxhall Songster for 1808*.[43] This contained twenty songs that Incledon was performing in London theatres at the time. Of these, fourteen are nationalist, naval songs; titles include 'England's Stout Man Of War', 'The Birth of Liberty', 'The Sailor's Epitaph' and 'May the King Live For Ever!'. The appeal of such sentiments, delivered by an authentic British Tar, is easy to imagine.

It is clear that Incledon's self-representation as an authentic sailor was constructed through music, performance, print, costume and life-writing. This image was disseminated far beyond the theatres of the metropolis, being accessible to anyone who frequented print shops, purchased sheet music or read the popular press. Both the tenor's visibility, and his leading role in productions that sought to share and celebrate news of recent naval events, meant that he became a prominent representative of the sailor in Britain during the Napoleonic period. His deployment of naval masculinity to create a positive public persona was clearly a popular success, but it was not without its complexities.

Models of naval masculinity: Jack Tar or joke?

Historians of the navy in Britain have argued that the popular image of the sailor started to shift in the mid-eighteenth century, becoming increasingly domesticated and patriotic.[44] This new idea of the sensitive yet manly sailor gradually replaced the earlier understanding of Jack Tar as a dissolute figure with a weakness for women and grog. Incledon's identity sat somewhere between these two ideas – though he presented himself to the public as a brave and respectable sailor, he was largely seen as more bawdy than brave, and more rakish than respectable. Commentators were acutely aware of the disjunction between these two competing images, often using it as the basis for mockery. Though other performers were frequently lampooned in the press, there does seem to have been a particular proclivity to target Incledon. These responses to the singer reveal that the earlier model of the wild and rugged Tar was frequently evoked to undermine Incledon's self-representation as a brave British sailor. Furthermore, these responses were overlaid with anxieties about music and performance, which further sought to undermine Incledon's desired patriotic image.

Mary Conley has described how the early Georgian sailor was typically imagined as having both a 'lust for women' and an 'unquenchable thirst for grog'.[45] These two stereotypical characteristics were often ascribed to Incledon. Just one example is the anecdote shared by fencing master Henry Angelo, who gives a humorous description of the occasion on which Incledon was shipwrecked whilst travelling to Ireland. Angelo explains that the singer and his wife had to cling to their sinking vessel for many hours until they were rescued. He describes the 'strange mixture of oaths, prayers, and confessions' that the singer uttered during this ordeal, including the following confessional monologue:

'O Heaven, save my soul – grant me forgiveness. I do confess my manifold sins – I have been a great scoundrel to this dear woman, my wife – I do confess that I got her to ask Mrs. – to our house, for my own purposes. I do confess my wickedness with her dear friends Mrs. –, and Mrs. –, and that dear innocent girl, Miss – I do confess and repent me of the liberties I have taken with our maid Susan and the maid we had last year, I forget her name'.[46]

Angelo continues:

> And so he went on, enumerating his sins, until the return of the day. The condition of the sufferers then discovered from the shore, boats put off, and they were speedily relieved and Mr. Incledon soon forgot his dangers and his repentance; but Mrs. Incledon took care that he should never forget his confessions![47]

This episode was a case of life imitating art; as we have seen, Incledon was best known for his shipwreck song 'The Storm'. He was quick to recognise the publicity value of his involvement in a real wreck, and announced performances of his famous song as soon as he arrived in Dublin. Unsurprisingly, these 'attracted large audiences'.[48] Incledon, then, used this unfortunate incident as a way to 'shore up' his status as an authentic sailor with real experience at sea. Angelo, in contrast, does not present this story as the survival of a brave and assured Tar, instead depicting Incledon as a 'scoundrel' whose womanising behaviour conforms to the idea of sailors as dissolute characters.

Incledon's drinking habits were also much commented on. Many of his contemporaries shared anecdotes about his fondness for drink in their memoirs, and these were often reprinted in newspapers and biographies. The oboist W. T. Parke, for example, reproduced a bar bill in his autobiography to demonstrate the singer's capacity for drink; whilst Parke and another companion ordered 'two glasses of brandy' each, Incledon enjoyed 'two bottles of Madeira'.[49] Again, these stories contribute to the idea that Incledon was more a wild rogue than a brave British Tar.

Many contemporaries offered descriptions of Incledon that conformed to the stereotype of unreconstructed Georgian sailor. One biographer described him thus:

> Nature had bestowed upon him the instinctive feelings of a gentleman, which were dashed if not neutralized by the portly person and rolling gait she had given to his outward man, by the simplicity approaching to fatuity of his mind, as well as by early habits and language drawn from vulgar and nautical associations in boyhood and youth; whilst mental and moral weaknesses rendered him a butt whom everyone laughed at, yet everybody liked. Such a compound of good feeling, vanity, humility, credulity, blasphemy, and devotion, never surely were assembled before.[50]

This is not a description of a respectable naval veteran; Incledon's 'nautical associations' are conflated with his vulgarity. Gillian Russell has discussed the perceived 'otherness' of the sailor in the eighteenth century, quoting Leigh Hunt's description of a sailor:

> [H]e goes treading in a sort of heavy light way, half waggoner and half dancing-master, his shoulders rolling, and his feet touching and going; the same way, in short, in which he keeps himself prepared for all the rolling chances of the vessel, when on deck. There is always, to us, this appearance of lightness of foot and heavy strength of upper works, in a sailor.[51]

Hunt's bodily description of a sailor is strikingly similar to the earlier description of Incledon; both use the term 'rolling', as if to suggest a body that is conditioned by the seas and uncomfortable on land. The way in which Hunt presents the sailor as a strange 'other' also resonates with the earlier claim that a man like Incledon had never been 'assembled' before. This description evokes nothing so much as Frankenstein's monster – a compelling parallel, as Mary Shelley's monster was famously portrayed on London stages by another former sailor, the dramatic actor Thomas Potter Cooke, in the decade before the description was offered.[52] It was not just monstrous bodies that were used to present Incledon as 'other'; he was also compared to animals. The theatre manager John Bernard, for example, remembered Incledon as 'a Newfound-land dog – compounded of courage, gratefulness, and love of the water'.[53] Casting Incledon in the role of 'grateful' canine suggests both an uncultivated personality and an implicit subservience – both characteristics that could be ascribed to the sailor.

Although it is clear that the reception of Incledon's naval identity was problematic, it was not wholly negative. Many of Incledon's contemporaries, including John Braham, performed in continental opera. As Incledon performed works in English only, several commentators suggested that he represented pure and untarnished British music and feeling, contrasting him favourably with his Italianate colleagues. The theatrical commentator William Robson, for example, argued, 'The character of English musical is perfectly national, and not to be mistaken – it is marine and pastoral – and every step it takes to approximate the Italians emasculates it.'[54] Robson draws on the familiar idea of the Italian style as an emasculating force, diluting British sentiment and rendering it effeminate. He uses Incledon and Braham to illuminate his point, continuing, 'no English public singer has ever had so fine a voice, taken in all its qualities and powers, as that of Incledon [...] there never was a sound, so rich, so powerful, so sweet an English voice as Incledon's'.[55] Braham, on the other hand, is described as Incledon's opposite; Robson tells us: 'No two singers could be more unlike; the voice seemed to flow from Incledon as from a copious spring, whereas, with Mr. Braham it was brought up as if it were by a forcing pump, and with, apparently, unpleasant efforts.'[56] In musical commentary of this period, these two singers are frequently imagined in this way; Incledon was a representative of a natural and respectable British style, while Braham was seen as symbolic of the forced and frivolous Italian school.

However, whilst Incledon's repertoire might have made him emblematic of a preferred musical style for some, this praise was not sufficient to eclipse the problematic elements of his constructed naval persona. It is clear that Incledon's self-representation was undermined by stereotyped characteristics of the sailor – dissolute behaviour, promiscuity and otherness – all of which he was accused of exhibiting himself. These same traits, though, also did something else: they conformed to widely held beliefs about singers. As I have argued elsewhere, the male singer in this period was viewed with suspicion – he was imagined as an effeminate figure with questionable morals, a love of ostentation and a lust for wealth.[57] Accounts of Incledon's sexual misadventures and proclivity for drink, then, not only represent an attempt to caricature him as a bawdy Georgian Tar – they also underscore his problematic status as a male singer. Anecdotes frequently commented on Incledon's ostentatious nature, with the diarist Henry Crabb Robinson typically describing him as having '[s]even rings on his fingers, five seals on his watch-ribbon, and a gold snuff-box'.[58] This image conforms to the visual code that was typically used to signify the effeminate, Italianate trappings of male opera singers during this period.[59] These ideas of ostentation directly undermined the singer's self-representation as a British Tar. In 1791, a reviewer commented on Incledon's performance of Charles Dibdin's popular naval ballad 'Poor Jack', arguing: 'The Poor Jack of INCLEDON has more voice than character – surely the Greenwich PENSIONER ought not to be decked out in all the Italian finery of a *laced* Jacket and *embroidered* Trowsers!'[60] It is notable that 'Italian finery' is the phrase used to describe the incorrect costume; the suggestion is that the costume was too effeminate, smacking of the Italianate trappings of the operatic profession and thus undermining the singer's representation of a brave naval veteran.

It was once said that Incledon was 'an egoist in the most liberal and extended sense of the word'.[61] Anecdotes frequently poked fun at the singer's ostentation and vanity. Just one example that did the rounds in various journals and newspapers related the story of Incledon going to buy some books to fill a shelf. He went about this by measuring the empty shelf, then asking for two feet of books. When the confused bookseller asked what sort of books he wanted, Incledon replied, 'I shall require them to have handsome bindings; but I'm not particular about their titles.'[62] The humour of this anecdote was derived from the fact that Incledon himself was seen much like these books – his finery falsely suggesting sophistication, when he was in fact lacking in substance. Many other tales similarly characterised him as uneducated and distastefully flamboyant.

The most repeated comical story about Incledon is also the most revealing. This anecdote skewers the singer's keenness to present himself as a brave veteran in a manner which makes it clear that audiences were keenly aware of the constructed nature of this identity. Furthermore, it reveals that Incledon's eagerness to portray himself in this way was nothing so much as comedic. In his memoirs, the actor Samuel William Ryley shares an extended account of an occasion on which Incledon was tricked by several of his theatre colleagues.[63] Knowing him to be something of a hypochondriac with an enthusiasm for quack medicines, they decide to play a trick on him that revolves around the 'Wellington lozenge'. Ryley explains that this was a small bar of soap bearing Wellington's profile that was used for removing stains from soldier's coats. The group of pranksters decided to convince Incledon that this bar of soap was in fact a throat lozenge. One man tells Incledon, 'Why, my good friend, the Wellington lozenge is a medicine, invented by that gallant general, who was so hoarse that he could not give the world of command on the plains of Waterloo, and this medicine cured him.'[64] After eating several of these bars of soap, Incledon is heard to say through a mouthful of foam, 'bloody nasty, my boy, but if it cured the first English general, it may cure the first English singer, and that will be serving the country'.[65] This anecdote presents the singer as both arrogant and stupid – he conflates himself with the general, despite foaming at the mouth as a result of his foolishness. Of course, it is difficult to prove the veracity of this story, and it could be entirely untrue. Nevertheless, the amount of times this story was reprinted and reproduced in newspapers and journals demonstrates that Incledon's keenness to present himself as a naval hero was recognised widely enough for this anecdote to resonate. His desperation to cling blindly to any Napoleonic association, no matter how tenuous, was clearly seen as ridiculous.

Experiencing martial masculinities

The Duke of Cumberland's Sharpshooters

In 1803, when Incledon was appearing regularly on London stages, he revived his martial career by joining the Duke of Cumberland's Sharpshooters. This was a fashionable new voluntary regiment formed in London in response to the threat of French invasion.[66] It appears that the tenor was an early member of this group; he sang the sea song 'The Bold Arethusa' to a group of assembled Lords at the regiment's ceremonial launch.[67] At this event, 210 members of the regiment (presumably including Incledon) demonstrated their military manoeuvres, including 'skirmishing, ambush fighting, covering battalions, and advancing in front of an enemy's line'.[68] Before a large crowd of supporters, Incledon appeared wearing the uniform of the regiment: 'a very high black cap with black feather, a dark green jacket and trousers made in one, relieved by light green trimmings, and small gilt buttons, with high shoes laced in front'.[69] The activities of the Sharpshooters were limited to drills, parades and shooting matches with other voluntary regiments. These often attracted large crowds of spectators – such drills have been described as 'an important entertainment genre that exerted a deep, sustained impact on British society'.[70] By joining this regiment, then, Incledon was able to publicly exhibit his military prowess to audiences and strengthen his reputation as a manly patriot. However, this effort backfired. Henry Angelo's memoirs included a humorous account of Incledon's time as a Sharpshooter. Angelo describes the 'picturesque' outfit donned by the regiment, but describes Incledon as one of a particular group of members whose 'spirits outlived their bodily capabilities'.[71] He goes on to describe Incledon's performance at a drill on Hampstead Heath:

> Charles Incledon, now become corpulent, brought up the rear at a little more than a walk. 'My lad' said he to a butcher boy, who followed the troops, 'carry this d-d gun for me, and I'll give you a shilling'. He then started off a little quicker, but was nearly thrown down by his sword getting caught between his legs; a little girl just then caught his eye: 'My little girl', said Charles, 'do carry this d-d sword for me, and I'll give you a shilling'. This, too, was done, and at the halt, Incledon made his appearance round and green as a cabbage, accompanied by his male and female armour bearers, to the no small amusement of his comrades, and of the by-standers. 'What a shame', exclaimed Cooke, 'that the first singer in the world should be the last soldier in the field!'[72]

This widely repeated anecdote ridicules the singer's efforts to present himself as a martial figure. As Matthew McCormack has demonstrated, satirical prints of this period often mocked the disjunction between the uniforms of volunteer militia men (designed to highlight the ideal masculine physique) and their aged or overweight bodies.[73] Incledon was being mocked in the same way. For the tenor, then, his stint as a Sharpshooter was yet another abortive attempt to lay claim to a respectable form of military manliness.

It is clear that Charles Incledon made a great effort to present himself as a brave and respectable British sailor during a period in which we might have expected this mode of self-representation to be especially effective. Though he became a prominent representative of the sailor on the British stage, and in doing so played a role in constructing ideas about the navy, the model of masculinity that he sought to claim eluded him. This is evident when considering the responses to Incledon given by his contemporaries – it is clear he was seen as a colourful and comedic figure who did not command the respect that he hoped to attract. Problematic ideas about the sailor as a wild, strange and dissolute character undermined the image that the singer sought to project. Incledon failed to lay claim to the more sanitised and respectable model of Jack Tar that scholars suggest had emerged by the period in which he was performing. There were two key reasons for this. First, negative ideas about male singers combined with and reinforced problematic elements of the sailor's identity – both groups were perceived as sharing problematic traits that directly undermined a respectable model of masculinity, including a tendency for dissolute behaviours such as womanising and drinking. Furthermore, perceptions of the singer as an Italianate, ostentatious and arrogant figure were also at play. Secondly, Incledon's own behaviours seemed to underscore the negative aspects of both the sailor and the singer's identity – his fondness for drink, women and fine clothes, teamed with his arrogance, caused his self-representation as a brave naval veteran to appear ridiculous.

Gillian Russell has drawn an illuminating comparison between the figures of the soldier and the actor in Georgian Britain. This comparison applies equally to the figures of the sailor and the singer. She argues, 'There are a number of reasons why the identities of the actor and the soldier should have been interchangeable in Georgian society.'[74] These reasons include their renunciation of family ties, their representation of 'an outside world that was attractive but also potentially threatening', their habits of touring and their perceived sexual threat.[75] She concludes, 'to become a soldier in late Georgian society was therefore to take on the identity of the actor (and vice versa) – stigmatized, dislocated, and exotic'.[76] In Incledon, both of these identities were combined – and the negative aspects of each ultimately destabilised the model of masculinity that he sought to project.

Notes

1　For more on music as a feminine art form, see Deborah Rohr, *The Careers of British Musicians, 1750–1850* (Cambridge: Cambridge University Press, 2001); Benjamin Walton, 'Rara Avis or Fozy Turnip: Rossini as Celebrity in 1820s London', in Tom Mole (ed.), *Romanticism and Celebrity Culture, 1750–1850* (Cambridge: Cambridge University Press, 2009); Derek B. Scott, 'The Sexual Politics of Victorian Musical Aesthetics', *Journal of the Royal Musical Association* 119:1 (1994), pp. 91–114.

2　Colley, *Britons*, pp. 33–5, 252.

3　Kennedy, *Narratives of the Revolutionary and Napoleonic Wars*, pp. 3–4.

4　Oskar Cox Jensen, *Napoleon and British Song, 1797–1822* (Basingstoke: Palgrave Macmillan, 2015), p. 2.

5　Susan Valladares, *Staging the Peninsular War: English Theatres 1807–1815* (Farnham: Ashgate, 2015); Gillian Russell, *The Theatres of War: Performance, Politics, and Society, 1793–1815* (Oxford: Clarendon Press, 1995).

6　Mark Philip, 'Music and Politics, 1793–1815: Introduction', in Mark Philip (ed.), *Resisting Napoleon: The British Response to the Threat of Invasion, 1707–1815* (Aldershot: Ashgate, 2006), p. 173.

7　Land, *War, Nationalism, and the British Sailor, 1750–1850*, pp. 77–104.

8　Begiato (Bailey), 'Tears and the Manly Sailor', pp. 117–33.

9　Oskar Cox Jensen, David Kennerley, and Ian Newman (eds), *Charles Dibdin and Late Georgian Culture* (Oxford: Oxford University Press, 2018).

10　Anna Maria Barry, 'The Dream of a Madman: Constructing the Male Opera Singer in Nineteenth-Century Britain' (PhD Thesis: Oxford Brookes University, 2017).

11　Trevor Herbert and Helen Barlow, *Music and the British Military in the Long Nineteenth Century* (Oxford: Oxford University Press, 2013), p. 15.

12　The only existing scholarly work on Incledon takes the form of entries in biographical dictionaries: John Rosselli, 'Incledon, Charles', in *Dictionary of National Biography*, 2004. Available at: www.oxforddnb.com.oxforddb rookes.idm.oclc.org/view/10.1093/ref:odnb/9780198614128.001.0001/ odnb-9780198614128-e-14377 (accessed 22 June 2018); Philip H. Highfill, Kalman A. Burnim, and Edward A. Langhans, 'Charles Incledon', in *A Biographical Dictionary or Actors, Actresses, Musicians, Dancers, Managers*

& Other Stage Personnel in London, 1660 – 1800, 16 vols (Carbondale and Edwardsville: Southern Illinois University Press, 1975), vol. VIII, pp. 86–99. Incledon is considered in other studies of the late Georgian stage, most notably Terence M. Freeman, *Dramatic Representations of Soldiers and Sailors on the London Stage, 1660–1800* (Lewiston, ME, Queenston, Lampeter: The Edwin Mellen Press, 1995).

13   See, for example, Anon., 'Incledon, Charles', in *The Thespian Dictionary, or Dramatic Biography of the Eighteenth Century* (London: T. Hurst, 1802), n. p.

14   Charles Incledon, 'Biographical Memoir of Mr. Incledon', in *Theatrical Inquisitor and Monthly Mirror* (London: Chapple, August 1817), pp. 85–94.

15   *Ibid.*, p. 85.

16   See, for example, Anon., 'Editor's Note', *Theatrical Inquisitor* (London, November 1816), n. p.

17   Incledon, 'Biographical Memoir', p. 86.

18   *Ibid.*

19   John Mendes, 'Thunderer Master's Journal, 1779 – 1780' (London: National Archives, 1779), ADM52/2042.

20   Incledon, 'Biographical Memoir', p. 87.

21   *Ibid.*

22   This ship is not named by the singer, but biographies of both Incledon and Captain Stanton make it clear that it was the *Formidable*. See, for example, Highfill, Burnim and Langhans (eds), 'Charles Incledon', *A Biographical Dictionary*, vol. VIII, p. 88.

23   Incledon, 'Biographical Memoir', pp. 87–8.

24   Anon., 'Royal Navy Ship's Musters: Formidable, January 1780–July 1783' (London: National Archives, 1780), p. 25, ADM36/9121. Note that this record is made up of three muster lists, and Incledon is listed on page 25 of each. Anon., 'Royal Navy Ship's Musters: Raisonnable, March 1783–July 1783' (London: National Archives, 1783), p. 11, ADM36/10068. Note that this record is also made up of three muster lists, and Incledon is listed on page 11 of each.

25   Quoted in Highfill, Burnim, and Langhans (eds), *A Biographical Dictionary*, vol. VIII, p. 96.

26   Incledon, 'Biographical Memoir', p. 87.

27   Rohr, *The Careers of British Musicians*, p. 20.

28   'Benjamin Charles Incledon', in Clarke (ed.), *The Georgian Era: Memoirs of the Most Eminent Persons, Who Have Flourished in Great Britain, from the Accession of George the First to the Demise of George the Fourth*, 4 vols (London: Vizetelly, Branston & Co, 1824), vol. IV, p. 290.

29   James Davey, 'Mutiny and Insecurity', in Quintin Colville and James Davey (eds), *Nelson, Navy & Nation* (London: Conway, 2013), p. 134.

30 *Ibid.*, pp. 145–51.
31 *Ibid.*, p. 148.
32 Michael Burden, 'Opera in the London Theatres', in Jane Moody and Daniel O'Quinn (eds), *The Cambridge Companion to British Theatre, 1730–1830* (Cambridge: Cambridge University Press, 2007), p. 205.
33 *Ibid.*
34 Susan Valladares has offered an insightful examination of this opera in the context of the Peninsular Wars: Valladares, *Staging the Peninsular War*, pp. 176–84.
35 Anon., 'Theatre Royal, Covent Garden', *The Times* (London, 14 December 1803), p. 3.
36 Described in an advert: Anon., 'Theatre Royal, Covent Garden', *The True Briton*, 19 October 1797, p. 1. Freeman also discusses this: Freeman, *Dramatic Representations*, p. 176.
37 Anon., 'Theatre Royal, Covent Garden', p. 1.
38 Freeman, *Dramatic Representations*.
39 *Ibid.*, p. 172.
40 *Ibid.*
41 Stevens was a well-known actor, playwright, author and songwriter.
42 Lithograph after Joseph Ayton, *Charles Incledon as He Appeared Singing 'The Storm'* (London: National Portrait Gallery, August 1826).
43 Various, *Fairburn's Incledonian and Vauxhall Songster for 1808* (London: John Fairburn, 1808).
44 Begiato, 'Tears and the Manly Sailor'; *Land, War, Nationalism and the British Sailor*; Lincoln, *Representing the Royal Navy*.
45 Conley, *From Jack Tar to Union Jack*, p. 2.
46 Henry Angelo, *Reminiscences of Henry Angelo*, 2 vols (London: Henry Colburn, 1828), vol. II, pp. 548–9.
47 *Ibid.*, p. 549.
48 Highfill, Burnim, and Langhans (eds), *A Biographical Dictionary*, vol. VIII, p. 93.
49 W. T. Parke, *Musical Memoirs*, 2 vols (London: Henry Colburn and Richard Bentley, 1830), vol. II, p. 22.
50 Anon., 'Memoirs of Charles Mathews', *The Spectator* (London, 22 December 1838), p. 15.
51 Quoted in: Russell, *The Theatres of War*, p. 9.
52 For more on Cooke, see: Ellie Miles, 'Characterising the Nation: How T. P. Cooke Embodied the Naval Hero in Nineteenth-Century Nautical Melodrama', *Journal for Maritime Research* 19:2 (2017), pp. 107–20. This is not the place for a comparative study of Incledon and Cooke, but such a study is surely called for.
53 John Bernard, *Retrospections of The Stage*, 2 vols (London: Henry Colburn and Richard Bentley, 1830), vol. I, p. 214.

54 William Robson, *The Old Play-Goer* (London: Joseph, Masters, 1846), p. 217.

55 *Ibid.*, p. 216.

56 *Ibid.*, p. 219.

57 Barry, *The Dream of a Madman*; see especially chapter 1.

58 Henry Crabb Robinson, *Diary, Reminiscences and Correspondence of Henry Crabb Robinson*, 2 vols (London: Macmillan and Co, 1872), vol. I, p. 179.

59 Barry, *The Dream of a Madman*, pp. 63–5.

60 Anon., 'The Poor Jack of Incledon', *The Times* (London, 18 January 1791), p. 2.

61 Anon., 'Anecdotes of Actors: Incledon's Madeira', *Fraser's Magazine for Town and Country* (April 1842), p. 437.

62 *Ibid.*, p. 437.

63 Samuel William Ryley, *The Itinerant*, 9 vols (London: Sherwood and Co, 1827), vol. VII, pp. 144–67.

64 *Ibid.*, p. 158.

65 *Ibid.*, p. 159.

66 For a history of the Sharpshooters, see Major John Eustace Anderson, *The Cumberland Sharpshooters* (London: R. W. Simpson and Co. Ltd., 1897).

67 *Ibid.*, p. 16.

68 *Ibid.*, p. 13.

69 *Ibid.*, p. 15.

70 Scott Myerly, *British Military Spectacle*, p. 139.

71 Angelo, *Reminiscences*, vol. II, p. 540.

72 *Ibid.*, pp. 537, 542.

73 Matthew McCormack, *Embodying the Militia in Georgian England* (Oxford: Oxford University Press, 2015), pp. 54–74.

74 Russell, *The Theatres of War*, pp. 180–1.

75 *Ibid.*

76 *Ibid.*

5

Visualising the aged veteran in nineteenth-century Britain: memory, masculinity and nation

Michael Brown and Joanne Begiato

Introduction

In December 1914, the British Parliamentary Recruiting Committee (PRC) issued a poster entitled 'The Veteran's Farewell' (figure 5.1). By this point of the First World War, following the First Battle of Ypres (October-November 1914), the small, professional British Expeditionary Force had effectively been wiped out, and the British army was increasingly reliant on civilian volunteers. The PRC had been established on 31 August 1914 to commission posters, leaflets and other materials calculated to encourage the enlistment of able-bodied men of fighting age. This particular poster was designed by Frank Dadd (1851–1929), a well-regarded commercial artist who had worked for the *Illustrated London News* and *The Graphic* and who had a penchant for military scenes. It portrays a new recruit being sent off to war by a red-coated, white-bearded Chelsea Pensioner with the words 'Goodbye, my lad. I only wish I were young enough to go with you!' In the background of the image is a recruiting sergeant, leading a group of newly enlisted men from different social classes. Here, then, the transition from civilian to soldier in the service of the state is given the stamp of approval - not simply by the older generation, but by the veteran professional soldier, the guardian of British military memory. Dadd's work was clearly effective. *The Graphic* described it as 'a powerful appeal to the manhood of the nation', and it was one of the most popular posters of the early war years.[1]

'The Veteran's Farewell' was not initially commissioned by the PRC, but rather by the British cigarette firm Abdulla and Co. It was not unusual for tobacco companies to capitalise on the appeal of martial masculinities to sell their products in time of war. Neither was it unusual

Figure 5.1   Frank Dadd for the Parliamentary Recruiting Committee, 'The Veteran's Farewell' (1914) – NAM. 1977-06-81-6.

for the image of the aged veteran to feature in advertisements for commercial products more generally. Indeed, 'The Veteran's Farewell' was part of an established visual lexicon which, from the later nineteenth century, was used to sell a range of products ostensibly unrelated to the military. This image for 'Provost Oats' (figure 5.2) from the early twentieth century, for example, portrays an elderly Chelsea Pensioner placing a paternal hand on the shoulder of a Guards drummer boy, suggesting that its product will help the young develop a robust constitution.

Figure 5.2   R. Robinson and Son, 'To Build Up the Constitution Eat Scotch "Provost Oats"' (c. 1900).

Both of these images share a common motif, in that they juxtapose age and youth. As we shall see, this cross-generational relationship was an important aspect of the representation of the aged veteran through-out the long nineteenth century, one which constructed the transmission of national, martial and moral values in familial terms, speaking in particular to young men and boys, but also to girls.

What is also notable about these images is that they represent a very particular subset of military veterans, namely Pensioners of the Royal

Hospital of Chelsea. This institution had been founded in 1682 to provide shelter and support for long-serving, retired members of the army.[2] Its naval equivalent, the Royal Hospital for Seamen at Greenwich, was established in 1692. These men thus embodied the ideal of a reciprocal relationship between the serviceman and the state. For this reason, as well as for their colourful uniforms and picturesque setting, Chelsea and Greenwich Pensioners became an established part of the visual culture and tourist landscape of London. But, of course, the cliché of the Pensioner that such images promoted glossed over the complexities not only of their own experiences, but also of the majority of aged veterans, who were not cared for by the state to anything like the same extent. Indeed, as we shall see, even in terms of visual and textual representation, the Pensioner shared space with other, more ambivalent, visions of the aged veteran.

Recent years have seen a significant scholarly interest in the figure of the veteran. Indeed, it is possible to speak of a distinct field of 'Veteran Studies', although it is mostly concentrated in the United States and draws on a range of disciplines, in which history is comparatively underrepresented.[3] Nonetheless, even in terms of historical writing, the interest in veterans has been marked. Much of the focus has been on mass military participation in the twentieth century. For example, there has been sustained analysis of the experience of wounded and disabled servicemen in the years following both world wars.[4] Likewise, there is considerable interest in the political role of veterans, particularly in the development of far-right nationalist movements in interwar Europe, but also in other contexts.[5] As regards the nineteenth century, the scholarship is most advanced in the United States, where there is a substantial historiography of 'veteranhood' related to the Civil War. This scholarship is notable for the ways in which it explores the experiences of veterans in post-war society, as well as the broader meanings ascribed to those who had participated in a conflict with complex legacies for national and racial identities.[6] For example, David Blight's *Race and Reunion: The Civil War in American Memory* (2002) argues that veterans were central to a Gilded-Age culture of 'reunion' in which the racial politics of the conflict were obscured by an image of shared white sacrifice and fraternal 'Blue-Gray' reconciliation across the stone walls of Gettysburg.[7] Others, meanwhile, have painted a more complex picture, in which veterans on both sides clung to very different, often antagonistic, understandings of the war and its meanings.[8]

Compared to the United States, the literature on veterans in nineteenth-century Britain is less developed. This is to be expected. The Civil War, on the one hand, constituted a huge social upheaval involving tens of thousands of fighting men, the vast majority of them civilian volunteers and draftees, rather than professional soldiers. Moreover, the legacy of the war, and hence of its living embodiments, was deeply contested and highly politicised. The experience of Britain, on the other hand, was almost the diametric opposite. In the near hundred years between the Battle of Waterloo (18 June 1815) and the First Battle of Ypres, Britain's conflicts took place at an often considerable spatial remove from the metropole and were fought by a small professional standing army (or by East India Company and colonial troops) and a larger navy. The number of veterans was thus nowhere near those of the United States, and the direct experience of war was shared by a much smaller group of individuals. Neither, for the most part, was their legacy as problematic as those veterans of the defeated, yet largely unrepentant, Confederate states. Even so, the imaginative power of the British veteran was still significant, and historians like Caroline Nielsen, who studies the Chelsea Pensioner in the long eighteenth century, are interested not only in the social history of these men, but also in their cultural representation.[9] The same is true of Lara Kriegel, who has explored the importance of Crimean War veterans to cultures of local remembrance in *fin-de-siècle* Britain.[10]

It is in terms of meaning, imagination and representation that we intend to make our intervention into the historiography. In one sense, although the study of the nineteenth-century British military veteran may not be especially well developed, the groundwork has already been laid by the remarkable flowering of scholarly interest in the cultural history of war, which we discussed in the Introduction to this volume. As Joan Hichberger's seminal *Images of the Army: The Military in British Art, 1815–1914* (1988) suggested, and as subsequent scholarship has confirmed, visual, literary and material cultures were central to shaping popular understandings of, and attitudes towards, the military and its members. Historians and literary scholars have likewise shown that Georgian and Victorian conflicts enjoyed an extended afterlife through objects, text and performance, many of which referred to, and often directly involved, the veteran soldier and sailor.[11]

In this chapter, we therefore want to explore some of the ways in which veterans came to – quite literally – embody a range of meanings about the conflicts in which they were themselves involved, as well as those which took place in their lifetime; the ways, in other words, in which veterans were made and remade to accommodate new narratives. As we have already suggested, while the figure of the Pensioner spoke of the veteran remembered and rewarded, the reality was rather more complex. In our first section, we therefore explore the dynamics of remembering and forgetting, showing how, while many aged veterans were indeed forgotten by both the public and the state, the figure of the forgotten veteran was, paradoxically, the subject of considerable literary and artistic meditation. Our second section examines the generational qualities of the representation of the veteran and the ways in which he was figured as an exemplar and progenitor for the inheritance of military, masculine and moral values. Our third and final section considers the issues of materiality and performativity, demonstrating how the imaginative power of the veteran was shaped by his body, his material adornment and even, on occasion, his public performance.

Remembering and forgetting

Among the most famous images of the British army in the nineteenth century, Henry Nelson O'Neil's twin paintings, *Eastward Ho!* (1858) and *Home Again, 1858* (1859), portray the embarkation of troops bound for India to supress the Sepoy Rebellion and their subsequent return. As Hichberger notes, these paintings draw on 'the stock characters of military genre painting', one of the most recognisable of whom is the Chelsea Pensioner.[12] In *Eastward Ho!*, he is seen waving goodbye to his son (or possibly grandson); in *Home Again*, he greets the same, who now proudly brandishes the Victoria Cross. As we shall see, such familial representations were central to the didactic functions of the aged veteran in popular culture. However, O'Neil's image also contains the seeds of a more ambivalent representation. According to Hichberger, *Eastward Ho!* was generally better received by critics than *Home Again*. Whereas the former stoked patriotic sentiments, the latter made for more uncomfortable viewing, in part because, according to the reviewer for the *Art Journal*, it was simply 'not true'. The returning soldier, particularly the sick and wounded one, was not greeted by the same dockside throng that had seen him off. Rather, he 'is sent home like a piece of live lumber ... His return is generally unknown until after his arrival ... broken health and penury, to be endured in obscurity, are all that remain'.[13]

It is unclear whether O'Neil sought to respond to such criticism of his work, or whether the intention had been there all along. Either way, rather than the diptych they are generally imagined to be, it seems that O'Neil's paintings actually form a triptych, of sorts, for in 1861 he painted a third work entitled *The Soldier's Return* (figure 5.3), which clearly portrays the same wounded sergeant who is pictured in *Home Again* being comforted by his daughter as he reads the last letter from his wife, who has died during his absence.[14] In *The Soldier's Return*, this man is presented as destitute, still in his uniform (though reduced to wearing slippers for want of boots) and with his arm still in a sling. This image draws on the established representational conventions of the soldier's and sailor's return. Traditionally, these kinds of images presented either a benign and domesticated picture of the serviceman restored to the bosom of his family (most frequently true of sailors) or a less heartening, though equally sentimentalised, image of the wounded or

Figure 5.3 Henry Nelson O'Neil, *The Soldier's Return* (1861) – NAM. 1995–06–18–1.

'broken' soldier.[15] O'Neil's image falls into this latter tradition, presenting a man forlorn, his lonely state compounded by the pitying faces of two young girls. Although not an aged veteran in the sense of the decrepit pensioner, his maturity is evident in his greying beard and his status as a senior non-commissioned officer. Doubtless, the pathos of the painting is enhanced by the fact that he is evidently a man of character and responsibility, but one whose prospects outside the army appear bleak.

This is not the place for a detailed social-historical discussion of the fortunes of ex-servicemen in nineteenth-century Britain. Nonetheless, what is clear is that discharged sailors generally found it easier, with their range of skills, to find work in cognate trades such as fishing or the merchant navy. Soldiers, by contrast, particularly those of line regiments, often struggled to find gainful employment, especially if they were old, incapacitated or 'worn out'. As Peter Reese notes, between 1855 and 1870, 707 men were discharged from the Royal West Surrey Regiment, of whom 'over two-thirds were discharged on medical grounds'.[16] In any case, ex-servicemen occupied an ambiguous place in British society. Most received a pension, although with the sheer numbers involved (the number of out-pensioners on the books of Chelsea Hospital stood at 84,000 in 1834) the government was always inclined towards parsimony.[17] Moreover, before the creation of the Reserve in 1870, discharged soldiers were never fully civilians and were required to perform military tasks in times of national emergency.[18] For the truly aged veteran, life could be particularly harsh. A lucky few might find refuge within the walls of Chelsea or Greenwich. However, even here there could be discontent. In 1843, for example, *John Bull* reported on the case of a sixty-five-year-old Chelsea in-pensioner who had died of a haemorrhage attributed to heavy drinking. The local coroner, the radical surgeon and editor of *The Lancet*, Thomas Wakley, declared that 'although he had lately held a great many inquests on the bodies of out-pensioners who … came to violent deaths through drunkenness, he had held none on the in-pensioners until the present case'.[19]

It has been suggested that the veteran soldier (the sailor was always a slightly different case) was viewed with relative indifference by the British public until around the time of the Crimean War, an indifference which stemmed from a more general disdain for the rank and file of the army.[20] This is something of an overstatement. Philip Shaw has shown that the sufferings of the soldier could function as a subject for sympathetic sentiment and moral reflection within the cultures of

Romanticism, while Simon Parkes and Caroline Nielsen have demonstrated how such emotions might be extended to veterans.[21] Nonetheless, while aged veterans from the Napoleonic Wars continued to feature in popular print deep into the nineteenth century, it is in the latter half of the century, particularly from the 1870s onwards, that one begins to see a marked proliferation of veterans in literary and visual culture. There are a range of potential explanations for this. Traditionally, historians might point to the improved image of the army in the years after the Crimean War, as it came to assume a heroic status equivalent to that of the long-valorised navy. What is also clear is that this period saw significant changes in the technologies of visual reproduction, as well as the growth of working-class readerships and the concomitant expansion of a graphically rich periodical press, all of which tended towards an increase in the production and circulation of images of all kinds, including those of military veterans. The appeal of aged veterans can, however, be linked to more specific social and cultural developments. In the United States, veterans of the Civil War assumed a particular prominence towards the end of the century. This was due not so much to their scarcity (their numbers were still considerable) as to their cultural appeal at a time of renewed military activity, notably the Spanish-American War of 1898, and during a period of rapid urbanisation, industrialisation and commercialisation when there was a marked anxiety about a loss of traditional masculine virtues - virtues that these men were thought (or made) to embody.[22] Similar patterns are evident in Britain, where the advent of New Imperialism, concerns about the physical prowess of the British soldier and the increasing technologisation of modern warfare all encouraged the drawing of reassuring parallels with the martial masculinities of old.[23]

As we shall see, the figure of the aged veteran, particularly the Chelsea Pensioner, was therefore regularly positioned in relation to contemporary conflicts. Conversely, however, the spectre of the forgotten veteran was also often invoked at such moments. In 1870, for example, *Punch* reported on the case of one Janes Kenning, an 'infirm, decrepit, half-bedridden' eighty-three-year-old veteran of the Peninsula and Waterloo. 'Ninepence a day is what a grateful country thinks of this veteran's worth and wounds', it declared. 'Munificent reward of valour! Generous encouragement to brave death or mutilation in fighting your country's battles my boys!' Reflecting on the army's recruiting crisis and the parsimony of the New Poor Law, *Punch* imagined, with bitter irony, the cost of his upkeep:

A man of eighty-three might live to be ninety-three ... and the amount which the old soldier's two pounds [of meat] a-week ... would cost the Union is too frightful to calculate ... A retiring pension of ninepence a-day is as bountiful a provision for old age as any private soldier can reasonably expect. Why, it is three pence more than an officer would pay for a good cigar! If such prizes will not induce the populace to enter the Army, we must resort to Conscription.[24]

In 1882, the same publication used the occasion of the Anglo-Egyptian War to reflect on the disparity between glorious youth and neglected old age. 'Our young Soldiers have been doing well in Egypt', it claimed, but 'How many of those who will be eager to applaud them on their return, will consider what becomes of "Our Boys", when old or disabled, and compelled to leave the Service.' Thankfully, *Punch* pointed out, there was a worthy exemplar in the late William Woodman, who had left £10,000 in his will for the relief of 'soldiers, of good character'. In comedic, pun-laden verse, it urged its readers to emulate his generosity:

Walk up, British public, your *Punch* will trouble you
To follow the lead of good W. W.
Kind care for Old Soldiers can't surely o'ertax you
So stump up and do as the Woodman would axe you.[25]

By the end of the nineteenth century, one particular group of aged veterans had come to stand as a synecdoche for the more general neglect of their kind. Celebrated in painting and verse, most notably Alfred, Lord Tennyson's *Charge of the Light Brigade* (1854), the survivors of Lord Cardigan's disastrous assault on the Russian artillery at the Battle of Balaclava (25 October 1854) were, in many ways, first among veterans. They had even formed their own 'Balaclava Commemoration Society' with strict entry requirements.[26] In 1890, however, *Punch* ran a satirical pastiche of Tennyson's ode, entitled 'The Last Charge of the Light Brigade', the 'charge' in this case being that 'bought by the survivors against those – who might have looked after them'. The poem was prefaced with a statement from the 'Secretary of the Balaclava Committee' which claimed that Lord Cardigan had assured those who had 'done a glorious deed ... that you will all be provided for. Not one of you fine fellows will ever have to seek refuge in the workhouse'! The reality was sadly different. 'We are all getting older every year', it read, 'and with the lapse of time, while many have died, a good number have fallen into dire misfortune'. The poem invoked the same dread institution to which Cardigan had referred:

> For here they grow old,
> With their grand story told,
> Left to the bitter cold,
> Starving Six Hundred!
> Workhouse to the right of them,
> Workhouse to the left of them,
> Workhouse in front of them!
> Has no one wondered
> That British blood should cry,
> 'Shame!' and exact reply,
> Asking the country why
> Thus it sees droop and die
> Those brave Six Hundred?[27]

The Light Brigade veterans' most high-profile spokesperson was perhaps Rudyard Kipling. In the same year that *Punch* ran its Tennyson-inspired satire, he too published a poem, entitled *The Last of the Light Brigade*, which contrasted the past celebration of these heroes with their current neglect. Kipling imagined the ragged remnants of the Brigade assembling before Tennyson's door:

> The old Troop-Sergeant was spokesman, and 'Beggin' your pardon', he said,
> 'You wrote o' the Light Brigade, sir. Here's all that isn't dead.
> An' it's all come true what you wrote, sir, regardin' the mouth of hell;
> For we're all of us nigh to the workhouse, an' we thought we'd call an' tell.
>
> No, thank you, we don't want food, sir; but couldn't you take an' write
> A sort of to be continued and see next page o' the fight?
> We think that someone has blundered, an' couldn't you tell 'em how?
> You wrote we were heroes once, sir. Please, write we are starving now.'[28]

As the particular case of the Light Brigade suggests, for the remembered veteran, as much as for the half-forgotten one, memory could serve a deeply ambiguous function. In a peculiar irony, the aged veteran reached his pathetic prime at the moment of his own passing. From the Waterloo veterans of mid-century, to the Crimean and Indian Mutiny veterans of the late nineteenth and early twentieth centuries, the veteran was perpetually poised, in the words of the *Punch* poem, to 'drop off the stage'.[29] In images such as Sir Hubert von Herkomer's celebrated painting *The Last Muster: Sunday at the Royal Hospital, Chelsea* (1875), much of the imaginative appeal of the aged veteran lay in his essential evanescence. Moreover, even those veterans who were more securely anchored in the land of the living remained, somehow, fixed in time. As an article on the Chelsea Pensioners from 1835 observed,

> No expectation lighted up their countenances during the ... morning's proceedings, and now that this had come to a close, the memory of it had fled at the same time. There is nothing inexplicable here. These grey-beards had no longer a part to play in the drama of life. Observation was dead within them. They had no motive to crave new sights, or treasure up fresh experiences. Hope for the future had departed from them. They were, and felt themselves, but 'sojourners by the wayside'.[30]

These aged veterans had no substantive presence. They were, rather, repositories of memory, monuments to their own past glories. Even so, they had a powerful didactic role to play.

Generators of feeling

As we have seen, visual and textual representations of veterans frequently juxtaposed aged soldiers and sailors with children and youths. In this way, they were part of a broader discourse which promoted the values of military service though appeals to masculinity and fatherhood, as well as to paternal and familial obligation. This representational culture configured the aged veteran in two key ways. In the first place, he was depicted as the literal progenitor of boys who would go on to enter the armed services.[31] This was a frequent feature of the reporting of veterans' funerals. For example, when the eighty-year-old Sergeant-Major Woodhouse was buried with full military honours in 1868, *John Bull* noted his service record, but dedicated most space to remarking on his family of eighteen children, six of whom served as soldiers, 'three of them non-commissioned officers in the 2nd Life Guards'.[32] Such familial links were likewise celebrated in art, such as C. T. G Formilli's painting *My Son's Regiment* (1903), which depicts seven Chelsea Pensioners avidly reading a poster outside a newspaper shop. To some extent, these forms of representation confirmed aged military men's manliness, connecting them with the laudatory characteristics of fatherhood, and demonstrating that they were exemplars of approved values for the next generation.[33]

The idea of veterans having fathered the next generation of soldiers and sailors was common in popular culture throughout the century and conveyed complex, and occasionally ambiguous, meanings. In a story from 1811, 'The Pensioner' tells his interlocutor that he had two sons and professed his wish for them 'to be something else than soldiers, for I knew the hardships of a soldier's life; but they liked it, and both fell, sir, fighting for their country'.[34] If the precise configuration of the veteran altered across the century, this maudlin representation of loss and sacrifice in the service of the state remained a consistent feature. Thus, in a much later poem, published in the *Ladies Monthly Magazine*, 'The Old Soldier' recounts that he had lost not only his brave comrades in war, but also his two sons. The first fought alongside him, saving his life by fighting off the enemy until his father's fainting form was carried away; he then fought 'his way to glory'. As the old soldier declared, 'My true son died in manhood's pride.' He then proceeds to explain that his 'second joy, my sailor boy ... lies dead, / Beneath the sun-kissed billow'. If these doleful accounts risked losing their force for recruitment purposes, they nonetheless stirred sentiment and reminded the reader that the soldier-father would find consolation at death, when he and his sons would be reunited.[35]

In situating the veteran as a father of soldiers, these accounts also reminded the male reader of the pleasures and obligations of filial duty, not just to an imagined father but also to the king and country he symbolised. In 'My Old Regiment' (1891), a stirring story for children set in 1880, an old pensioner and veteran of the First Anglo-Afghan War (1839–42), Peter Harwood, watches the soldiers from his old regiment return to their village with glory from the Second Anglo-Afghan War (1878–80).[36] He muses that, though his comrades are all gone, '*my boy* wears the old uniform and keeps up the old name amongst them' (original italics). One of the colour sergeants, bearing the encased regimental colours, gives him a 'quick smile' as he passes the old soldier's gate, the moment captured in a beautiful illustration (figure 5.4). Later, when permitted to drop out of the ranks, Colour Sergeant Jim Harwood visits his father, who is seated on the bench outside his cottage, beside the hollyhocks. The old soldier feels exceeding joy as his son 'reverently touching the medals on his father's breast, points to his own heart, above which hung on a similar scrap of rainbow ribbon the six-pointed star which commemorated the world-famous march from

Figure 5.4   'One of the Colour Sergeants turned with a quick smile', *Our Darlings*, 1 April 1891, p. 203.

Kabul to Kandahar'. Deploying all the cultural motifs of British life - families gathered around their cottage doors, hollyhocks blazing - and the emotional tropes of father-son relationships, this story indicated to its imagined male reader that to fill his father with joy and preserve his beloved nation, he needed to fulfil his manly duties in the service of his country and perpetuate the British imperial project.

As we saw in the introduction, Chelsea Pensioners were regularly depicted alongside young, uniformed soldiers. As with 'My Old Regiment', these images often explicitly linked past and present conflicts, as the title of an engraving for the *Illustrated London News* (1882) indicates: 'After the review: Waterloo and Tel-el-Kebir – a sketch on the Chelsea Embankment'. Arm in arm, the aged veteran and young cavalryman stroll along, watched by a young girl, distracted from gazing at the Thames (figure 5.5). These motifs reached their peak in 1914, when the PRC issued this poster, part of a series by Lawson Wood (1878–1957), which portrays a young recruit being seen off to war by an old soldier (figure 5.6). The phrase 'Chip of the Old Block' implies a father–son relationship and reiterates the connection between the veteran's military past and the martial valour of the volunteer, as well as between Britain's historic glories and its current endeavours. As James

Figure 5.5 'After the review: Waterloo and Tel-el-Kebir – a sketch on the Chelsea Embankment', *Illustrated London News*, 2 December 1882, p. 575. Picture no. 12029904.

Marten observes, the drilling together of young and old soldiers in the decades after the American Civil War provided 'a symbolic bridge from the bloody battlefields of the past to the possibility of future sacrifice'.[37] And with its tagline 'Your King and Country Need You / To Maintain the Honour and Glory of the British Empire', Lawson's poster is even more explicit in its appeals to national memory than the Dadd image with which we began.

In the second place, as well as being the literal progenitors of future servicemen, veterans were also visualised as the disseminators of values across generations. Luke Fildes' illustration 'The Greenwich Pensioner' (1879), from *The Boy's Own Paper*, is a particularly notable example (figure 5.7). The pensioner is seated on a bench in Greenwich Park, surrounded by boys ranging in age from about three to fifteen. The older boy is dressed in naval attire. All are transfixed by the old sailor, who

Figure 5.6 Lawson Wood for the Parliamentary Recruiting Committee, *Your King and Country Need You* (1914) – NAM. 1977–06–81–15.

Figure 5.7 Luke Fildes, 'The Greenwich Pensioner', *The Boy's Own Paper*, 8 February 1879, p. 65.

is pictured in the act of telling a story, gesticulating with stick and hand; except the little one, who, like all little boys in such pictures, is focused on his toy boat.[38] Their dispositions evoke the images, so popular from the eighteenth century onwards, of labourers returning home to be greeted by their young children gathered at their knee and the baby dandled in their arms.[39] Clearly these men were imagined in a paternal-like role, transmitting values to a younger generation. If the images evoke fathers, however, their age suggests that they were grandfathers. Grandfathers often acted as substitute parents, carrying out very similar duties, and they were culturally perceived to be loving – even doting.[40] Elderly folk (in their 'dotage') were understood to prattle and tell tales, and this is gestured to in images of old veterans, who are often depicted as inveterate storytellers. *Bell's Life* gently mocked the Chelsea Pensioner's garrulousness in 'enumerating the various battles he had been in'. In the description of the pensioner's stories, however, one glimpses the pleasures for children listening: 'long-prosing stories, hair-breadth escapes, extraordinary adventures, services unrequited, mines exploded, forlorn hopes, fatigues undergone, hardships endured, marches and counter-marches, plunder, patience, and prize-money, forming the sources from whence you must be entertained'.[41]

The values transmitted to the young varied. In the earlier part of the period, some old veterans are depicted telling the young the truth about the hardships of war. This is the case with the mid-century story 'The Old Veteran; His Wooden Leg, and His War Stories'. While playing at being soldiers and beguiled by the imagined glories of war, a group of children spy a 'soldierly looking man' sitting at the foot of a tree, identifiable by his military cap, medal and wooden leg. This story would appear at first to be a straightforward depiction of boys spellbound by the tales of the aged veteran, yet the text is far more cautionary in tone. Engaging him in conversation to indulge their military fantasies, the boys are instead told, in graphic detail, how his leg was blown off at Waterloo and how he was trampled by a French horse. He tells them that being a 'hero' did not ease the agony, nor does it stop the blood he still coughs up or the pain in his missing leg and foot. He refutes the glory of battle, describing the dead soldiers that littered the battlefield, until one of the boys, Marmaduke, begs him to stop, tears up his paper cocked hat and breaks his wooden sword. Another boy, Manby, asks why his cousin tells jolly tales of the Crimea and the glorious deaths of his comrades, sporting his Victoria Cross at church every Sunday. The old veteran insists that the children must know the misery that war brings to peoples and nations and that 'one quiet peaceable night by your own fireside is worth twenty victories'.[42] In the rather more jingoistic context of the later nineteenth century, however, such images of age and youth were easily harnessed to a sentimentalised glorification of war. For example, Arthur Elsley's *A Young Briton* (1895), which hangs in the Royal Hospital at Chelsea, depicts an elderly pensioner helping a delighted child to draw his sword from its scabbard (figure 5.8).

Aged veterans not only served a purpose in teaching boys about war; they also provided more general instruction, conveying moral and religious messages. In 'The Withered Oak' (1830), a desperately dour story which plays on the familiar trope of the forgotten veteran, a 108-year-old soldier's sheer longevity serves as an object lesson to a child who hoped to live a long life. The boy's father explains that the veteran is a shadow of a man, who had buried his wife and all his children; only one of his grandchildren survives, a soldier in India. As such, he singularly proves that long life is not sufficient for happiness.[43] As well as providing a lesson in their own selves, old soldiers' tales more often than not had didactic intentions. For example, in 'Always Speak the Truth, Boy' (1871), a grandfather who is also 'an old soldier, with a pension for good and faithful service' teaches his grandson not to lie. While the large accompanying illustration of 'Grandfather Quayle' seated on a stool,

Figure 5.8 *A Young Briton*. Chromolithograph by Grover and Co. after Arthur J. Elsley (1895) – Picture No. 11096707.

with a small boy standing in front of him, does not have him dressed as a soldier, his status as a veteran clearly strengthens his message.[44] Girls were often present on the periphery of these depictions, and they too were intended to be recipients of the general values of filial duty, obedience and piety that they imparted. In *The Children's Treasury* (1870), for example, an old, blind soldier is the means by which 'little' Mary's heart is opened to Jesus.[45] By the late nineteenth and early twentieth centuries, however, images of pensioners and young girls had, for the most part, become clichéd and highly sentimentalised. A typical example is *Grandad's Garden* by Rose Maynard Barton (1856–1929), which plays on the associations between the Hospital and gardening - an association solidified by the inauguration of the Royal International Horticultural Show in 1912 and evident in this wartime poster from 1915 (figure 5.9). In such images, the veteran is simply is a bearer of a nostalgic patriotism, and much of the former moral content is lost.

Figure 5.9 'Vee Bee', 'Royal Horticultural Society War Relief Fund Floral Fête' (1915).

Materiality and performativity

The veteran's moral message was frequently conveyed through his body. Thus, the readers of *The Penny Satirist* in 1840 were reminded that, during their active service, Greenwich Pensioners were literal barriers between the British and their enemies; it was thanks to their 'walls of stout and honest flesh, [that] we have lived securely, participating in every peaceful and domestic comfort, and neither heard the roar of the cannon nor seen its smoke'. The sailor (and soldier) often fought at a considerable spatial and imaginative remove from the metropole, but here the author brings the bodily sacrifice of the serviceman directly into the homes of the British middle classes:

if it had not been for his leg, the cannon-ball might have scattered us in our tea-parlour – the bullet which deprived him of his orb of vision, might have stricken *Our Village* from our hand, whilst ensconced in our study; the cutlass which cleaved his shoulder might have demolished our china vase, or our globe of golden fish.[46]

Textual representations dwelled on the physical form of the veteran to serve a number of ends. The aged veteran's body could, in some cases, stand for all soldiers, past and present. In an article entitled 'The British Soldier' in *The Ladies Cabinet* (1844), the 'soldier of a hundred battles is stamped upon the veteran's aspect'! The medals on his breast, the scar on his brow from Waterloo, the bronzed skin, the 'blue and peppery tinges of "foul priming"' on the right of his face: all, the author suggests, remind one of the 'thousands – the hundreds of thousands – who, in the buoyancy of hope and youth, commenced their military career with our hero. Alas! how very few survive'.[47]

At the same time, veterans were also the literal embodiment of their specific service record. In *The Boys' Own Paper* of 1897, for example, eighty-three-year-old Chelsea Pensioner William Simcock is interviewed about his service since joining the army in 1834. The piece offers details of his injuries and hardships while serving in India and during the conquest of Burma and the Andaman Islands. But it also shows how this experience was inscribed on his body, noting that he was tattooed all over, like Burmese soldiers. Simcock explains, with a flourish, that the Burmese thought such tattoos protected them from being wounded but, once the British troops appeared, 'they did not believe in it any longer'.[48] This simultaneous appropriation and dismissal of the colonial other's culture doubtless added to the glamour of military conquest and imperial adventure for its impressionable young readers.

In many instances, the veteran's body, though aged and often injured, was still seen as active and appealing. In *Bell's Life* (1830), a semi-fictional Chelsea Pensioner was described thus:

This warm-hearted son of Mars was as fine a piece of weather-beaten anatomy (of seventy-five years' standing) as you would meet with … his limbs, unlike his comrades, perfect; and, although they bore stronger symptoms of ossification than sleekness, yet had they been well-formed – his head erect, and a martial fire in his eye that seemed to bid defiance to time … a deeply furrowed brow (ornamented with a few professional scars)[49]

The author linked his service in arms with his body, including his silver hair, 'spared by the tropical climate of the east and swampy vapours of the west'. He was wounded in at least twenty-three places with 'two balls *quartered* in his body'; he had been in as many engagements as he had received wounds, 'and which wounds, he said, would serve him, when his memory began to fall, as an "Orderly-Book," to the number'![50] Such veterans were a living mnemonic of historic battles.

As well as being intriguing in its own right, the aged veteran's body was also often contrasted with his youthful self. One old soldier was described as 'lit up with not a little portion of his youthful fire', when recounting his life.[51] In some ways, this noble past counterbalanced the cultural association of old age with garrulousness. In 'Old Soldiers, and Old Sailors' (1843), for example, the author ruminates that elderly storytellers, on one hand, are generally boring or insufferably self-satisfied. Soldiers and sailors, on the other hand, along with players, travellers and retired highwaymen were, he claimed, amusing raconteurs. In this account, an old soldier recalls the scene as the 'clangour of the trumpet rings through the air, and the cold, clear, cruel bayonets flash and glisten in the sun'. The author then contrasts his story of excitement, turmoil, terror and passions with its teller, prostheses and all:

> and as you look at the crippled narrator of all this, – old, infirm, mutilated, 'curtailed of man's fair proportions', a mere piece of patch-work made up for the great part of cork, or common timber, – it requires some exercise of the imaginative faculty to bring it home to you, that this is the creature who has been an actor in these things; that this is the veritable man who has stood ancle-deep [*sic*] in blood … As you look at him you cannot help coinciding with the psalmist, that 'all flesh is grass'.[52]

The veteran's damaged body had long been a problematic reminder of the risks of military service.[53] An article in *Punch*, reflecting on the recent *Report on the Recruiting of the Army* (1866), warned that 'There is no object that more tends to counteract the eloquence of the recruiting sergeant than the sight of a ragged and famishing old soldier, or of a veteran in the workhouse.' Their empty sleeves and wooden legs were a discouragement to martial impulse, 'deterring all reasonable spectators from adventuring to tread the path of glory in which he got mutilated'.[54] And yet, what the popular literature of the period suggests is that the disabled veteran's body could still be presented as manly, displaying its owner's valour though its scars, skin, limbs and dress. Thus, Thomas

Kelly's engraving of three Greenwich Pensioners, each lacking one or two limbs, produced for *The Good Child's Reward* (c. 1860), is accompanied by the text: 'The wooden substituted limb, / The eye, tho' sightless, never dim; / The armless body proudly wears / The laurel gain'd – the laurel shares.'[55]

Indeed, the aged veteran could often serve as a glamorous, if poignant, reminder of manly beauty and courage. In the same *Bell's Life* article as the 'warm-hearted son of Mars' appears, another Chelsea pensioner is connected to his younger self and glorious deeds in perhaps the most material form imaginable. The narrator explains that he was the 'identical Serjeant [sic] that received the lamented Abercombie in his arms', when he died on the battlefield of Alexandria in 1801:

> Yes, reader; in the sculptured figure in St. Paul's of the Highland Serjeant [*sic*], receiving in his arms the dying hero of Alexandria, you behold the once athletic form of the brave veteran, a sketch of whom I am now endeavouring to draw, mixed up, it is true, with the characteristics of the whole Pantheon of Chelsea.[56]

In some cases, the aged veteran was imagined as still virile. W. C. Safford Esq.'s 'Old Soldier' in *La Belle Assemblée* (1830) was described as 'hale and hearty in body', though missing an arm and leg and with a scar above his left eye, which 'did not add to the beauty of his countenance', which was bronzed by exposure to other climes. With grey hair, and intelligent eye, he had some fire of youth left in him and 'proved that he *had been* what may be termed a gay man amongst the lasses' (original italics). When the narrator looks with interest on what he takes to be the soldier's pretty daughter, the veteran informs him that she is in fact his wife. Thirty years younger than him, they had been married for nearly ten years and he is, he says, 'as happy as the King'.[57] Such virile veterans stood somewhere between the twin poles of the youthful, gay soldier/sailor and the decrepit and dependent pensioner, still merely an echo of the former, yet not so readily sentimentalised as the latter. Perhaps this particular representation imagined one way in which veterans might be rewarded for armed service and bodily damage in the service of king and country.

If veterans' bodies functioned as a metonym for sacrifice and valour, then so too did the objects with which they were associated, notably medals, uniforms and regimental colours. Like the veteran himself, these objects created an imaginative bridge between past, present and future conflicts.[58] A particularly powerful example of this can be found in 'Nearly Forty Years Ago. A Reminiscence of a Waterloo Veteran' (1895), from the adolescent paper *Chums*, which tells the tale of John, an elderly veteran of Waterloo, who ends his life in a small Canadian village. The author recalls that, as a boy, he would see this 'antique and martial figure', who sold fresh fish, tap his left breast proudly when he had served his customers. The boy realises that he wore his Waterloo medal under his coat, a gesture which 'restored him from trade to his soldiership'. His father tells him that a customer had once asked John if he would sell that 'bit of pewter'. The old soldier was so insulted that he thereafter wore it beneath his coat where it would be 'always felt by the heart of the hero'. In 1855, however, the author meets John walking erect with the medal on his coat; since war had been declared on Russia, the veteran felt it 'right to show it' as his son had gone with the regiment. John displays his medal until the end of the Crimean War, when he leads a torch-lit procession 'in full regimentals, straight as a ramrod, the hero of the night'. The narrator recalls, 'We boys thought the old army of Wellington kept ghostly step with John Locke, while aerial drums pealed and beat with rejoicing at the new glory of English-speaking men.'

Then comes the 'Sepoy Mutiny', and as that conflict unfolds, John and his medal become a barometer for British military fortunes: 'Week after week, month after month, as hideous tidings poured steadily in, his face became more haggard, gray, [*sic*] and dreadful. The feeling that he was too old for use seemed to shame him. He no longer carried his head high, as of yore.' He was despondent in part because his son was not marching behind Havelock, having sailed to join Outram in Persia before the rebellion. After some months, news comes that his son's regiment has gone to India to fight the 'mutineers', and thus 'John marched into the village with a prouder air … His medal was again displayed on his breast.' The story ends tragically, however, with the village postmaster reading aloud the press report of the capture of a sepoy fort. The veteran's son is named as a member of the forlorn hope, leading the assault, but as the report unfolds, his son is described dying in action, riddled with bullets. When the report ends, the veteran announces that his son had 'died well for England and duty', nervously fingers the medal on his chest, wheels around and marches to his cabin. The next day, the minister finds him dead upon his straw bed in 'his antique regimentals, stiffer than at attention, all his medals fastened below that of Waterloo above his quiet heart'.[59] Here, then, the medal is a remarkably powerful emotional object intended to convey the generational links of duty and self-sacrifice in the military.[60] Even divested of such explicitly generational meaning, moreover, veterans' medals acted as material cultural reminders of the continuity of national military endeavour. An account of Chelsea Hospital, for example, describes a case of medals in the great hall: 'When a pensioner dies, should no relatives appear to claim his effects, his medals are put into this case, and here are dozens, representing service in every battle since the days of the Peninsular War.'[61]

Indeed, when Chelsea Hospital was described in popular texts, authors often focused on those spaces that were most intimately linked to the materiality of war. For example, in 'Chelsea Pensioners at Home' (1886) from *The Boy's Own Paper*, the adornment of the chapel is described in highly evocative terms:

> captured flags ... form the chief decoration ... Torn to tatters, most of them tender as tinder, they are now sewn on to silken nettings to support them in their decay; but often tiny pieces of the rotting silk come floating into the brown oak pews that line the walls.[62]

The captured flags in the Great Hall are illustrated on the frontispiece (figure 5.10). The account explains that every seven years when the chapel is cleaned, the 'precious trophies' are wrapped and laid in store, 'so delicate are they that slightest draught would blow them into dust'. These trophies are then delineated, naming the battles they were taken in and their various states of decay, including the French Imperial Eagle ('the sacred standard') captured by the Scots Greys at Waterloo.[63] This paradoxical allusion to the ephemerality of the trophies of war, their combination of glory and decay, captures the passage of time, both in the artefacts of war and the bodies of the men themselves.

In addition to medals and flags, veterans' uniforms also had an evocative power. Indeed, part of the appeal of the Chelsea and Greenwich Pensioners was that their uniforms tied them irrevocably to their martial past. In 1830, *Bell's Life* observed that the 'dress of your Chelsea Pensioner ... adds very materially to the veteran-like appearance of the man'. With its long red coat and tricorn hat, it evoked the 'Guardsmen's dress of 1745', and, 'although somewhat antiquated' presented a 'more warlike and martial appearance than your more dandyfied and bedizened one of the present'.[64] Of course, although they might proudly display their medals, most veterans did not wear their old service uniforms as a matter of course, rarely even on special occasions. However,

Figure 5.10 'Chelsea Pensioners at Home', *The Boy's Own Paper*, 16 October 1886, p. 40.

there are examples, which parallel the famous images of the veterans of Napoleon's *Grande Armée* taken in c. 1859, where aged British veterans also wore full regimental uniform for the record.[65] For example, in c. 1880, Robert Turner, formerly a sergeant in the Royal Artillery and a veteran of the Crimea, was photographed in full dress uniform in his capacity as Master Gunner at Fort Belvedere, Windsor, with the inscription 'the oldest soldier in the Royal Artillery'. (figure 5.11). Likewise, while most of the photographs taken of the members of the Bristol Crimean War and Indian Mutiny Veterans Association in the

Figure 5.11 Photograph of Master Gunner Robert Turner, Fort Belvedere, Windsor Park (1880) – NAM. 1988-03-93-1.

later nineteenth century show them in civilian dress, albeit with their medals on display, this remarkable image of J. E. Wright of the 46th (South Devonshire) Regiment of Foot presents him in full field dress, complete with Kilmarnock cap, bedroll and musket (figure 5.12).

The appeal of seeing aged veterans in uniform was multi-faceted. At one level, as Scott Hughes Myerly has demonstrated, nineteenth-century military uniforms were designed to be spectacular in their own right and so their display had an intrinsic appeal.[66] This was certainly the case for the images of the *Grande Armée* veterans, which included such impressive and 'exotic' uniforms as those of the 1st Hussars and the Mamelukes of the Imperial Guard. In the British context, it is likely that the increasingly utilitarian nature of army field dress, which, by the 1880s, had fully dispensed with scarlet finery in favour of drab khaki, lent the uniforms of the past a particular mystique. This was especially true when, as with the veteran more generally, past glories could be linked to present concerns. In this sense, it is notable that the image of J. E. Wright, which is clearly a carefully composed studio portrait, contains not only a large, draped Union flag, but also an African-inspired pedestal atop which sits a light-coloured Foreign Service helmet, an allusion, perhaps, to the contemporary Anglo-Zulu (1879) or First Anglo-Boer Wars (1880–81). In addition to this, it is clear that the sight of elderly men re-enacting, through dress or action, the prime of their

Figure 5.12   Contact print of J. E. Wright, Bristol Crimean War and Indian Mutiny Veteran's Association (1870–80) – NAM. 1994-11-169.

youth had a peculiar frisson. The large-scale later nineteenth- and early twentieth-century reunions of Civil War veterans on the battlefield of Gettysburg are a remarkable case in point, but, in Britain too, certain veterans, most notably the survivors of the Light Brigade, were induced to relive their experiences, often for commercial gain.[67] For example, Sergeant Frederick Peake of the 13th (Light) Dragoons used regularly to don the tattered and torn coatee he had worn during the battle and even had it let out as he aged.[68] Similarly, Nehemiah William Eastoe of the 11th Hussars offered to recite Tennyson's poem while dressed in 'full uniform' for a 'moderate fee', while Trumpeter Martin Landfried of the 17th Lancers would often accompany the actress Amy Sedgwick's dramatic recitals of the same poem, dressed in his uniform and playing a trumpet. In 1890, Landfried was even recorded by the Edison Company, playing the regimental bugle which had allegedly sounded at both Waterloo and Balaclava.[69] This latter example captures the remarkable potency not only of the aged veteran's self, but also of his material accoutrements. This bugle, which had served in two historic conflicts, was only one of a number of claimants to be the 'authentic' instrument which had sounded the fateful charge and, together with Peake's coatee, was the kind of powerful emotional object to be preserved for posterity in both local and national museum collections.[70]

The case of Landfried's recording also demonstrates how the performance of veteranhood was shaped by technological innovation. Of course, this performance had deep roots. Chelsea and Greenwich Pensioners had long provided a public spectacle, especially on occasions such as Founders' Day, when the former would be inspected by a member of the royal family. No wonder that the veteran was understood as a 'type' to be painted. One, it was noted in 1811, 'would have furnished an excellent subject for an artist; his features were fine, and strongly marked; a few white hairs were scattered over a brow which had seen many years; his beard had not lately been shorn of its honours, which added greatly to his venerable appearance'.[71] As with Lanfried's bugle, military accoutrements also provided a performative aspect to the pensioner's identity. One of the 'postcards' represented on the frontispiece to 'Chelsea Pensioners at Home', for example, depicts two pensioners marching side by side, one playing a fife, the other a drum (figure 5.10). These immediately recognisable instruments symbolised battle and its supposed glories. In the poem 'The Air That Led to Victory' (1884), the 'time-worn Chelsea pensioner', in his long coat and cocked hat, draws a fife from his breast and plays it for his fellow pensioners. As they listen they are transported into battle, dashing across the plain on their horses, until they hear the 'stirring trumpet-blast'; 'then there comes / The memory of muffled drums; / Unbidden rise the silent tears / When sounds "The British Grenadiers."'[72]

However, it was the development of photography from the 1840s onwards that provided an especially potent means for the performance of veteranhood. The Crimean War had seen the innovative use of photography on the battlefield and, on their return, a number of soldiers were famously captured in the series 'Crimean Heroes 1856' by Robert Howlett and Joseph Cundall (one of these images appears on the cover of this book).[73] As the century wore on, photography was similarly used to capture veterans in their aged state. Despite the various 'small wars' of empire fought around mid-century, it was veterans of the Crimean War and Indian 'Mutiny' who proved the most enduring in this respect, although veterans from the Waterloo campaign were also photographed as late as 1880.[74] Individual and group portraits of veterans abounded, ranging from members of memorial societies and 'native' troops in

India to a photograph taken in front of the Chelsea Hospital in 1910 of 'Mutiny' veterans which included such luminaries as Field Marshalls Frederick Roberts and Garnett Wolseley as well as rank-and-file pensioners.[75] Even so, at least one example, of uncertain origin, sought to capture the sheer range of conflicts in which British veterans participated. Dating from sometime after 1906, this panoramic photograph consists of veterans, many of them aged, some of whom are carrying poles onto which have subsequently been superimposed somewhat crudely drawn placards bearing the name and medal of each major British military land campaign from the Crimean War to the Natal Rebellion (1906) (figure 5.13).

Such attempts to memorialise the veterans of mid-century conflicts peaked in the early twentieth century as their numbers began to dwindle and as renewed conflict and popular militarism encouraged patriotic reflection. Perhaps the most remarkable instance of this was the dinner held at Christmas 1907 to commemorate the golden anniversary of the Indian 'Mutiny'. This took place in the imposing surroundings of the Albert Hall, and while invited dignitaries such as Rudyard Kipling joined the veterans inside, members of the public crowded in the rain to witness 'the arrival of the veterans and their subsequent inspection

Figure 5.13 Panoramic photograph, in two parts, of veterans of campaigns, 1852–1906 – NAM. 1985–04–52.

by Lord Roberts'. The occasion was reported on by the *Daily Telegraph*, which had sponsored the event, in remarkably florid prose. 'We have seen them', it wrote, 'In the weakness of their age and the glory of their honour, they have come together for the last time on earth, and they have melted again into the mist.' Reflecting on the emotions aroused by these aged men, it claimed, 'Vain are the human triumphs untouched by the sense of tears in mortal things. That sense was present and penetrating yesterday, as in few scenes ever witnessed upon English soil.'[76]

Conclusion

In many ways, the *Daily Telegraph's* celebratory dinner for the 'Mutiny' veterans encapsulates much of what we have sought to highlight in this chapter about the representation of the aged veteran in the long nineteenth century. In its combination of mass media, sentimentalism and nationalism, it both represents the culmination of nineteenth-century trends as well as anticipating certain cultural forms that would shape aspects of the twentieth- and twenty-first-century conceptualisation of the veteran soldier in Britain. For example, commentators were moved to contrast the bodily infirmity of these men with the time when they had 'fought and bled for England, when the blood was fresh in their arteries and youth was in their cheeks'. Similarly, veterans were encouraged to perform their identities though the wearing of old uniforms and medals and, in the case of 'Angus Gibson, of the Black Watch, the last surviving piper of the Mutiny', through the emotive re-enactment of former duties. The *Telegraph* even used the opportunity to remind its readers that the 'most pathetic' fact about the celebration was that 'of all the Indian Mutiny veterans who were eligible to be present at the Albert Hall, at least a hundred are inmates of workhouses'. Most notably of all, however, the entire event was assimilated into a jingoistic discourse in which these aged veterans served not simply as memorials to their own past, but also as exemplars for current and future generations of imperialists As a poem, especially commissioned for the occasion, read,

To-day, across our fathers' graves
The astonished years reveal
The remnants of that desperate host,
Which cleansed our East with steel.
Hail and farewell! We greet you here,
With tears that none will scorn –

O keepers of the house of old,
Or ever we were born!
One service more we dare to ask.
Pray for us, heroes, pray,
That when Fate lays on us our Task
We do not shame the day.[77]

Notes

1 *The Graphic*, 27 February 1915, p. 278; *St Andrew's Citizen*, 15 May 1915, p. 7.

2 The history of the institution was set out in several contemporary periodicals, including *The Ladies Cabinet*, 1 December 1845, p. 379 and *The Boys' Own Paper*, 16 October 1886, p. 41.

3 The *Journal of Veteran Studies*, for example, was launched in 2016, but very few of its articles to date are historical in approach.

4 There is a voluminous literature on this topic but, for an example from each of the two world wars, see Deborah Cohen, *The War Come Home: Disabled Veterans in Britain and Germany, 1914–1939* (Berkeley: University of California Press, 2001) and Julie Anderson, *War, Disability and Rehabilitation in Britain: 'Soul of a Nation'* (Manchester: Manchester University Press, 2011).

5 For the European context, see Ángel Alcalde, *War Veterans and Fascism in Interwar Europe* (Cambridge: Cambridge University Press, 2017). For an example of extra-European contexts, see Norma J. Kriger, *Guerrilla Veterans in Post-War Zimbabwe: Symbolic and Violent Politics, 1980–1987* (Cambridge: Cambridge University Press, 2003).

6 An excellent introduction to this literature is provided by Larry M. Logue and Michael Barton (eds), *The Civil War Veteran: A Historical Reader* (New York: New York University Press, 2007). For work on the social history of veterans, see James Martens, *Sing Not War: The Lives of Union and Confederate Veterans in Gilded Age America* (Chapel Hill: University of North Caroline Press, 2011).

7 See also, Stuart McConnell, *Glorious Contentment: The Grand Army of the Republic, 1865–1900* (Chapel Hill: University of North Carolina Press, 1997).

8 Caroline E. Janney, *Reunion and the Limits of Reconciliation* (Chapel Hill: University of North Carolina Press, 2013); M. Keith Harris, *Across the Bloody Chasm: The Culture of Commemoration Among Civil War Veterans* (Baton Rouge: Louisiana State University Press, 2014). For the differential experiences of black soldiers, see Donald Robert Shaffer, *After the Glory: The Struggles of Black Civil War Veterans* (Lawrence: Kansas University Press, 2004).

9   Caroline Nielsen, '"Continuing to Serve?": Representations of the Elderly Veteran Soldier in the late Eighteenth and early Nineteenth Centuries' in Stephen McVeigh and Nicola Cooper (eds), *Men after War* (London: Routledge, 2013), pp. 18–35. See also, Caroline Nielsen, 'The Chelsea Out-Pensioners: Image and Reality in Eighteenth-Century and Early Nineteenth-Century Social Care' (PhD thesis: Newcastle University, 2014).

10 Lara Kriegel, 'Living Links to History, or, Victorian Veterans in the Twentieth-Century World', *Victorian Studies* 58:3 (2016), pp. 289–301.

11 The Crimean War (1854–56) has come in for especial attention in this regard. For example, see Lara Kriegel, 'Who Blew the Balaklava Bugle? The Charge of the Light Brigade and the Afterlife of the Crimean War', *19: Interdisciplinary Studies in the Long Nineteenth Century*, 2015 (20), DOI:10.16995/ntn.713; Rachel Elizabeth Bates, 'Curating the Crimea: The Cultural Afterlife of a Conflict' (PhD thesis: University of Leicester, 2015).

12 Hichberger, *Images of the Army*, p. 169.

13 Quoted in *Ibid.*, p. 170.

14 In fact, O'Neil produced a number of images around this theme, but most are studies rather than exhibited paintings.

15 Begiato (Bailey), 'Tears and the Manly Sailor', pp. 117–33; Parkes, 'Wooden Legs and Tales of Sorrow Done', pp. 191–207; Nielsen, 'The Chelsea Out-Pensioners', pp. 236–9.

16 Peter Reese, *Homecoming Heroes: An Account of the Reassimilation of British Personnel into Civilian Life* (London: Leo Cooper, 1992), pp. 34–5.

17 Nielsen, 'The Chelsea Out-Pensioners', p. 4.

18 Reese, *Homecoming Heroes*, pp. 36–7.

19 'Sudden Death of a Chelsea Pensioner', *John Bull*, 18 February 1843, p. 102.

20 For example, see Kenneth Hendrickson, *Making Saints: Religion and the Public Image of the British Army, 1809–1885* (London: Associated University Presses, 1998).

21 Shaw, *Suffering and Sentiment*; Parkes, 'Wooden Legs and Tales of Sorrow Done'; Nielsen, 'The Chelsea Out-Pensioners'.

22 David W. Blight, *Race and Reunion: The Civil War in American Memory* (Cambridge, MA: The Belknap Press, 2001), pp. 208–9; Marten, *Sing Not War*, pp. 249–52.

23 Brown, 'Cold Steel, Weak Flesh', pp. 155–81.

24 *Punch*, 2 April 1870, p. 133.

25 *Punch*, 21 October 1882, p. 90.

26 National Army Museum, London, NAM.1998-06-107, 'Rules of the Balaclava Commemoration Society' (1877).

27 *Punch*, 26 April 1890, p. 196.

28 www.kiplingsociety.co.uk/poems_brigade.htm (12 March 2019).

29 *Punch*, 26 April 1890, p. 196.

30 'The Chelsea Pensioners "at Home"', *The Court Magazine*, 1 December 1833, p. 253.

31 For the earlier period, see Nielsen, 'The Chelsea Pensioners', pp. 242–4.

32 *John Bull*, 28 March 1868, p. 228.

33 Begiato (Bailey), *Parenting in England*, pp. 174–98; Begiato (Bailey), '"A Very Sensible Man"', pp. 267–92. See also, Trev Lynn Broughton and Helen Rogers (eds), *Gender and Fatherhood in the Nineteenth Century* (Basingstoke: Palgrave Macmillan, 2007).

34 *Lady's Monthly Museum*, 1 April 1811, p. 229.

35 *Ladies Monthly Magazine*, 1 July 1870, p. 8.

36 'My Old Regiment', *Our Darlings*, 1 April 1891, p. 199.

37 Marten, *Sing Not War*, p. 23.

38 *The Boy's Own Paper*, 8 February 1879, p. 64.

39 Begiato (Bailey), *Parenting in England*, chapter 4. See also, Christiana Payne, *Rustic Simplicity: Scenes of Country Life in Nineteenth-Century British Art* (Nottingham: Djanogly Art Gallery, 1998).

40 Bailey (Bailey), *Parenting in England*, p. 203.

41 *Bell's Life*, 11 July 1830, p. 3.

42 'The Old Veteran; His Wooden Leg and his War Stories', *Peter Parley's Annual* (date unknown), pp. 35–43.

43 *Child's Companion*, 1 October 1830, p. 289.

44 *Chatterbox*, 26 January 1871, p. 65.

45 *The Children's Treasury*, 1 October 1870, p. 181.

46 *The Penny Satirist*, 21 March 1840, p. 3.

47 'The British Soldier', in *The Ladies Cabinet*, 1 January 1844, p. 30.

48 The story is illustrated by a rather fine engraving of the veteran telling his story, from a painting by Arthur Robinson. *The Boys' Own Paper*, 4 December 1897, p. 145.

49 *Bell's Life*, 11 July 1830, p. 3.

50 *Ibid.*

51 'The British Soldier', p. 30.

52 The old sailor, says the author, is 'more discursive' and speaks of all sorts of subjects. He tells of the parts of the world he has visited from the North Cape, to the Bay of Bengal, to Sierra Leone, California, and New Zealand. His tales revolve around women he loved, a 'score of Pollys and Mollys'. His sea-battles are recounted with more coolness, with the loss of limbs alluded to as 'rather unlucky circumstances'. 'Old Soldiers and Old Sailors', *Ladies Cabinet*, 1 September 1843, p. 196.

53 Parkes, 'Wooden Legs and Tales of Sorrow Done'.

54 *Punch*, 1 December 1866, p. 221.

55 'Greenwich Pensioners', Henry Sharpe Horsley, *The Good Child's Reward* (London: Thomas Kelly, c. 1860).

56 *Bell's Life*, 11 July 1830, p. 3.

57   *La Belle Assemblée*, 1 September 1830, p. 114.

58   For the role of battlefield relics and the artefacts and memorabilia of war that were kept and then later given monetary or emotional value in the post-Civil War period in the United States, see Marten, *Sing Not War*, pp. 138–46.

59   *Chums*, 6 February 1895, p. 369.

60   Stephanie Downes, Sally Holloway and Sarah Randles (eds), *Feeling Things: Objects and Emotions through History* (Oxford: Oxford University Press, 2018).

61   'Chelsea Pensioners at Home', *The Boys Own Paper*, 16 October 1886, p. 41.

62   *Ibid.*

63   *Ibid.*

64   *Bell's Life*, 11 July 1830, p. 3.

65   For the French images, see the Anne S. K. Brown Military Collection, Brown University Library. Available at: https://repository.library.bro wn.edu/studio/collections/id_619/?selected_facets=genre_aat%3Apho tographs&selected_facets=keyword%3AVeterans (accessed 21 February 2018).

66   Myerly, *British Military Spectacle*.

67   Harris, *Across the Bloody Chasm*.

68   NAM. 1956-10-44-1, Short-tailed coatee worn by Sergeant Frederick Peake of the 13th (Light) Dragoons at the Battle of Balaklava, 1854.

69   Roy Dutton, *Forgotten Heroes: The Charge of the Light Brigade* (Oxton: InfoDial, 2007), p. 307; Kriegel 'Balaklava Bugle', p. 8. Oddly, Dutton and Kriegel disagree on the spelling of Landfried/Landfrey's name, while the 'Rules of the Balaclava Commemoration Society' (1877), p. 12 lists him (surely incorrectly) as 'T. Landfred'.

70   Kreigel, 'Balaklava Bugle'.

71   'The Pensioner', p. 229.

72   *The Boys Own Paper*, 25 October 1884, p. 62.

73   NAM. 1964-12-154-6, Robert Howlett and Joseph Cundall, 'Crimean Heroes 1856'. See also, Ulrich Keller, *The Ultimate Spectacle: A Visual History of the Crimean War* (Basingstoke: Palgrave, 2003), chapter 4.

74   Royal Collection Trust, RCIN 2907241, Last survivors of Waterloo at the Royal Hospital, Chelsea, June 1880.

75   For an example of the memorialisation of 'native' troops, see NAM. 1985-07-27-1, Indian Mutiny veterans of the 2nd (Prince of Wales' Own) Gurkha Regiment, c. 1880. For the 1910 group portrait, see NAM. 1991-02-49, Indian Mutiny Veterans, Royal Hospital Chelsea, July 1910.

76   *Daily Telegraph*, 24 December 1907, pp. 9–10.

77   *Ibid.*

Part II

Imagining martial masculinities

6

Hunger and cannibalism: James Hogg's deconstruction of Scottish military masculinities in *The Three Perils of Man or War, Women, and Witchcraft!*

Barbara Leonardi

The anonymous reviewer of the *Monthly Censor*, feeling rather uncomfortable with the depiction of the violence of war in *The Three Perils of Man* (1822), claimed that James Hogg did

> more to disgust us with that abominable species of border warfare, which historians are glad to pass over with brevity, or in silence, than any of his contemporaries. In fact he has entered, with such appalling minuteness, into details of wanton and aggravated barbarities committed upon each other, by his combatants, that we must protest against such narratives at once; and say, if the picture be correct if this was the spirit of the age, and the practice of the period to which Mr. Hogg has assigned the date of his story, then such enormities ought, for the honour of human kind, to be committed to oblivion. If he has over-done the thing, he ought to blush for having painted the race from whom his countrymen are sprung, in such black and hideous colours.[1]

This reviewer must have strongly disagreed with Hogg's blatant depiction of the skirmishes between the English and the Scots for the conquest of the castle of Roxburgh as, in *The Three Perils of Man*, they

> fought like baited bears, with recklessness of life and the silence of death. … When the day light arose, the English fought within a semicircular wall of mangled carcasses; for, grievous to relate, they were not corpses; yet were they piled in a heap higher than a man's height, which was moving with agonized life from top to bottom, and from the one end to the other; for the men having all fallen by sword wounds, few of them were quite dead.[2]

Jill Rubenstein points out that at the time of Waterloo, 'the chivalric model remained the accepted literary ... paradigm for war', emptied of 'the brutal details of individual suffering' to convey the ideology of self-sacrifice.[3] Contrary to this vogue, the chivalrous warriors in *Perils of Man* die violently, and their hunger symbolises the destructiveness of tyrannical power inherent in the myth of the Highland soldier. The vivid picture 'of mangled carcasses'[4] in the previous extract evokes a cannibalistic act, where the hunger for power of self-interested individuals like Sir Ringan is inversely proportional to a real hunger suffered by his soldiers, who die for the former's success. In *Perils of Man*, the characters' robberies and fixation on meat are a consequence of their lords' ambition, while the warriors' never-satisfied hunger is a metaphor for 'the thirst of military fame' that 'is never quenched'.[5] This chapter contends that hunger and cannibalism are extended metaphors that Hogg utilises to denounce the human losses in the Napoleonic Wars and to convey an indirect critique of 'the slaughter of so many millions' in 'the campaign of Buonaparte', as Hogg claims more explicitly in his essay 'Soldiers', published a decade later.[6] In so doing, Hogg deconstructs the potent stereotype of Highland masculinity, so pivotal in the militaristic discourse of the British Empire.

Considering that Hogg viewed history as a cyclical phenomenon, rather than a progressive one, where wars are 'originated in the evil and malevolent passions of our nature'[7] and then reiterated by the same logic through time, I propose that in Hogg's medieval 'chivalric romance', cannibalism and hunger deconstruct the ideology of self-sacrifice of the British soldier. The anonymous reviewer of the *Monthly Censor* might have feared the impact that Hogg's novel could have had on the public's opinion about British militarism which, at the time, was promoted through the myth of the Highland warrior. Heather Streets contends that though 'most Britons were perfectly aware that the Highland regiments were not ethnically "pure" ... the superlative qualities of Highland soldiers functioned as an inspirational tool, an image of ideal masculinity and racial superiority to which all potential recruits could aspire' – a 'martial race' that would still be current in the Indian revolt of 1857 and well beyond the nineteenth century.[8]

Deconstructing this martial ideology in his essay 'Soldiers', Hogg observes that his generation may have been enjoying 'a wider range of ... intellectual improvement than our fathers did; yet we are no less destructive in fields of battle than they were, but have rather improved in our modes of general destruction'.[9] The following section discusses the various types of masculinities that shaped the construction of Scottish, English and British identities as well as their relation to war in the early nineteenth century. The analysis then highlights how Hogg played with these stereotypes in some of his works to expose the devastation stemming from the arbitrary power that in the Napoleonic Wars served the purposes of a few privileged men in the social hierarchy. Hogg highlights explicitly the ideology of self-sacrifice in two poetical works: 'The Pilgrims of the Sun' (1815) and 'The Field of Waterloo' (1822), the first published and the second composed in the same year of Napoleon's defeat at Waterloo, while conveying the same critique more implicitly some years later in his novel *The Three Perils of Man* (1822), where the hunger for meat is a ubiquitous trope meant to expose the destructiveness of tyrannical power.

Before proceeding with the discussion, it must be noted that when Hogg first published *Perils of Man*, he had to rename the character 'Sir Walter Scott of Rankleburn' as 'Sir Ringan' on the suggestion of Walter Scott, who feared that the guardians of the juvenile 5th Duke of Buccleuch, whose father had provided Hogg with Yarrow's farm free of rent for life, could feel offended at Hogg's depiction of one of his ancestors as having such opportunistic traits.[10] Yet Scott probably objected to this name because it was an unflattering portrait of himself – at the time one of the most famous Scottish literary figures. Hogg and Scott had previously fallen out for a while, after Scott refused to contribute a poem to a repository containing the works of the period's best poets, which Hogg had in mind to publish to overcome his financial straits. Hogg's adoption of the name of Sir Walter Scott of Rankleburn for the self-interested Borders chieftain in *Perils of Man* could thus have been Hogg's little personal revenge for Scott's refusal to provide a poem for his repository. In their recent edition of *Perils of Man*, Judy King and Graham Tulloch have reinserted Hogg's earlier choice, arguing that 'the portrait of the fictional Sir Walter Scott, a hard-headed chief only concerned for the advancement of his clan, is very different from the way Scott would have seen himself, as a modern inheritor of the values of disinterested medieval chivalry'.[11] Re-adoption of the fictional name 'Sir Walter Scott of Rankleburn' emphasises Hogg's deconstruction of the real Walter Scott's rhetoric of idealised chivalric masculinity. To avoid confusion between the fictional and the real Walter Scott among scholars who are not familiar with *Perils of Man*, this chapter will adopt the name of Sir Ringan to refer to the ambitious Borders chieftain of

Hogg's novel, and it will thus refer to Douglas Gifford's edition for extracts and quotations.

A brief outline of the plot focused on the themes of hunger, food and cannibalism is now necessary to provide some background context to a reader unfamiliar with the text. *Perils of Man* consists of two main narratives: the siege of Roxburgh castle, and the delegation to the castle of Aikwood. Both castles are set in the Scottish Borders at the time of Robert II, in the fourteenth century. The Aikwood narrative also gives space to a tale-telling contest which allows the setting of five other short stories. The beginning of the novel has a chivalric tone. It starts with the English Lady Jane Howard demanding that Sir Philip Musgrave conquer the castle of Roxburgh as a test of his love. The Scottish Princess Margaret Stuart requests the same of her suitors, adding a further demonstration of love: the winner of Roxburgh will have her hand in marriage, but should he lose, he will also lose all his possessions. The only suitor who accepts these conditions is Lord Douglas. The early chapters relate the first attempt of the Scots guided by Lord Douglas to dislodge Sir Philip Musgrave and his English garrison from the castle of Roxburgh. Meanwhile, the Borders chieftain Sir Ringan Redhough is unsure of which side to stand up for: either the Scottish Lord Douglas or the English Sir Philip Musgrave. The weird encounter of Sir Ringan with an old man who tells him a prophecy of Thomas the Rhymer, a figure of folk legend, motivates Sir Ringan to send an embassy to the castle of Aikwood. This castle is held by an obscure character: the wizard Michael Scott, who is asked to interpret the prophecy that the old man has told Sir Ringan.

One of the themes most discussed in twentieth-century criticism of *Perils of Man* is the ubiquitous hunger with which the characters are constantly faced and which, according to W. G. Shepherd, functions as an overarching, unifying trope of Hogg's novel.[12] The castle of Roxburgh proves to be the site where the English suffer hunger 'staring them in the face'[13] and posing the threat of starvation – which could lead to the extremity and moral peril of cannibalism – as all provisions are being blocked by Sir Ringan's men. Significantly, Richard Maxwell contends that the siege metaphor in the historical novels published in the same period was seen as 'an apt description of the Bastille's fall', where '[t]he most direct connection between sieges and food is that people in a besieged city sometimes starve to death – or even devour one another'.[14] In Hogg's novel, the threat of cannibalism is a constant, and is likewise suffered by the delegation sent by Sir Ringan to the castle of

Aikwood. One of its members – the friar – blows up with gunpowder the seneschal who holds the keys of the castle, with the result that they are all left there to perish from hunger as well. As the members have only two alternative courses of action, either to throw themselves from the walls of the castle or to remain and feed on each other, the wizard Michael Scott proposes a tale-telling contest: the best storyteller will win the maid Delany, offered to him by Sir Ringan as a reward for a prophecy, while the worst storyteller will become food for the others.

Shepherd contends that the threat of cannibalism menacing the characters in both castles suggests a vivid 'vision of creatures devouring each other',[15] thereby alluding to fighting and war, while Ian Duncan views it as a metaphor for disintegration – a place where domination of instinct and appetite converge.[16] Duncan contends that '[t]he tale-telling contest locks together the topoi of narration and cannibalism', and that since '[a]ll drives, in extremis, become reflexes of an original hunger, the drive to fill an empty mouth', in Hogg's novel '[n]arration and devouring are oral acts' mirroring a 'carnal society … that reduces your fellow to prey'.[17] Significantly, 'Marion's Jock', one of the stories that the characters tell, narrates the voracious hunger suffered by a young servant, mistreated and abused by his master.

Jason Marc Harris holds that the passages in Hogg's novel dealing with food convey a social critique. He sets the example of Sandy the fisherman who, finding meat in the river flowing upstream in the direction of Roxburgh castle, discovers the English garrison's trick for receiving provisions. Sandy starts stealing their food and, eventually, is discovered by the English and punished by death. Harris views this episode as representative of food as both a vital and lethal source of sustenance: meat in the water mirrors a world that has been turned upside-down, where the balance between life and death has been broken by the Borders conflict.[18] In *Perils of Man*, war is even more dangerous than witchcraft, because the fights between the English and the Scots cause more deaths than the compact between the devil and the wizard Michael Scott. When the latter transforms Sir Ringan's warriors into oxen, Hogg exposes the interests of selfish lords, suggesting that men 'are all potentially oxen to be slaughtered when ruled by feudalism'.[19] A similar devastation of human lives was still occurring in Hogg's time and visible in the recent Napoleonic Wars.

Twentieth-century critics of *Perils of Man* have also discussed Hogg's deconstruction of the chivalric code as represented, for instance, in Walter Scott's *Ivanhoe* (1819). King and Tulloch have argued that Hogg's vision of chivalry was 'very different from Scott's. Scott recognised the violence endemic to the age of chivalry but he nevertheless believed that the idea of chivalry could inspire generous and noble actions'.[20] In his 'Essay on chivalry', first published for the *Encyclopaedia Britannica* in 1818, Scott argues that 'it was peculiar to the institution of Chivalry, to blend military valour with the strongest passions which actuate the human mind, the feelings of devotion and those of love', maintaining that 'from the wild and overstrained courtesies of Chivalry has been derived our present system of manners'.[21] Alice Chandler observes that in his medieval novels, Scott promotes 'a consistent ideal of human conduct', an absolute 'dedication to a cause in the face of danger' which, though set in a medieval past, exposed 'the growing nineteenth-century conflict between utilitarian and anti-utilitarian modes of behaviour … the contrast between calculation and chivalry':[22] a contrast that in *Ivanhoe* Scott embodies in the dialogue about chivalry between Rebecca, the secondary heroine, and the title character, '"and what is it [chivalry], valiant knight, save an offering of sacrifice to a demon of vain-glory … what remains to you as the prize of all the blood you have spilled[?]" … "What remains?" echoed Ivanhoe; "glory, maiden, glory! which gilds our sepulchre and embalms our name"'.[23] Scott was promoting a chivalric rhetoric of self-sacrifice and, at the same time, questioning that rhetoric, even though through the words of a Jewish woman, an apparently less authoritative secondary character.

Maxwell notes that in *Ivanhoe*, Scott endorses an ideal of 'controlled chivalric violence'[24] as his 'knights in armor who have internalised a Christian concept of honor can fight for a worthy purpose: to subdue corruption within their own ranks'.[25] On the contrary, King and Tulloch contend that in *Perils of Man*, 'Hogg's willingness to portray extreme violence allows him to tear the mask off chivalry and to expose the dark forces of self-interest that underlie its professions of noble ideals.'[26] Maxwell contends that 'in Hogg's view, chivalry and romance are incapable of containing violence', and that in both castles 'a fight for possession of a woman is set against a rising wave of cannibalistic hunger'.[27] No scholar, however, appears to have engaged to any degree with Hogg's exploitation of hunger and cannibalism to prompt reflection on the violence of the Napoleonic Wars arising from the ideology of chivalric patriotism. Sharon Alker and Holly Faith Nelson have discussed the figure of the soldier in various Hogg texts (among them *Perils of Man*), arguing that while contemporary writers such as Wordsworth in *The Prelude* (1805) or Charlotte Smith in *The Old Manor House* (1793) 'mitigate' 'Britain's complicity' in the 'brutality of war', 'Hogg's inclusion of martial violence in the British or Scottish consciousness is an important corrective for Scottish Enlightenment narratives of progress. By embracing painful elements of national history, Hogg opens up a space to consider precisely what a nation asks of its soldiers … when it sends them to war.'[28] As a matter of fact, the Highland regiments employed for imperial expansion during the Napoleonic Wars, which Scott supported, were constituted largely by soldiers whose lives were wasted as a consequence of the ideology of patriotism. A writer in the *Newcastle Magazine* (July 1829), feeling 'at a loss to give a distinct and intelligible definition' of patriotism, gives a vivid idea of how this ideology works in the mind of 'men of great talent … who have sacrificed their earthly all, and even their life itself, to testify their belief in it, that we are compelled to allow that it must be something … which, like the gift of warlike destruction, dazzle the eyes of the beholder, and bedim their vision so much, that its true nature cannot be distinctly observed'.[29] In *Perils of Man*, Hogg utilises hunger for meat and the threat of cannibalism to critique the ideology of patriotism.

Maureen Martin in her book *The Mighty Scot* discusses the significance of Highland masculinity for the British Empire, arguing that although in the eighteenth century the Scottish Enlightenment had played an important role in the cultural achievements of the sophisticated Lowlands, by the nineteenth century Scotland was identified with a wild hyper-masculinity located in the Highlands.[30] Kenneth McNeil contends that Highlandism, a 'set of anthropological assumptions', was 'crucial to the rise in popularity of the figure of the Highland soldier-hero in the late eighteenth and early nineteenth centuries', because the remote and harsh nature of the land itself 'produces a "natural warrior" who from childhood develops a propensity for warfare'. Though the martial deification of the Highlander really comes of age in the Crimea and Indian Mutiny, McNeil contends that '[t]he origins of highlandism' though in evidence in the Napoleonic Wars 'predate war with France', originating when 'travel writers had remarked on their [the Highlanders'] tenacious, warlike character' in the middle of the eighteenth century.[31]

Walter Scott – a committed supporter of the union between Scotland and England – played an important role in developing the notion of romantic Highland Scotland. Martin maintains that in his works, he recreated the Jacobite risings as heroic romances set in a mythical past, while glossing over the military attacks by the Highland clans, whose courage and unconditional loyalty to the chief he re-channelled into the service of the British Union.[32] In *Waverley* (1814), for instance, Scott depicts a safe representation of a turbulent moment in Scottish history by exploiting the marriage plot, the function of which was pivotal to the new genre of the national tale and its narration of a stable and secure concept of a British Union founded on erotic and sentimental as well as political bonds. Scott's novel, in fact, simultaneously encompasses the 1746 Jacobite defeat in the battle of Culloden and the assimilation of Scotland into a Britain dominated by England through the cross-national wedding of the two main characters: the Scottish Rose Bradwardine and the English titular character.

In *Rob Roy* (1817), McNeil explains, Scott engages in a more sophisticated representation of the Highlanders as less restricted and isolated by their land, highlighting instead their 'participation in a globalising economy that necessitates a constant movement within and across regional boundaries', thereby representing the relations between Highlanders and Lowlanders in more fluid terms.[33] Ian Duncan points out that in *Rob Roy*, Scott portrays 'the historical simultaneity of different worlds … [in which] savagery and commerce sustain rather than cancel one another, constituting the uncertain, cryptic field of the present'.[34] After *Waverley*, Scott undoubtedly rearticulated a more fluid relation between Highlanders and Lowlanders as Scots who, by sharing a less threatening Highland imagery for the union, kept a distinctive national identity from the English with whom they now were equal partners in the imperial project. However, Scott's rethinking of this relationship was rather classist, as he did not expose the negative effects of the British enterprise on the margins of both Scottish regions.

Lowland Scots, who already had to bear the political supremacy of England and the cultural invasion of the Highland myth, were further affected by the stereotype of the money-oriented Lowlander. Martin contends that the English felt threatened by the Scots' economic potential in the British Empire, and that the

> penny-pincher … caricature, popular in English newspapers and music halls especially towards the end of the [nineteenth] century, deflate[d] both the intimidating masculinity of the untamed Scottish warrior figure and the commercial success of the ambitious Scottish entrepreneur with whom Englishmen had found themselves in competition since the Union [in 1707].[35]

This cultural stereotype, however, mirrored only a portion of the Scottish social spectrum. On the one hand, Douglas Mack has argued that it exposed the avaricious nature of the 'lucrative but slavery-based "sugar and tobacco-trade" which allowed Glasgow to flourish in the eighteenth century'.[36] On the other hand, Martin has observed that it showed 'the lucrative renting of Highland estates throughout the [nineteenth] century, first to sheep farmers and then to English sportsmen'[37] by the Highland landlords who were involved in the clearances of their lands and who forced their farmers either to emigrate to Canada or to enrol in the Napoleonic Wars. This is an issue well described by Christian Isobel Johnston in her novel *Clan-Albin: A National Tale* (1815). Undeniably, the lower classes of both Scottish regions were not enjoying the financial gains offered by the empire either as migrants or as metropolitan/countryside inhabitants of Britain and, as argued later in this chapter, Hogg wanted to make his readers aware of this point.

Martin explains that the mystique of the Highland soldier did not affect English masculinity because England was a solid economic and political force.[38] Juliet Shields maintains that at the beginning of the nineteenth century, English manliness began to be rather characterised by the discourse of sensibility. Shields emphasises the 'crucial eighteenth-century distinctions between sentiment, sensibility, and sympathy in order to explore the gendered implications of these forms of feeling': while 'sentiment' referred to 'virtuous feeling', and sympathy was a 'learned rather than innate' 'complex social behaviour' to feel with someone, 'sensibility', Shields explains, 'connoted "extremely refined emotion"', and it was considered a 'feminine virtue' that distinguished bourgeois women and made them suitable mothers and wives. Yet, it also indicated 'weakness, justifying women's confinement to the safety of the domestic sphere'. For this reason, Shields continues, '[a] man who was too compassionate and too easily moved to tears was considered effeminate'. Nevertheless, by the start of the nineteenth century there was a cultural shift, and a type of tamed sensibility came to be assimilated into an idealised 'benevolent patriarchy' supposedly exercised by men of the middle and upper classes.[39] This shift contributed to shaping a less violent sense of manhood than the one symbolised by the rugged Highlander. According to Adam Smith, sensibility and self-control work together in the formation of manhood, as the former restrains the roughness of martial features while the latter deters the emotional overindulgence that would 'destroy the masculine firmness of character', hence melding the feeling and the physical, where self-control converts sensibility into a less passive quality 'founded on humanity'.[40] However, Martin points out that 'to feel authentic ... modern masculinity had to incorporate older measures of masculinity too', and 'Scottish wildness was an attempt to ensure that, beneath the manly self-control, that crucial volcanic core of masculinity still burned.'[41]

Walter Scott's re-appropriation of the Highland myth during King George IV's visit to Edinburgh in August 1822 served this purpose. McNeil remarks that during the King's visit, Scott played the 'pageant master' promoting the '"Celtification" of Scotland' through a 'gaudy overuse of "tartanry"'.[42] For Douglas Mack, the King's visit represents a significant moment in the history of Scotland, a return of the King to his ancient origins, as George IV descended from 'a daughter of James VI, one of the Stuart Kings of Scots'.[43] McNeil explains that by exploiting the cultural trope of 'kinship ties' in 'Highland social identity',[44] and having the Hanoverian king wear the Stuarts' tartan, Scott presented George IV as a modern, updated version of the absolute monarchy of the past. Mack contends that the king thus appeared as 'the legitimate heir of the Stuarts and of Scotland's hero-king, Robert I (the Bruce)', whose memory was still alive among the Scots for having 'secured the country's pre-Union independence' in the 1314 battle of Bannockburn.[45] In this way, Scott re-established Scotland's position within the British Union not just as an equal partner with England but as a fundamental one, from which the King was descended. Mack contends that by asserting people's loyalty to the Hanoverian king, Scott also reaffirmed the status quo, kept at bay any revolutionary threat from France, and 'weaken[ed] support for radical political change ... establish[ing], instead, an understanding of Scottish identity based on loyalty to George IV as King of Scots, and as a monarch of the united kingdom of Britain'.[46] In Scott's royal spectacle, the Highland militaristic discourse posited Scotland as an indispensable partner for the virilisation of the more feminised commercial England, the centre of the British Empire.

Nevertheless, Hogg viewed these representations of masculinities as unfair depictions of the lower classes of Scotland. In an essay published in the *Quarterly Journal of Agriculture* (1831–32), he maintains that not only did the peasantry of the Scottish Lowlands not enjoy any material benefit from the colonial enterprise, but they also suffered the negative consequences of a deteriorated relationship between master and servant, feeling 'no more a member of a community, but a slave; a servant of servants, a mere tool of labour'.[47] Though Hogg seems to be arguing for a benevolent feudalism and hence may be criticised as backward-looking, he claims that the new imperial economy had enriched the Scottish landlords, who were now 'expect[ing] feudal obedience without assuming feudal responsibility', as Katie Trumpener observes in her analysis of the Irish condition in Maria Edgeworth's *Ormond* (1818).[48] In other words, as Mack explains, 'the economic and social changes that took place in rural Scotland around the time of the Napoleonic Wars d[id] not necessarily add to Progress'.[49] In *Perils of Man*, Hogg exploits hunger and cannibalism to reveal how ethnic and masculine stereotypes foment the violence of both the English and the Scottish chivalric warriors, who fight for the sole advantage of their medieval lords in the fourteenth century – a cyclical historical theme, the negative consequences of which were still evident in the aftermath of Waterloo.

Food, particularly the absence of meat – a symbol of prosperity – is Hogg's tool for critiquing the consequences of arbitrary power of such privileged lords in *Perils of Man*. The English Sir Philip Musgrave, the Borders chieftain Sir Ringan, and the Scottish Lord Douglas keep their soldiers motivated to fight the enemy through martial ideology, namely, as Streets explains, through an 'image of ideal masculinity and racial superiority'[50] which causes them to starve to death. The two banquets at the castle of Aikwood attended by the members of Sir Ringan's delegation and the wizard Michael Scott offer some of the most hilarious passages of Hogg's novel, thanks to a comical mixture of enchantment and hunger in what has been defined by Ian Duncan as magic realism in its embryo.[51] In the first banquet,

> [t]he dishes of meat were ... of good quality, and well mixed with fat and lean; yet none of them knew exactly what they were, neither would the sullen steward deign to give them the least information on that head. There was even one large shapeless piece, of a savour and consistence so peculiar that no one of them could tell whether it was flesh or fish. Still they continued their perseverance, devouring one dish after another, and drinking off one stoup of wine after another, without any abatement of appetite on the one side or any exhilaration of spirits on the other[.][52]

In a parallel scene which shows a similar situation, Sir Ringan's men engage, once again, in a feast with the wizard, joined this time by the devil in person disguised as an abbot. But, as in the previous banquet, our yeomen's voracious hunger is never assuaged: 'There was great variety on the table of every kind of food, yet there was no one of our yeomen knew of what the greater part of the dishes consisted. … The feast went on, and the wine flowed; but, as on a former occasion, the men ate without being satisfied.'[53] Similar phrases, alluding to the ignorance of Sir Ringan's warriors concerning the origin of their food, characterise these two parallel scenes which occur at two crucial moments in the novel, signalling the beginning and the end of the peril of witchcraft. The warriors' lack of interest in questioning the source of their food – as long as they can satisfy their voracious hunger – symbolises their unwillingness to discover their lord's real motives for fighting as long as they are 'fed', even though their hunger is never appeased. Sir Ringan is the epitome of self-regarding lords whom Hogg describes in his essay 'Soldiers' as behaving like those 'princes and great men, who are the means of stirring up wars and commotions among their fellow-men' and who are 'generally … little sensible of the miseries that accompany the wars that they themselves have raised'.[54] Some years before the writing of Hogg's novel, those 'princes and great men' had been responsible for the wasted lives of soldiers in the Napoleonic Wars, the negative consequences of which were still affecting the stability of Europe at the time when Hogg published *Perils of Man* in 1822.

Indeed, in *Perils of Man* Sir Ringan is responsible for the hunger suffered in both castles since his warriors are blocking the provisions sent by the English to Roxburgh, while the Scots members of his delegation are held on the top of Aikwood. Sir Ringan's 'philosophy' is revealed when the wizard Michael Scott provides his enigmatic interpretation of the prophecy of Thomas the Rhymer, the old man whom Sir Ringan encounters at the beginning of the novel and who advises him to '[a]ct always in concert with the Douglasses, while they act in concert with the king your master … It is thus and thus alone, that you must rise and the Douglas fall'.[55] Since this prophecy is contained in Michael Scott's book of fate, Sir Ringan sends a delegation to Aikwood to ask for elucidation; but rather than providing a clear interpretation, Michael Scott transforms Sir Ringan's warriors into bulls which are then returned to human shape thanks to an antidote provided by the wizard himself. This carnivalesque transformation suggests to Sir Ringan the 'Trojan horse gambit',[56] through which he conquers Roxburgh: he disguises his men as cattle to 'feed' the English who are perishing there from famine. However, the conquest of Roxburgh causes an equal devastation of both Scots and English warriors, a devastation anticipated by the never-quenched hunger they suffer in both castles.

The narrator informs the reader that on learning the words of the mysterious prophecy in the book of fate, Sir Ringan did not seem to be worried about its truth or fulfilment, as his 'philosophy ... taught him to estimate facts and knowledge as he found them developed among mankind, *without enquiring too nicely into the spirit of their origin*'.[57] Yet, the 'spirit' of such 'origin' is witchcraft, a metaphor for opportunistic alliances and source of the seemingly 'nourishing' food provided by the wizard in the two banquets which leaves the voracious hunger of Sir Ringan's men unquenched. The hunger for power of self-interested individuals like Sir Ringan is inversely proportional to a real hunger suffered by those in less powerful positions who, blinded by the ideological assumptions of ethnicity, martial valour and self-sacrifice, and ignorant of the real purpose of the wars they fight, are unleashed like 'dogs'[58] 'yelping and yowling',[59] to empower the magnificence of a few potent men.[60] The Borders conflict in Hogg's novel proves to be a great source of destruction for both the English and the Scots, as the European conflicts had been shortly before Hogg's time of publication in 1822.

Nonetheless, as Linda Colley explains, in the period when Hogg wrote *Perils of Man*, the ideology of British patriotism was pivotal for the Scots to claim 'the right to participate in British political life, and ultimately a means of demanding a much broader access to citizenship'.[61] In 1815, after Waterloo and the end of the Napoleonic Wars, the British Empire had achieved colossal dimensions, providing prodigious opportunities to Scotland. The Glaswegian merchants involved in the tobacco trade had been quite reluctant to join the political union with England in 1707 for fear of losing their commercial power in competition with the English traders. At the beginning of the nineteenth century, however, the economic advantages of the Union were unquestionable and pivotal to the modern development of Scotland because, as Tom Devine contends, 'virtually every other sphere of Scottish life, from economy to emigration, from rural transformation to political development, was fashioned in large part by engagement with empire'.[62]

Hogg's novel mirrors the dynamics of the birth of Britain which Colley describes as an 'invented nation superimposed ... onto much older alignments and loyalties' and 'forged above all by war'.[63] These opportunistic alliances between a few powerful men who exploit ethnic ideology at the expense of their subaltern warriors are at work on both sides of *Perils of Man*. The English in the castle of Roxburgh

bound themselves by a new and fearful oath never to yield the fortress
to the Scots while a man of them remained alive. Every new calamity
acted but as a new spur to their resolution; and their food being again
on the very eve of exhaustion, their whole concern was how to procure a
new supply. Not that they valued their own lives or their own sufferings,
– these had for a good while been only a secondary consideration, – but
from the excruciating dread that they should die out, and the Scots attain
possession of the fortress before Christmas.[64]

Hogg here describes the dynamics of a militaristic ideology of self-sacrifice nourished by ethnic assumptions which, by feeding the soldiers'
blind instinct for violence, increases the personal gain of a few men who
reduce the former to starvation and death.

'[T]here will mony ane o' us throw away our lives to little purpose',[65]
claims Will Laidlaw o' Craik, one of Sir Ringan's warriors, when reflecting upon the worth of disguising themselves as oxen to conquer the castle of Roxburgh. This subaltern, *heteroglot* voice anticipates the negative
consequences of such disguise on both the English and the Scots, whose
slaughter Hogg depicts through the 'semicircular wall of mangled carcasses',[66] a scene that 'shock[s]' the Borders chiefs, and which makes
one of them exclaim 'Gude faith, Sirs, it strikes me, that this is rather
carrying war to an extremity.'[67] The vivid image of 'mangled carcasses'
evokes an impressively dramatic picture in the reader's mind, recalling another visual representation of the destructiveness of wars, which
Hogg quotes at the end of his essay 'Soldiers': 'Let me conclude this
rambling discourse by a quotation', Hogg writes, 'which I have always
deemed powerful':

> The dreadful harass of the war is o'er,
> And Slaughter, that, from yestermorn till even,
> With giant steps passed striding o'er the field,
> Besmeared and horrid with the blood of nations;
> Now weary sits among the mangled heaps,
> And slumber o'er her prey.[68]

Hogg implies that wars are vain and useless, as their negative consequences affect both winners and losers. Although the carnivalesque
disguise of Sir Ringan's men as oxen puts an end to the skirmishes
with the English, it also reveals that the warriors of both sides
are mere tools in their lords' hands, and that they all end up in a
mixed heap of corpses, where the 'recklessness of life' in the name

of martial valour and ethnic difference is nullified by the 'silence of death'.[69]

Walter Scott would allude to a similar waste of human lives and provision through the anecdote of the Douglas Larder, 'a never to be forgotten record of horror and abomination', in *Castle Dangerous* (1831) some years after the publication of *Perils of Man*.[70] Likewise, Scott narrates a chivalric competition for the conquest of Castle Douglas to gain an English lady's hand,[71] where the two-year gathering of provisions has been stored for the King of England. Young James Douglas, enraged by the death of his Scottish father who had never yielded 'to become Anglocised [*sic*]',

> caused the meat, the malt, and other corn or grain to be brought down into the castle cellar, where he emptied the contents of the sacks into one loathsome heap, striking out the heads of the barrels and puncheons, so as to let the mingled drink run through the heap of meal, grain, and so forth. The bullocks provided for slaughter were in like manner knocked on the head, and their blood suffered to drain forth into the mass of edible substances; and lastly, the quarters of the cattle were buried in the same mass, in which were also included the dead bodies of those in the castle, who, receiving no quarter from the Douglas, paid dear enough for having kept no better watch.[72]

This is indeed quite a change in Scott's tamed chivalric violence. Now, Scott seemed to have grown more in line with Hogg's aesthetics, exposing a 'base and ungodly abuse of provisions intended for the use of man',[73] when personal revenge takes the lead and the lives of so many warriors are lost as a consequence of a blind and arbitrary military power.

When working on *Perils of Man*, Hogg was also involved in the collection of his *Poetical Works* (1822), which he published in four volumes – the second of which was recently edited as *Midsummer Night Dreams and Related Poems* (2008). In this volume, Hogg conveys very explicit considerations of the shocking consequences of the recent European conflicts, specifically in 'The Pilgrims of the Sun' (1815) and 'The Field of Waterloo' (1822). Recurrent phrases and motifs representative of the soldiers' exploitation through the ideology of martial honour support the intertextual relations between these two works and *Perils of Man*, thereby suggesting that the latter's chivalrous world of potential or magical cannibalism communicates the same reflections on Hogg's contemporary wars, though in a more implicit way.

'The Pilgrims of the Sun', published for the first time 'by William Blackwood in Edinburgh in December 1814 and by John Murray in London in January 1815', relates Mary Lee's dreamy 'long trance', through whose 'erratic pilgrimage'[74] in the worlds around the sun Hogg provides a pointed critique of his society.[75] As Fiona Wilson observes, the visionary worlds that Mary Lee experiences are 'possible versions' of Hogg's contemporary reality, where Mars, the planet devoted to war in the collective imagination, is the field of 'eternal war, ... much as Europe must have appeared after its recent battles'.[76] In her enchanted dream, Mary Lee beholds an apocalyptic vision of the martial world:

> Now oped a scene, before but dimly seen,
> A world of pride, of havock, and of spleen;
> A world of scathed soil, and sultry air,
> For industry and culture were not there;
> The hamlets smoked in ashes on the plain,
> The bones of men were bleaching in the rain,
> And, piled in thousands, on the trenched heath,
> Stood warriors bent on vengeance and on death.[77]

While the second line recalls Hogg's own critique of wars in 'Soldiers', as well as intertextually alluding to the Shakespearean trope of havoc and war, the last two lines recall language from Hogg's same essay where, after a destructive battle, a personified 'Slaughter ... / Besmeared and horrid with the blood of nations; / Now weary sits among the mangled heaps'.[78] This quotation alludes to the pulsing image 'of mangled carcasses', 'piled in a heap higher than a man's height' and 'moving with agonized life' which Hogg describes in *Perils of Man*.[79]

Hogg wrote 'The Field of Waterloo' quite soon after the defeat of Napoleon on 18 June 1815 in the famous battle which concluded a twenty-year period of European wars with France – an event that, as Jill Rubenstein observes, 'sparked an explosion of celebrations in Scotland in which Hogg participated in various ways'.[80] Rubenstein contends that Hogg must have been aware of 'the heavy losses sustained by Scottish regiments in the battle'.[81] In a letter to Walter Scott of 16 November 1815, Hogg writes: 'since ever I saw you and heard your enthusiastic sentiments about the great events of late taken place in the world and of our honour and glory as a nation lately won I have been busily engaged with a poem on Waterloo as a small tribute to our heros [*sic*] which I think not unbecomes every British Bard'.[82] Hogg's poem mirrors the effects of Europe's macro-history on a Borders soldier from Yarrow through which Hogg 'deconstructs military glory and undermines the widely-accepted ethic of sacrifice'.[83] Rubenstein claims that Hogg's failure to publish this poem in the aftermath of Waterloo was probably motivated by his questioning of the martial values so much endorsed by other contemporary poems.[84]

Class prejudices and Hogg's identity as the Ettrick Shepherd were certainly at the heart of the negative reception of Hogg's works dealing with the violence of war, as shown by the anonymous reviewer of the *Monthly Censor* at the beginning of this chapter. Valentina Bold points out that in the early nineteenth century, the Scottish reviewers of the literary periodical press considered Hogg as a 'peasant poet' and regarded him only 'on their own terms'.[85] They accepted Hogg's writing when, in the Ettrick Shepherd's persona, he engaged in rural genres such as ballads and songs because this was in line with the Romantic figures of the 'bard' and the 'rustic peasant-poet'. Ian Duncan contends that Hogg's image as the Ettrick Shepherd, however, struggled against 'a historiography which at once valorized the poet as voice of a primordial stage of society close to nature and depreciated him as an uncouth relic doomed to extinction by the logic of economic and cultural improvement'.[86] Scottish reviewers had problems with accepting Hogg's attempts at writing more urban and sophisticated literary genres, such as the national tale and the historical novel, because here Hogg's 'indelicacies' (when dealing with prostitution or out-of-wedlock pregnancy) and his willingness to expose the ideology of patriotism disturbed the imperial ideology which these works were meant to convey.

In the poem 'The Field of Waterloo', for example, Hogg's soldier describes his experience as follows:

> I've had no knowledge what hath been,
> Nor thought, nor mind – a mere machine.
> I only viewed it as my meed (reward),
> To stand or fall, as heaven decreed;
> For honour's cause to do my best,
> And to the Almighty leave the rest.
> Blessed be his hand that swayed the fight
> For mankind's and for freedom's right![87]

Contrary to the ideology of self-sacrifice in 'Pilgrims' and 'Waterloo', Hogg dismisses the military institution 'as devoid of purpose and merely self-serving'.[88] A soldier is 'a mere machine',[89] 'an abject fool! / A king's, a tyrant's, or a stateman's [*sic*] tool!'.[90] A parallel line can thus be drawn with the Scots and the English chivalrous warriors of *Perils of Man*, who die fighting for their lords. This is the direct result of a 'blindfold levity', nurtured by the ideology of patriotism, which 'directs' a soldier's military action, thereby rendering him a 'licensed murderer that kills for pay!', as Hogg states in 'Pilgrims',[91] when more blatantly critiquing the Napoleonic Wars. Hogg's writings questioned the assumptions of the modern progress implied by his post-Enlightenment historical phase because the financial gains of the British Empire, sustained by the potent stereotype of Highland masculinity, entailed the loss of many soldiers blinded by the rhetoric of war who had 'no knowledge what hath been' nor 'thought, nor mind', 'a mere machine'.[92]

Notes

1   Anon., '[Review of] *The Three Perils of Man*', *Monthly Censor* 1 (1822), pp. 467–9 (pp. 467–8).
2   James Hogg (ed. Douglas Gifford), *The Three Perils of Man: War, Women and Witchcraft*, (Edinburgh: Canongate Classics, 1996 [1822]), p. 454.
3   Jill Rubenstein, 'Introduction' to 'The Pilgrims of the Sun', in *Midsummer Night Dreams and Related Poems*, written by James Hogg, ed. by the late Jill Rubenstein and completed by Gillian Hughes with Meiko O'Halloran (Edinburgh: Edinburgh University Press, 2008), pp. xliv–lxxvi (p. xlviii).
4   Hogg, *Perils of Man*, p. 454.
5   James Hogg, 'Soldiers', in Gillian Hughes (ed.), *A Series of Lay Sermons on Good Principles and Good Breeding* (Edinburgh: Edinburgh University Press, 1997 [1834]), pp. 40–7 (p. 47).
6   *Ibid.*, p. 41.
7   *Ibid.*, p. 44.
8   Heather Streets, *Martial Races: The Military, Race and Masculinity in British Imperial Culture, 1857–1914* (Manchester: Manchester University Press, 2004), pp. 4, 8.
9   Hogg, 'Soldiers', p. 46.
10 See Hogg's letter to Walter Scott of 10 December 1821, *The Collected Letters of James Hogg*, ed. by Gillian Hughes, associate editors Douglas S. Mack, Robin MacLachlan and Elaine Petrie, 3 vols (Edinburgh: Edinburgh University Press, 2004–8), vol. 2 (pp. 129–30), and the editorial note on p. 130.
11 See Judy King and Graham Tulloch, 'Introduction' to *The Three Perils of Man: A Border Romance*, written by Hogg, ed. by King and Tulloch (Edinburgh: Edinburgh University Press, 2012 [1822]), pp. xi–lxiii (pp. xv–xvi).

12 W. G. Shepherd, 'Fat Flesh: The Poetic Theme of *The Three Perils of Man*', *Studies in Hogg and his World* 3 (1992), pp. 1–9.

13 Hogg, *Perils of Man*, p. 443.

14 Richard Maxwell, *The Historical Novel in Europe, 1650–1950* (Cambridge: Cambridge University Press, 2009), pp. 185, 196.

15 Shepherd, 'Fat Flesh', p. 3.

16 Ian Duncan, 'Scott, Hogg, Orality and the Limits of Culture', *Studies in Hogg and his World* 8 (1997), pp. 56–74.

17 Ian Duncan, *Scott's Shadow: The Novel in Romantic Edinburgh* (Princeton, NJ: Princeton University Press, 2007), pp. 197, 204, 207.

18 Jason Mark Harris, 'National Borders, Contiguous Cultures, and Fantastic Folklore in Hogg's *The Three Perils of Man*', *Studies in Hogg and His World* 14 (2003), pp. 38–61 (p. 52).

19 *Ibid.*

20 King and Tulloch, 'Introduction to *Perils of Man*', pp. xvi–xvii.

21 Walter Scott, 'Essay on Chivalry', in *Essays on Chivalry, Romance, and the Drama* (Edinburgh: Robert Cadell, 1834), pp. 8, 47. Available at: http://books.google.com (accessed 22 January 2016).

22 Alice Chandler, 'Chivalry and Romance: Scott's Medieval Novels', *Romanticism* 14:2 (spring 1975), pp. 185–200 (pp. 187, 190).

23 Walter Scott (ed. Graham Tulloch), *Ivanhoe* (Edinburgh: Edinburgh University Press, 1998 [1820]), p. 249.

24 Maxwell, *Historical Novel*, p. 192.

25 *Ibid.*, p. 191.

26 King and Tulloch, 'Introduction to *Perils of Man*', pp. xvi–xviii.

27 Maxwell, *Historical Novel*, pp. 194, 195.

28 Sharon Alker and Holly Faith Nelson, '"Ghastly in the Moonlight": Wordsworth, Hogg and the Anguish of War', *Studies in Hogg and His World* 15 (2004), pp. 76–89 (pp. 77, 83, 86).

29 J. M., 'What Is Patriotism?', *The Newcastle Magazine*, n.s., 8:7 (July 1829), pp. 305–7 (p. 306).

30 Maureen M. Martin, *The Mighty Scot: Nation, Gender, and the Nineteenth-Century Mystique of Scottish Masculinity* (Albany: State University of New York Press, 2009), p. 2.

31 Kenneth McNeil, *Scotland, Britain, Empire: Writing the Highlands, 1760–1860* (Columbus: The Ohio State University Press, 2007), p. 86.

32 Martin, *The Mighty Scot*, pp. 20, 82.

33 McNeil, *Scotland, Britain, Empire*, p. 53.

34 Duncan, *Scot's Shadow*, p. 110.

35 Martin, *The Mighty Scot*, p. 110.

36 Douglas S. Mack, *Scottish Fiction and the British Empire* (Edinburgh: Edinburgh University Press, 2006), p. 155.

37 Martin, *The Mighty Scot*, p. 110.

38 *Ibid.*, p. 84.
39 Juliet Shields, *Sentimental Literature and Anglo-Scottish Identity, 1745–1820* (Cambridge: Cambridge University Press, 2010), pp. 8–9.
40 Adam Smith (ed. D. D. Raphael and A. L. Macfie), *The Theory of Moral Sentiments*, Glasgow Edition of the Works and Correspondence of Adam Smith (Oxford: Clarendon Press, 1976 [1759]), p. 204.
41 Martin, *The Mighty Scot*, p. 6.
42 McNeil, *Scotland, Britain, Empire*, p. 52.
43 Douglas S. Mack, 'Introduction', in *The Bush aboon Traquair and The Royal Jubilee*, written by James Hogg, ed. by Douglas S. Mack (Edinburgh: Edinburgh University Press, 2008), pp. xi–lv (pp. xxx, xxxiii).
44 McNeil, *Scotland, Britain, Empire*, p. 71.
45 Mack, 'Introduction to *The Royal Jubilee*', pp. xxxiv–xxxv.
46 *Ibid.*, p. xxxiv.
47 James Hogg, 'On the Changes in the Habits, Amusements and Condition of the Scottish Peasantry', in Judy Steel (ed.), *A Shepherd's Delight: A James Hogg Anthology* (Edinburgh: Canongate, 1985), pp. 40–51 (pp. 44–5), first published in the *Quarterly Journal of Agriculture*, vol. 3 (February 1831–September 1832).
48 Katie Trumpener, 'National Character, Nationalist Plots: National Tale and Historical Novel in the Age of *Waverley*, 1806–1830', *ELH* 60 (1993), pp. 685–731 (p. 694).
49 Mack, *Scottish Fiction*, p. 60.
50 Streets, *Martial Races*, p. 4.
51 Duncan, *Scott's Shadow*, p. 194.
52 Hogg, *Perils of Man*, p. 202.
53 *Ibid.*, p. 389.
54 Hogg, 'Soldiers', p. 40.
55 Hogg, *Perils of Man*, p. 9.
56 Shepherd, 'Fat Flesh', p. 3.
57 Hogg, *Perils of Man*, p. 458, emphasis mine.
58 Hogg, 'Soldiers', p. 47.
59 Hogg, *Perils of Man*, p. 285.
60 Hogg, 'Soldiers', p. 40.
61 Colley, *Britons*, p. 5.
62 T. M. Devine, *Scotland's Empire 1600–1815* (London: Penguin Books, 2004 [2003]), p. 360.
63 Colley, *Britons*, p. 5.
64 Hogg, *Perils of Man*, p. 443.
65 *Ibid.*, p. 420.
66 *Ibid.*, p. 454.
67 *Ibid.*
68 Nicholas Rowe, *Tamerlane, a Tragedy*, II, lines 1–6. See note on p. 131 of Hogg's *Lay Sermons*, ed. by Hughes; Hogg cites it on p. 47.

69 Hogg, *Perils of Man*, p. 454.
70 Walter Scott (ed. J. H. Alexander), *Castle Dangerous* (Edinburgh: Edinburgh University Press, 2006 [1831]), p. 35.
71 For the germ of *Castle Dangerous* see Scott's 'Essay on Chivalry', pp. 35–6.
72 Scott, *Castle Dangerous*, pp. 35–6.
73 *Ibid.*, p. 36.
74 See Hogg's own 'Notes to "The Pilgrims of the Sun"', in *Midsummer Night Dreams and Related Poems*, written by James Hogg, ed. by the late Jill Rubenstein and completed by Gillian Hughes with Meiko O'Halloran (Edinburgh: Edinburgh University Press, 2008), pp. 148–52 (p. 148); they first appeared in his *Poetical Works* in 1822.
75 Meiko O'Halloran, '"Circling the Pales of Heaven": Hogg and Otherworld Journeys from Dante to Byron', in *Midsummer Night Dreams and Related Poems*, written by James Hogg, ed. by the late Jill Rubenstein and completed by Gillian Hughes with Meiko O'Halloran (Edinburgh: Edinburgh University Press, 2008), pp. lxxvii–ci.
76 Fiona Wilson, 'Hogg as Poet', in Ian Duncan and Douglas S. Mack (eds), *The Edinburgh Companion to James Hogg* (Edinburgh: Edinburgh University Press, 2012), pp. 96–104 (p. 101).
77 James Hogg, 'The Pilgrims of the Sun', in *Midsummer Night Dreams and Related Poems*, ed. by the late Jill Rubenstein and completed by Gillian Hughes with Meiko O'Halloran (Edinburgh: Edinburgh University Press, 2008), pp. 3–50, lines 239–46, p. 31.
78 Hogg, 'Soldiers', p. 47.
79 Hogg, *Perils of Man*, p. 454.
80 Jill Rubenstein, 'Editorial Notes to "The Field of Waterloo"', in *Midsummer Night Dreams and Related Poems*, ed. by the late Jill Rubenstein and completed by Gillian Hughes with Meiko O'Halloran (Edinburgh: Edinburgh University Press, 2008), pp. 212–21 (pp. 212–13); see also Gillian Hughes, 'James Hogg, and Edinburgh's triumph over Napoleon', *Scottish Studies Review* 4:1 (Spring 2003), pp. 98–111, where she argues that the celebrations held in Edinburgh after the defeat of Napoleon in 1815 prepared the ground for Scott's pageantry during the 1822 King's visit.
81 Rubenstein, 'Editorial Notes', p. 213.
82 Hogg, *Collected Letters*, vol. 1, p. 256.
83 Rubenstein, 'Introduction', in *Midsummer Night Dreams and Related Poems*, written by James Hogg, ed. by the late Jill Rubenstein and completed by Gillian Hughes with Meiko O'Halloran (Edinburgh: Edinburgh University Press, 2008), pp. xliv–lxxvi (p. xliv).
84 *Ibid.*, p. xlv.
85 Valentina Bold, *James Hogg: A Bard of Nature's Making* (Oxford: Peter Lang, 2007), p. 19.
86 Duncan, *Scott's Shadow*, p. 149.

87 James Hogg, 'The Field of Waterloo', in *Midsummer Night Dreams and Related Poems*, ed. by the late Jill Rubenstein and completed by Gillian Hughes with Meiko O'Halloran (Edinburgh: Edinburgh University Press, 2008), pp. 123–41 (lines 150–63, p. 127).

88 Rubenstein, 'Introduction', p. xliv.

89 Hogg, 'Waterloo', line 157, p. 127.

90 Hogg, 'Pilgrims', lines 323–4, p. 33.

91 *Ibid.*, lines 327–8, p. 33.

92 Hogg, 'Waterloo', lines 156–7, p. 127.

7

Model military men: Charlotte Yonge and the 'martial ardour' of 'a soldier's daughter'[1]

Susan Walton

Introduction

Throughout her life, Charlotte Yonge (1823–1901), author of the best-selling novel *The Heir of Redclyffe* (1853), not only adopted the mind-set of the military members of her family but moulded her fictional heroes in their likeness to create templates of desirable characteristics for her readers to emulate. The experiences of her father and her uncle in the Peninsular War and at Waterloo remained a fundamental feature of her life and will occupy a central role in this essay. Thanking an American woman for some books in 1896, Yonge wrote, 'My father fought at Waterloo and I grew up to many army traditions from him, and his Colonel, Lord Seaton' – thus, eighty-one years after the Battle of Waterloo, forty-two since her father had died, she still identified herself as the daughter and niece of soldiers who had fought at this significant battle.[2] Unable herself to follow in her father's footsteps or those of her celebrated uncle, Lord Seaton, she believed that people of all classes, in their daily lives, should display the sort of courage and discipline instilled in soldiers.[3] Neither did she reserve such military characteristics as essential only for grown men; she believed both boys and girls could act with resolution in difficult situations, and she encouraged women to embrace a similar gritty fortitude. For Yonge, military manliness was non-gendered and cross-generational, imbibed initially through childhood stories and reinforced by the retelling of factual and fictional tales which prompt imaginative participation. Joshua Goldstein, in his examination of the complex relationship between war and gender, suggests that 'the single main lesson … for those interested in gender is to pay attention to war', since the 'war system influences the socialization of children into *all* their gender roles'.[4] In this process, women play a crucial role in the 'making of militarized masculinity' by helping to model male members of their families into potential warriors 'shaping their sons for war'.[5] Yonge's stories provided an upright version of martial manliness - one that could be replicated by both men and women, boys and girls, in the everyday battles of life as well as on the field of combat.

As well as considering Yonge's contribution to nineteenth-century imaginings of military masculinities, I claim a space for women such as Yonge in discussions on the literary and social developments that resulted in new notions about soldiers and their status in the nation. In his thought-provoking book, *The Ultimate Experience: Battlefield Revelations and the Making of Modern War Culture*, Yuval Noah Harari argues that an unprecedented revolution took place between 1780 and 1860, whereby participation in war was elevated to an opportunity for a quasi-mythical experience of revelation, where higher truths are discovered which are otherwise inaccessible: 'Under the influence of the Enlightenment and Romanticism, Western war culture was being transformed, and the battlefield was becoming a privileged site for learning the truth.'[6] One aspect of Romanticism maintained that sensitivity to new and unusual experiences was essential for the gaining of wisdom. Of particular importance was the mind-altering effect of encounters with the sublime, together with the belief that military combat not only fitted perfectly the Romantic definition of the sublime but transformed it into the ultimate experience. Such analyses tend to exclude women, who are relegated to an appreciation only of beauty rather than the sublime, and presuppose that they cannot partake in opportunities for transcendent knowledge, particularly those gained in the midst of battle. Yet Harari recognises the similarity between religious revelation and the idea of the sublime, though he assumes this no longer has relevance: 'the sublime may be seen as a vacuum in the field of human knowledge once the Enlightenment removed God from the scene'.[7] Such a statement is inappropriate for families such as the Yonges, living as they did in John Keble's parish of Hursley, deeply absorbed with him and others in the crusade of the Oxford Movement to restore religious reverence. Various scholars have commented on the close relationship, first identified by Stephen Prickett in 1976, between Romanticism and the Oxford Movement.[8] Keble and his associates were not only in sympathy with the attitudes of the Romantic poets but personally acquainted with them. Indeed, George Herring asserts that Keble's *The Christian Year* played a significant role in channelling the ideas of the Romantics into the mainstream of religious thought. For these committed supporters of the Oxford Movement, God was certainly not, in Harari's words, 'removed ... from the scene'. They perceived the Christian life to be one of perpetual warfare against the rising tide of liberalism and secularism, with themselves in midst of battle, besieged and on the defensive against their many critics, and both men and women employed the language of combat to describe their resistance. In *Musings over 'The Christian Year'*, Charlotte Yonge remembered how Keble 'thoroughly liked an account of a battle' and how 'war in its allegorical aspect, could not fail to win his imagination, as the type of Church Militant here on earth'.[9]

Charlotte Yonge's father, William Crawley Yonge, was a member of a large Devonshire gentry family also related to the Coleridges. He became an ensign in the army in 1812, aged sixteen, serving in the 52nd Regiment under the command of his relative, John Colborne, who later became Lord Seaton. His first experience of battle was at the siege of San Sebastian in the Peninsula. He earned four battle medals, fought at Waterloo and served in France in the Army of Occupation and in Ireland, before reluctantly retiring on half-pay in 1822.[10] Charlotte revered her father, remembering him in 1892 as 'the hero of heroes to both my mother and me. His approbation was throughout life my bliss; his anger, my misery'.[11] Her fixation on military matters is usually ascribed to this close bond with her father, forged during the first six years of her life before the birth of her only sibling, Julian, but it is just as likely that it was nurtured by her mother, Frances Bargus, a stepsister to Colborne. The letters Colborne wrote to his three sisters during the Peninsular War are remarkable for the military and political details he shared with them about the progress and setbacks of the war. His warning, 'Remember my letters are sacred and must not be repeated', emphasised the confidential nature of this epistolary dialogue with his family.[12] Thus Frances, while still a teenager, had been imaginatively involved with the military exploits of her step-brother before she became attached to William Yonge. Neither is there any record of her opposing William Yonge's continued career in the army; the objections that delayed their marriage for five years came not from her but from her mother, Mary Bargus, who 'would not hear of her daughter marrying into a marching regiment'.[13] Indeed it is possible that Frances empathised with William's father, Mr Duke Yonge, who was 'averse to his son relinquishing his profession' and 'vexed that so fine a young man should throw up his profession, and settle down on a small estate of his mother-in-law's, with nothing to do, except what he made for himself'.[14] William Yonge eventually capitulated to Mrs Bargus's demands and, for the rest of his life, lived in Otterbourne near Winchester with his family, a conscientious member of the gentry and a keen participant in the welfare projects of Keble and Sir William Heathcote in Hursley. Yet his military creed remained at the heart of his identity, and his friends and family remained aware of the great sacrifice that he had made when he married.

The 52nd Light Infantry and the Battle of Waterloo

The particular regiment in which William Yonge served under his relation Sir John Colborne is highly significant, as it represented a different type of soldiering than had been the typical pattern of the past. The 52nd Light Infantry had been reformed on new principles by Sir John Moore in the early years of the century. Instead of soldiers being drilled into submission under threat of extreme punishment, its members were expected to show initiative, take personal responsibility and demonstrate a superior type of restrained behaviour. The aim was to create troops capable of fighting in small independent groups over rough terrain, to be sharpshooters and skirmishers who needed therefore to be thinking soldiers, not automatons.[15] Also unusual was the stipulation that the officers themselves must take part in the drills so that 'when they became perfectly acquainted with the system, they could teach the men, and by their zeal, knowledge, and above all, good temper and kind treatment of the soldier, make the regiment the best in the service'.[16]

Concomitant with the new methods of training was the notion that officers had a duty 'to do everything in our power to *prevent* crime, as then there would be no occasion for punishment'.[17] Self-discipline was to be inculcated rather than the fear of the lash. According to Sir John Moore, 'it is evident that not only the officers, but that each individual soldier, knows perfectly what he has to do; the discipline is carried on without severity, the officers are attached to the men and the men to the officers'.[18] In her chapters of autobiography, Charlotte Yonge wrote how 'the 52nd was unanimously declared one of the most distinguished regiments in the service, and the high tone of many of the officers for all the qualities of true chivalry made it remarkable'.[19] Her use of 'chivalry' in this context is striking and at odds with the kind of dashing, pleasure-loving soldiers often portrayed in nineteenth-century fiction – Thackeray's Rawdon Crawley and Hardy's Sergeant Troy, as well as those typical of the military novels of W. H. Maxwell, Charles MacFarlane and Charles Lever. The military masculinity expected of the men of the 52nd demanded bravado but also self-discipline. This is a quality Yonge frequently identified in her fictional heroes and heroines as self-devotion, meaning the dedication of oneself to a cause and a willingness to sacrifice one's own interests for others.

The new system instituted by Moore suited perfectly the personality of Charlotte Yonge's uncle, John Colborne, who became a senior officer in the 52nd and later its commander.[20] What is striking in descriptions of his ability as a leader is the evidence of his diligence and scrupulous attention to detail. We gain an insight into the high moral and intellectual standard he set himself from the memoranda he wrote in 1835 for his eldest son, James, aged nineteen and about to follow in his father's footsteps as an army officer. After first 'intreating' (*sic*) him to pray daily and be 'fervent in spirit, serving the Lord', Colborne emphasises the need to 'acquire a perfect knowledge of every part' of his military profession. James should master not only the drills and manoeuvres, but the financial arrangements of a regiment, to become 'a good engineer and artillerist, and also fit for the Quarter-Master-General's department'. He should continue to study mathematics but also the classics, modern languages, grammar and history, especially the war historians. He rounds off this challenging list with a more homely, paternal request, 'Write to us often, at least once a week.'[21] The plaudits for Colborne's exceptional skills and upstanding character in military memoirs provide proof that this catalogue of advice to his son was an accurate representation of his own punctilious methods rather than an unrealistic wish-list. Sir Harry Smith stated that Colborne 'had more knowledge of ground, better understood the posting of picquets, ... knew better what the enemy were going to do, and more quickly anticipated his design than any other officer; with that coolness and animation, under fire, no matter how hot, which marks a good huntsman'.[22] Similarly, Sir George Napier talks of Colborne's 'coolness of head in the very heat of action which never fails him, and thus he penetrates with eagle eye into the enemy's intentions, and is sure to baffle his designs when least expected'.[23] Colborne gained each of his promotions, right up to his appointment as field marshal, on personal merit and not by purchase.

At the Battle of Waterloo, the conduct of the 52nd Regiment under the command of Colborne (ennobled later as Lord Seaton) exemplifies the exceptional characteristics of this band of soldiers and their officers and had an abiding influence on Charlotte Yonge, even though she was not yet born. On the late afternoon of 18 June 1815, Colborne noticed that Napoleon had brought up his elite Imperial Guard and that they were about to attack the hard-pressed British Guards, who were running out of ammunition. Recognising the seriousness of the situation, acting on his own initiative, without waiting for orders and in spite of being greatly outnumbered by the French, Colborne wheeled the 52nd to the left to come against the flank of the advancing French, who were thus caught by surprise and had their lines broken. This was an extraordinary, original manoeuvre, not previously practised and only possible because of Colborne's excellent relationship with his soldiers, many of them Peninsular veterans ready to trust in their commander's unusual orders even in the midst of battle. Colborne then wheeled his regiment back and pursued the retreating French, who fled the field in complete disorder.

This crucial action helped to turn the tide and was a major factor in the British victory at Waterloo. Indeed, in the eyes of the men of the 52nd and Lieutenant William Yonge, it was 'not only the decisive action of the day, but ... it was one of the most gallant feats ever performed'.[24] On that evening, Colborne wrote to his step-sister Frances (later to be the mother of Charlotte Yonge), giving scant details but ending with, 'You will be surprised at the Gazette', in the confident expectation that she would soon be reading an official account of his glorious contribution to the overthrow of Napoleon.

> But, the Gazette came out without any special recognition of the service, and a statement got about, not from the despatch, which was vague, but from gossip at Brussels, that the Guards had made the charge, and the story arose of the Duke's crying "Up Guards, at them." Sir John Byng, the Guards' colonel, actually said to Sir John Colborne, "How do your fellows like our getting the credit of what you did at Waterloo? I could not advance when you did because all our ammunition was gone."[25]

To the horror of the officers and soldiers of the 52nd, Wellington's despatch failed to acknowledge the momentous role played by their regiment's dramatic manoeuvre. This injustice rankled then and forever among the men and their families and became an event argued about in clubs and dining rooms and in print.[26] Apart from a sense of grievance at the lack of credit for their contribution to a victory that was to acquire a mythic importance in the history of the nation, there was a significant practical effect in terms of their salaries compared to the enhancement granted to the Guards for their participation at Waterloo.

This is not the place to examine the reasons for Wellington's omission, but this injustice remained a running sore within the Yonge household, replayed and anatomised on numerous occasions over the years. While the family's resentment was on behalf of Colborne, he himself was the embodiment of humility and restraint. Although deeply disappointed by the oversight, he refused to protest and even suggested reasons to excuse Wellington's snub – how difficult it is to write a dispatch after a battle and how the Duke had been distressed by the sufferings of his wounded staff-officer in the room as he wrote. For years, Colborne refrained from reading accounts of Waterloo to avoid painful recollections.[27] He loyally accepted various difficult diplomatic and military appointments abroad and, for this work, was ennobled in 1839, taking the title of Baron Seaton. The death of Wellington in 1852 followed by his lavish state funeral revived the arguments and the memories. As one of the eight pallbearers accompanying Wellington's coffin on its massive carriage, Seaton was reunited with his military contemporaries from the war against Napoleon. Also in the funeral procession was William Yonge, marching with the elite group of officers who had fought at Waterloo. It is possible that it was this experience that prompted Yonge in 1853 to revisit the battlefield in Belgium, where he was upset to discover that the area where the 52nd had been positioned had been dug up for the monument of the Belgic Mound: 'It is very grievous, for perhaps no other so effectual a mode could have been devised for mutilating so interesting an historical record, as the place itself would otherwise have always afforded.'[28] His short memoir about Seaton, written at this time, not only details the 'true' events of that day but is damning about alternative versions with their 'figurative descriptions of unrealities, so these inventions have become the staple of almost every subsequent account of Waterloo, and this trash has been handed on from one to the other, till by force of repetition, there is risk that at a future day, when none remain to contradict, it may be recognised as authentic'.[29] Charlotte Yonge would see it as her duty to take up this challenge; after the death of her father in 1854 and her uncle in 1863, she took it on herself to be their spokesperson. In this guise, unusual for a woman, she was asked by *The Christian Remembrancer* in 1867 to review four books about Lord Seaton and the 52nd Regiment, including the brief memoir written by her father. Throughout the rest of the nineteenth century she acted as Keeper of the Flame for the 'authentic' account of the 52nd at Waterloo and fashioned fictional individuals, both male and female, that embodied the military virtues demonstrated by the officers of that regiment.

Charlotte Yonge's military know-how

John Colborne's distinguished career, not only as a soldier but as an administrator and a diplomat, provided Charlotte Yonge with an exemplar of a life lived honourably devoted to public service, an archetype of a military man who combined courage and authority with modesty and generosity. Moore Smith's biography of Colborne, compiled mainly from his letters and records of his conversations, enables us to eavesdrop on typical acts of valour recounted in drawing-rooms of the wider Yonge family.[30] From other memoirs we know that such tales of derring-do were frequently accompanied by discussions about military tactics. The Yonges' neighbour and close friend, George Moberly, headmaster of Winchester College, loved to discuss the details of the Peninsular War with his brother Richard whenever he visited.[31] A letter from Mary Yonge testifies to Charlotte's active and informed engagement in such conversations: 'I can remember ... that it was most interesting to hear her discussing the Waterloo time with Lord Seaton, and again, after his return from Canada, all that time of the Rebellion and Church matters there, in which he took so great a part.'[32]

Throughout her life, Charlotte Yonge enthusiastically pursued knowledge of military campaigns, amassing information on the tactics used through extensive reading and careful listening to the discussions between soldiers within her family, imaginatively participating in the experience of battle. Until recently, scholars largely overlooked the flood of military memoirs in the post-Napoleonic Wars period; indeed, by the twentieth century such memoirs had become a niche interest for a coterie of military re-enactment enthusiasts and were not seen as significant from a historical or literary standpoint. Such an attitude has been challenged by new scholarship, particularly that of Neil Ramsey and Catriona Kennedy, who highlight both the role of such accounts within literary history and the large number of such publications.[33] Ramsey has alerted us to the need to consider these accounts as part of a British Romantic culture that demonstrated a new and influential way of representing warfare: 'Embroiled in distant wars, the soldier was a figure remote from his civilian counterpart, yet sentimental writing could enable the reading public to bridge this gap through forms of sympathy. ... The dramatic changes in the writing of military memoirs during this time can be seen as a reflection of this broader shift, as the affective eye-witness account emerged as a popular element in British cultural responses to the nation's wars.'[34] Ramsey examines some memoirs in detail, including G. R. Gleig's *The Subaltern* (1825), an account of a young man's first experiences of battle in the Peninsular War. Like William Yonge, Gleig had joined the army aged sixteen. Although he describes gruesome, frightening incidents and was himself wounded three times, he calls his time in the Peninsula 'one of the happiest in my life'.[35] We know this book to be a favourite with Charlotte Yonge, as Albinia Kendal in *The Young Stepmother* (1861) recommends it as wholesome reading for her disaffected teenage stepson, Gilbert, to inspire him to be more manly; Albinia, like Yonge herself, as 'the daughter of a Peninsular man, ... thought nothing so charming'.[36] The circulation of such memoirs contributed to a continued dialogue about the wars in the early nineteenth century, formative years in Charlotte Yonge's life. The authoritative six volumes of Sir William Napier's *History of the War in the Peninsula*, published over the years 1828 to 1840, added to this narrative bank of stories, supplying a source-book and a stimulus for yet more memories.

Yuval Noah Harari distinguishes between those who are actively involved in combat and those who study battles afterwards. He has invented the term 'flesh-witnesses' for the former, meaning they who had 'learned their wisdom with their flesh' by their actual presence in a battle; the latter, however much they scrutinise the details and relive the events in their imagination, can never be more than eye-witnesses: 'Eschewing the rationalist authority of logical thinking and the scientific authority of objective eye-witnessing, veterans lay claim to the visceral authority of "flesh-witnessing". They are neither thinkers nor mere eye-witnesses. Rather, they are men (and occasionally women) who have learned their wisdom with their flesh.'[37] In these terms, Charlotte Yonge clearly cannot be a 'flesh-witness'. A lifetime of immersion in the accounts of these battles, however, had made her an expert through her mind's eye, infused with the ethos of her father's regiment. In the 1888 Christmas Number of her own magazine, the *Monthly Packet*, she narrated the actions of the 52nd in 'the decisive moment of Waterloo' to illustrate the motto, 'Virtue has its own reward'; how 'Sir John Colborne ... never thought fit to utter a word of complaint of being deprived of the lustre of the crowning measure of the greatest victory of the time.' What is startling is that she writes as if she herself had been present at Waterloo: 'I cannot help here telling you what I have actually seen myself, and which is no mere tale.'[38] With both her father and uncle dead, it is as if she is speaking for them as a 'flesh-witness', not a mere eye-witness.

Charlotte Yonge's fictional exemplars

Yonge depicted her first attempts at story writing as 'perpetual dreams of romance ... in which somebody was always being wounded in the Peninsular War and coming home with an arm in a sling'.[39] Revering the military spirit of both her father and her uncle, Yonge perceived the perfect temperament to be one that combined contrasting elements: action and restraint, initiative and discipline, fortitude and gentleness. Although based on the moral fibre of soldiers, she believed such qualities were equally suitable for women and girls of all classes as well as men and boys, because everyone needs to soldier on as a participant in the battlefield of life. Through all her writings, she provided subtle illustrations of how to acquire these characteristics, assuming that it was possible to assimilate such attitudes through reading stories and by mentally rehearsing how to react courageously when confronted with both physical and moral challenges.

A typical example of Yonge's belief that stories of military heroism equip us for such situations in civilian life occurs in *Scenes and Characters* (1847), a novel about the Mohun family of eleven children. Phyllis Mohun, aged seven, yearns to be a knight in shining armour but can initially only find dragonflies, thrushes and tadpoles to rescue. She tells an older brother, Claude, 'do you know there is nothing I wish so much as to save somebody's life'.[40] Such an opportunity arises when some gunpowder, which her ten-year-old brother has acquired to make fireworks, almost causes a major fire. Acting with great presence of mind, Phyllis throws the horn of gunpowder out of the window just in time: 'A light in the midst of the smoke made Phyllis turn, and she beheld the papers on the table on fire. Maurice's powder-horn was in the midst, but the flames had not yet reached it, and, mindful of Claude's story, she sprung forward, caught it up, and dashed it through the window', thus saving her little sister from serious injury.[41] 'Claude's story', which Phyllis had internalised and which triggered her swift response, was an account of a real event in the Peninsular War of two English soldiers who had prevented the explosion of an arsenal by just such a courageous action.[42]

Yonge herself included a retelling of the original for 'Claude's story' – the prompt action of two soldiers of the 52nd in Ciudad Rodrigo in 1812 – in her very popular work, *A Book of Golden Deeds*.[43] This volume of tales, republished many times over and used in schools in shortened versions, consisted of stories of courageous action throughout history, collected by Yonge and re-told:

as a treasury for young people ... in the trust that example may inspire the spirit of heroism and self-devotion. For surely it must be a wholesome contemplation to look on actions, the very essence of which is such entire absorption in others that self is not so much renounced as forgotten; the object of which is not to win promotion, wealth, or success, but simple duty, mercy and loving-kindness.[44]

Her opening chapter 'What is a Golden Deed?' begins with the blunt declaration, 'We all of us enjoy a story of battle and adventure', and proceeds to analyse both why such stories delight and what type of bold deeds truly merit our admiration.[45]

A Golden Deed must be something more than mere display of fearlessness. ... it is the spirit that gives itself for others – the temper that for the sake of religion, of country, of duty, of kindred, nay, of pity even to a stranger, will dare all things, risk all things, endure all things, meet death in one moment, or wear life away in slow persevering tendance and suffering. ... if ever it be your lot to do a Golden Deed, it will probably be in unconsciousness that you are doing anything extraordinary, and that the whole impulse will consist in having absolutely forgotten self.[46]

For Yonge this was the essence of manly military virtue, to be emulated in all spheres of life by women as well as by men - what Christopher Coker calls 'the heroic version of history'.[47]

Phyllis's bold action in *Scenes and Characters* closely resembles a feat of heroism described in Yonge's novel, *The Clever Woman of the Family* (1865), where Captain Alexander Keith (Alick) carries a burning shell away from a tent full of wounded soldiers in India. Awarded the Victoria Cross, he returns to England to recuperate in a seaside town from the injuries sustained in the explosion. Rachel Curtis, the 'clever woman', assumes he is merely an idle soldier on leave and lectures him on true valour, retelling the courageous incident from the recent siege in Delhi to illustrate her meaning, unaware that Alick was the very man whose deeds she is describing.[48] Like Colborne, this hero is a man of extreme modesty so he does not enlighten Rachel as to his real identity. How to perform 'golden deeds' in ordinary life as well as in battle is one of the many themes of this multi-layered novel. Rachel believes she is acting nobly in setting up her charitable work-scheme to train girls in wood engraving, but fails to maintain sufficient oversight over the enterprise. It is not the independent-minded, 'modern' Rachel but the motherly Lady Fanny Temple, a widow of a general, who shows the required initiative and courage to rescue the young girls from this sweat-shop.[49] Typically, Yonge entitles the chapter in which Fanny liberates the children 'The Forlorn Hope', a military term for a small group of soldiers who volunteer to lead a hazardous assault, while the previous chapter was 'The Siege'.

Military themes permeated Yonge's writings – her contemporary domestic fiction, her historical novels, her books for children, her history textbooks. Some are set during periods of war: *Kenneth; or the Rear-Guard of the Grand Army* (1850) takes place during the Retreat from Moscow in 1812; *The Chaplet of Pearls; or the White and Black Ribaumont* (1868) takes place in sixteenth-century France at the time of the Massacre of St Bartholemew. *The Young Stepmother* (1861) incorporated the events of the Crimean War into a novel of contemporary domestic life. This conflict had brought the reality of war into the lives of the Yonge family in unpleasant ways. On 26 February 1854, William Yonge died of a stroke probably brought on by helping Julian, his only son and an officer in the Rifle Brigade, embark for the campaign. A few days before his death, Charlotte Yonge had written to her cousin Anne, 'Papa has been over working himself with spending whole long days without dinner upon Julian's preparations, and yesterday after going to Portsmouth to take leave of him, and coming home very late, a sort of seizure came on like an exaggerated headache.'[50] His demise meant William Yonge would never know how his son would cope on the battlefield and so was saved from the knowledge of his son's inglorious record. Julian, whom Charlotte had wanted to be called Alexander Xenophon, not only withdrew from the campaign in November 1854 but, to his mother's dismay, resigned his commission.

The Young Stepmother reflects the confusion in Charlotte Yonge's emotions about young men whom she knew well, involved in an actual war – both those like her own brother who earned no battle medals and others who fought with distinction, such as Colborne's eldest son Francis and Denzil Chamberlayne, the son of a neighbour in Otterbourne. Albinia Kendal, the eponymous young stepmother, and her brother, Maurice Ferrars, belong to an army family with strong similarities to Charlotte's own. Albinia, like Charlotte, has the 'martial ardour' of a 'soldier's daughter'.[51] This military background gives Albinia and Maurice a wholesome energy and courage with which to address family and parish problems, in sad contrast to Albinia's depressive non-military husband and her lacklustre stepson, Gilbert. Eventually Gilbert redeems himself by enlisting as a soldier, which thrills Albinia's 'soldier-spirit' when she sees 'the light in his eyes and the expression on his lips, making his face finer and more manly than she had ever seen it'.[52] It is likely that Denzil Chamberlayne's real-life *sang-froid* during the Charge of the Light Brigade provided Yonge with the inspiration for Gilbert's role in the battle.[53] In the novel, Gilbert, like Denzil but unlike her own brother, fights with honour at Balaclava, endangering his life to rescue his cousin Frederick. Gilbert's health has been strained, and he dies on the way back home. Mourning her stepson, Albinia feels guilty about the pressure she had put on him to enlist due to her belief that the only professions 'worthy of a man's attention [were] the clerical or the military'.[54] 'Had I but silenced my foolish pride, he might have been safe … now.'[55] The abrupt resignation of her brother from the army softened Charlotte Yonge's view of men who fail to live up to her high standards. When writing *Clever Woman* in the 1860s, her notions about warfare and heroism had already shifted slightly so that her manly soldier-hero Alick Keith declares, 'it is the discipline and constant duty that make the soldier, and are far more valuable than exceptional doings'.[56]

Charlotte Yonge believed the Christian life was one of perpetual warfare and vigilance, making all Christians, whatever their gender or age, into warriors. In *The Pillars of the House* (1873), Yonge's complex account of an orphaned family of thirteen children as they face the challenges of growing into adulthood, some words in a funeral sermon encapsulate this notion: 'warring as one band against darkness, foulness, cruelty, and all other evils, each fighting his own individual battle in private'.[57] The character of Guy Morville, the attractive hero of the phenomenally successful *The Heir of Redclyffe* (1853), who battles not on the war field but against his own temperament, seems to be very similar to that of her own virtuous but short-tempered father.[58] In *Heartsease* (1854), a non-soldier employs military terms to describe 'the turning-point of his life', his 'call to arms', whereby he understood 'where lies modern chivalry'.[59] Writing to her friend Elizabeth Wordsworth in 1892, Charlotte Yonge commented on a review of her fiction in the High Church paper *The Guardian*: 'One thing that pleased me in the … article … was the recognition that my good men were really imitations of the good men of the day, not mere ideals.'[60] Yonge embedded patterns of heroic conduct and self-discipline, modelled on the soldierly worthiness of the men in her family, into all her writings. The liveliness and authenticity of the dialogue of her fictional families allowed the inspirational messages buried within her stories to infiltrate the minds of the numerous male and female readers of her bestselling novels and to motivate their readiness to demonstrate true manliness.

Notes

1   Quotations in my title are from Charlotte M. Yonge, *The Young Stepmother; or A Chronicle of Mistakes* [1861] (London: Macmillan, 1889), pp. 80, 282. Some themes of this essay are discussed in 'Charlotte Yonge and the Aftermath of Waterloo: Military Men in Reality and Imagination', *Journal of the Charlotte M. Yonge Fellowship*, Special Issue on CMY and Waterloo, 12 (2017), pp. 49–63, and in Susan Walton, *Imagining Soldiers and Fathers in the Mid-Victorian Era: Charlotte Yonge's Models of Manliness* (Farnham: Ashgate, 2010).

2   Charlotte Mitchell, Ellen Jordan and Helen Schinske (eds), *The Letters of Charlotte Mary Yonge (1823–1901)*. Available at: https://c21ch.newcas tle.edu.au/yonge/3317/to-mary-elizabeth-wormeley-latimer (accessed 4 March 2016). Yonge is thanking Elizabeth Wormeley Latimer for her book, *England in the Nineteenth Century* (Chicago, IL: McClurg, 1894).

3   John Colborne was ennobled as First Baron Seaton, of Seaton in Devon, in 1839. Both of Charlotte Yonge's parents were related to him – her mother was his step-sister, and her father was first cousin to Colborne's wife. Colborne's military career was one of extraordinary distinction rewarded with a sequence of promotions on merit up to full general (1854) and field marshal (1860). In 1861 he became Commander in Chief of the Rifle Brigade, an illustrious position held previously by the Duke of Wellington (1820–54) and Prince Albert (1854–61). He also served as a proactive colonial governor in Guernsey, Canada and the Ionian Islands.

4   Joshua S. Goldstein, *War and Gender. How Gender Shapes the War System and Vice Versa* (Cambridge: Cambridge University Press, 2001), pp. 410–11; italics as in the original.

5   *Ibid.*, p. 309.

6   Harari, *Ultimate Experience*, p. 1.

7   *Ibid.*, pp. 154–5.

8   See George Herring, *What Was the Oxford Movement?* (London: Continuum, 2002), p. 21, for summary of the views of Prickett, Aidan Nichols and himself.

9   Charlotte M. Yonge, *Musings over 'The Christian Year' and 'Lyra Innocentium' Together with a Few Gleanings of Recollections of the Rev. J. H. Keble, Gathered by Several Friends* (Oxford: James Parker, 1872), p. xxxv.

10 Christabel R. Coleridge, *Charlotte Mary Yonge* (London: Macmillan, 1903), pp. 20–6.

11 Ethel Romanes, *Charlotte Mary Yonge. An Appreciation* (London: A. W. Mowbray, 1908), p. 16.

12 G. C. Moore Smith, *The Life of John Colborne, Field-Marshal Lord Seaton, Compiled from His Letters, Records of His Conversations and Other Sources* (London: John Murray, 1903), p. 147.

13 Coleridge, *Yonge*, p. 31.

14 *Ibid.*, pp. 31, 34–5.

15 Arthur Bryant, *Jackets of Green. A Study of the History, Philosophy and Characters of the Rifle Brigade* (London: Collins, 1972), pp. 23–8, 39–40, 56; W. S. Moorsom (ed.), *The Historical Record of the Fifty-Second Regiment (Oxfordshire Light Infantry) from the Year 1755 to the Year 1858* (London: Richard Bentley, 1860), pp. v–vi.

16 General W. C. E. Napier (ed.), *Passages in the Early Military Life of General George T. Napier, K.C.B. Written by Himself* (London: John Murray, 1884), p. 13.

17 *Ibid.*, p. 14; italics as in the original. See Harari, *Ultimate Experience*, pp. 166–70, for discussion of this 'revolution in military education'.

18 Sir J. F. Maurice (ed.), *The Diary of Sir John Moore*, 2 vols (London: Edward Arnold, 1904), vol. II, p. 155.

19 Coleridge, *Yonge*, p. 21. See Moorsom, *Historical Record of the Fifty-Second Regiment*, p. vi, for a description of the 52nd as 'A regiment never surpassed in arms since arms were first borne by men', made by William Napier in his *History of the Peninsular War*.

20 Colborne was Military Secretary to Moore from 1808. Accompanying him during the retreat to Corunna, Colborne was one of the small group who buried Moore in secret before embarkation. Moore's dying wish was for Colborne to be promoted to lieutenant-colonel.

21 Moore Smith, *Colborne*, pp. 268–9.

22 G. C. Moore Smith (ed.), *The Autobiography of Lieutenant-General Harry Smith*, 2 vols (London: John Murray, 1902), vol. I, p. 130.

23 *Ibid.*, p. 221.

24 William Crawley Yonge, *Memoir of Lord Seaton's Services* (Privately published, 1853), p. 13.

25 Charlotte M. Yonge, 'Preface: Arachne's Web', in Charlotte M. Yonge (ed.), *Christmas Number of the Monthly Packet*, 1888, p. vi.

26 Charlotte M. Yonge, 'Field Marshal Lord Seaton', *The Wykehamist* (June 1896), pp. 206–8. The debate continues to this day; see Nigel Sale, 'The Waterloo Secret Revealed'. Available at: http://waterlooassociation.org .uk/The%20Waterloo%20Secret%20Revealed.pdf (accessed 18 March 2015).

27 Moore Smith, *Colborne*, pp. 420–1, from a Memorandum by 2nd Lord Seaton.

28 Rev. William Leeke, *The History of Lord Seaton's Regiment (the 52nd Light Infantry) at the Battle of Waterloo*, 2 vols (London: Hatchard & Co, 1866), vol. II, p. 423.

29 Yonge, *Memoir*, pp. 14–15.

30 Moore Smith, *Colborne*, pp. 187–8.

31 C. A. E. Moberly, *Dulce Domum. George Moberly, His Family and Friends by his Daughter* (London: John Murray, 1911), p. 153.

32 Coleridge, *Yonge*, p. 142.
33 Ramsey, *The Military Memoir*; Kennedy, *Narratives of the Revolutionary and Napoleonic Wars*.
34 Ramsey, *The Military Memoir*, p. 10.
35 In Gleig's opening dedication to the Duke of Wellington.
36 Yonge, *Young Stepmother*, p. 48.
37 Harari, *Ultimate Experience*, p. 7.
38 Yonge, *Christmas Monthly Packet* 1888, pp. vi–vii.
39 Charlotte M. Yonge, 'Lifelong Friends', *Monthly Packet*, NS VIII (December 1894), p. 695.
40 Charlotte M. Yonge, *Scenes and Characters; or Eighteen Months at Beechcroft* [1847] (London: Macmillan, 1889), p. 176.
41 *Ibid.*, p. 241.
42 *Ibid.*, pp. 179–80.
43 Charlotte M. Yonge, *A Book of Golden Deeds of All Times and All Lands Gathered and Narrated by Charlotte Yonge* [1864] (London: Macmillan, 1871), p. 230, in a chapter entitled 'The Perils of Gunpowder'.
44 *Ibid.*, pp. v–vi.
45 *Ibid.*, p. 1.
46 *Ibid.*, pp. 4, 5, 9.
47 Christopher Coker, *The Warrior Ethos: Military Culture and the War on Terrorism* (Abingdon: Routledge 2007), p. 3. Ernest Hemingway chose Yonge's account of the Battle of Thermopylae from *Golden Deeds* for his anthology *The Best War-Stories of All Time* (1942), published to rally American willingness to fight in the Second World War.
48 Charlotte M. Yonge, *The Clever Woman of the Family* [1865] (London: Macmillan, 1902), p. 82. See also Susan Walton, 'Suitable Work for Women? Florence Claxton's Illustrations for *The Clever Woman of the Family* by Charlotte Yonge' in *Nineteenth-Century Gender Studies* 11:2 (Summer 2015). Available at: www.ncgsjournal.com/issue112/walton.htm (accessed 7 November 2017).
49 Yonge, *Clever Woman*, p. 217.
50 Mitchell *et al.*, *Letters of Charlotte Mary Yonge*. Available at: https://c21ch.newcastle.edu.au/yonge/3317/to-mary-elizabeth-wormeley-latimer (accessed 4 March 2016).
51 Yonge, *Young Stepmother*, pp. 80, 282.
52 *Ibid.*, pp. 310–11.
53 See Obituary of Chamberlayne, 13th Light Dragoons, 1833–73, for a vivid account of the part he played in that battle. Available at: http://chargeofthelightbrigade.com/allmen/allmenC/allmenC_13LD/chamberlayne_d_13LD.html (accessed 4 February 2016).
54 Yonge, *Young Stepmother*, p. 82.
55 *Ibid.*, p. 428.

56   Yonge, *Clever Woman*, p. 179.
57   Charlotte M. Yonge, *The Pillars of the House; or Under Wode, Under Rode* [1873] 2 vols (London: Macmillan, 1896), vol. II, p. 404, a sermon for some young men drowned in a boating incident.
58   Holly Furneaux, 'Victorian Masculinities, or Military Men of Feeling: Domesticity, Militarism, and Manly Sensibility', in Juliet John (ed.), *The Oxford Handbook of Victorian Literary Culture* (Oxford: Oxford University Press, 2016), pp. 224–6, for discussion of the popularity of Yonge's fiction with soldiers, especially *The Heir of Redclyffe* and *Heartsease*.
59   Charlotte M. Yonge, *Heartsease; or the Brother's Wife* [1854] (London: Macmillan, 1902), p. 409.
60   Elizabeth Wordsworth, *Glimpses of the Past* (London: A. R. Mowbray, 1912), p. 188.

8

'And the individual withers': Tennyson and the enlistment into military masculinity

Lorenzo Servitje

Tennyson, peering into the future, was attempting to see great forests – the big picture – without singling out individual trees. He had more luck than most of us today, who seem to find individual trees obscuring our vision. —William Turner

When Lieutenant General William Turner, commander of the United States' large-scale military airlift operations during the Second World War, suggests that Alfred Lord Tennyson aimed to see the larger context rather than focusing on the granular in his 1842 'Locksley Hall', he touches on a central problem in the poem: the place of the poem's speaker within his martial milieu and larger social sphere. This question of the one versus the many is indeed one of the central tensions of the Victorian period, as a number of scholars have suggested.[1] However, what is most interesting about Turner's reference is that when we consider his position as a military commander in context, we are prompted to ask how exactly 'Locksley Hall' might be working through a specifically martial iteration of this question.

In the form of a dramatic monologue, the poem narrates an unnamed protagonist's call to his comrades to leave him on a shore near his childhood home—Locksley Hall. Shifting between the past, present and future, he reflects on a primal scene of unrequited love with his cousin Amy. The speaker reveals that he was rejected by Amy's father, who favoured a match of higher social status. He consequently joins the military to partake in the march of progress toward a utopian future, having earlier been left an orphan with little social or economic capital after his father died on a foreign battlefield. The speaker processes the hopes and anxieties of the mid-century zeitgeist: industrialisation, urbanisation, technology, colonialism, gradualism, social and class hierarchies.

Prophesising a vision of a world to come, the speaker oscillates within a spectrum of emotions from nostalgia, hope and excitement to jealousy and rage, ultimately deciding to throw himself into imperialism's breech: letting Europe lead the 'great world['s]' spin forever down 'the grooves of change'.[2]

As evidenced by the epigraph, Tennyson's 'Locksley Hall' is often quoted both in and out of academic registers with respect to progress and wisdom. It has been identified as a favourite poem of a number of historical figures: Winston Churchill was said to be able to quote the poem at length, and Harry Truman kept a selection of the poem in his wallet.[3] 'Locksley Hall' is at heart a military poem, and as such, it must be considered within this context. The obfuscation of the poem's military narrative is indicative of a crucial element of the poem's cultural work. While the way in which the poem represents and complicates masculinity has been discussed by scholars such as Herbert Sussman, it is easy to overlook the poem's relevance to military history. When focusing on masculinity and progress in more abstract terms, we can forget that the speaker is a soldier and neglect to consider how 'Locksley Hall' works through the intersection of masculinity and the military during the first half of the nineteenth century. Moreover, within the scope of Tennyson's poetry, the military and masculine valances of this dramatic monologue are commonly overshadowed by works like 'On the Death of Duke of Wellington' (1852), 'The Charge of the Light Brigade' (1854), 'Maud' (1855) and the sequel of 'Locksley Hall', 'Locksley Hall Sixty Years After' (1887).[4] The poem's contemporary and historical overshadowing by Tennyson's other military poems resembles its engagement with the Victorian enlisted man's own occultation into narratives of progress and empire. The poem reveals how the early Victorian military's making of the man 'recruits' the individual into the whole but at the same time obfuscates the difficulties and consequences of actualising this masculine subjectivity.

This chapter contextualises 'Locksley Hall' within the manly braving of the vicissitudes of Victorian military life for the future of the nation. I contend that when read in the light of the British soldier's precarious socioeconomic position in the early Victorian period, 'Locksley Hall' articulates some of the complications in how the military made the man. Midway through the poem, the speaker emblematises this very thesis when processing his vision of the future: where 'the individual withers, and the world is more and more'.[5] Like the abstract concept of progress, the process of masculinisation is never fully realised; it

requires continual fashioning and development. This processual masculinisation facilitated the individual soldier's 'withering' into what the
Duke of Wellington called 'the scum of the earth',[6] a vital corporeal
undifferentiated mass that fuelled the empire's expansion 'more and
more'. Considering that marital rejection drives the speaker to become
a soldier, the poem shows how the military capitalised on the desire
for masculine subjectification, when men failed to achieve the marital
and familial ideals set by the middle-class cult of domesticity. In this
capacity, while the British military did not enforce conscription until
the First World War, it becomes clear that 'Locksley Hall' was part of
a larger cultural movement that recruited men into this narrative, to
direct their identity formation and labour power into the progress of
nation and empire.

At stake in this reading is a revelation of the poem's role as an ideological mechanism during the Victorian era, one that continued into
the twentieth and twenty-first century, as is evident in its continued
citation out of the context of its production and its ambivalent reading of military masculinity. While following some of the conflicting
accounts of masculinity in autobiographical narratives of enlisted
men,[7] on a broader scale, this reading reveals how the poetic form provided Tennyson the means to deploy a specifically classed masculinity
in support of the military's participation in the grand narrative of progress and empire, while at the same time providing a form to critique
the resulting effects.

While 'Locksley Hall' appears to be about a single man, in the single
moment of his utterance, the poem resists such discretising by situating
the individual in a longer diachronic temporality and the larger social
context of the military and the Victorian state to which it pertained. The
relationship between the part and the whole, moreover, itself becomes
effected in the poem's afterlife. Part of the problem with addressing
the poem's quotable individual lines, such as the infamous 'Woman is
the lesser man',[8] is that it obscures the specific subject position of the
speaker and cultural work of the poem. Certainly, a line like this speaks
broadly to the kind of patriarchy operative in the Victorian era at large;
however, when read within the context of the entire poem and its historical milieu, it addresses a more nuanced take on the role that kind of
misogyny played in the making of this specific military man, and how
such a position was related to the ideology behind such problematic
aphorisms. Masculinity in the Victorian period was neither monolithic
nor homogenised, as a number of studies have documented.[9] Rather, it

was contingent on the historical and socioeconomic context, and had both hegemonic and divergent iterations. What we see in 'Locksley Hall' are the contradictions and challenges that the speaker faces when aspiring to a kind of masculinity determined by his working-class status, and the resulting transference of that energy and self-fashioning to a grand narrative of progress.

The role, material conditions and perception of the enlisted man were mutable and overdetermined during the Victorian period: sometimes a figure of sympathy, other times of scorn. Yet, he remained an essential cog in the British imperial machine, both an effect and a contingent factor of industrialisation and empire. The military acted as a policing force for the empire's expanding colonies, and the enlisted man bore the brunt of this colonial work.[10] While he was essential to the sustenance and expansion of the nation and its increasing possessions, he was, for much of the century, but especially during the first half of the century, rarely the benefactor of it. The rank-and-file soldier in the early Victorian period was not always a hero in the popular imagination. At times despised by broader British culture, he was frequently caricatured as a drunk, a brute or a semi-reformed criminal, as the enlisted soldier came from the lowest social strata and was often forced into enlistment by poverty or as an alternative to prison. Besides being driven to the military by desperation, men were tricked and enlisted while under the influence of drink. To this effect, for the working classes, the images the common soldier conjured were often of abandoned, pregnant women and hungover young men, waking to find themselves freshly minted property of the army.[11] In these ways, the common lot of the enlisted man was likely a dreary one. While the image of the drunk, criminal and carouser was present during the eighteenth and early nineteenth century, other sentiments such as pride and espousal during the 'scarlet fever' after the French Wars emerged when many of their less describable qualities were 'scrubbed clean', especially in the case of the sailor, as Joanne Begiato has convincingly argued.[12] By the 1840s, the public began to see a much more prescient concern for army reform, which reflected their increased sympathy for the common soldier.[13] At the same time, however, the connotations attached to the Duke of Wellington's notorious moniker remained operative. Published memoirs of enlisted soldiers during the first half of the century recount 'the corporeal horrors of soldiering, its "terrible and sickening privations" and the soldier's appalling "powerlessness" in the face of military hierarchies and war's violence'. These memoirs of the early nineteenth century, contends Neil Ramsey, confirmed contemporary perceptions that 'the soldier had "relinquished the freedoms of civilian existence for slavery, exile, and (very likely) horrible death"'.[14] The memoirs of the common soldier, in contrast to that of the officer, revealed a kind of deindividualisation at work in these accounts of the self, as the stories of enlisted men 'reflected on war in universal terms, associating it with horrors and miseries in ways that did not need to include the private soldier in concepts of the nation'.[15] This erasure by means of assimilation into the larger mass of the army is precisely the process at work in 'Locksley Hall'.

While military life afforded economic and quartering opportunities, soldiers faced socioeconomic challenges that made their lives precarious, as Ramsey's readings document. They were fed little, were forced to provide many of their necessities themselves and, more often than not, had worse health than the poorest paupers of the metropole. On average, soldiers were hospitalised every thirteen months; one death occurred per every sixty-seven hospitalised.[16] In addition to dire living conditions, the process of becoming a military man could pose a significant burden on the individual, in effect representing a total submission of one's life to the military. Early in the century, the period of enlistment was 'for life' or twenty-one years; effectively the adult life of an individual who, if he was lucky, could hope to live to age fifty. After the introduction of Edward Cardwell's reforms and the Enlistment Act 1870 onward, enlistments were somewhat shorter – twelve-year enlistments were allowed.[17] As many soldiers had no skills transferable to civilian life, however, most reenlisted. The ambiguity and narrative play that the poetic form affords allow Tennyson's poem to explore the varied and sometimes competing social forces at work – like class and biopolitics – in the enlisted man's formation of masculinity.

While 'Locksley Hall' presents the complexities of the speaker's class origins, affective fulfilment and loss of individual identity in the process of becoming a military man, it hones in on marriage. The speaker narrates the process of moving from civilian to military life non-linearly, going back and forth between his present soldierly status, the past conditions that led him to join and the future he imagines it holds. As a member of the lower class, evidenced by the rejection of his marriage proposal, among other allusions to lack of access to pleasures of middle-class life, the speaker of 'Locksley Hall' finds himself unable to actualise this masculine role in the domestic context as a breadwinner who could come home for respite from working life in the comfort of his wife and family.[18] Therefore, while the soldier's lot was a tough burden to bear, it did create opportunities and a space – social and affective – to actualise his masculinity in another form besides the ideal set by the cult of domesticity.[19] In the military, the speaker is able to find a sense of alliance and purpose. If, like the speaker, the enlisted man found himself a social pariah, then, he could still find pride in his uniform. Many soldiers' memoirs suggest, in fact, that the right to wear the military uniform influenced their decision to enlist.[20] This sense of national pride and belonging with respect to his uniform reflects the process of military inclusion prompted by a preceding social exclusion, as is the case with the speaker in 'Locksley Hall'.

The poem narrates the conditions that shaped this particular enlisted man's contribution to a nation that in a certain capacity excluded him. The poem achieves this end through both its formal construction and its representation of the speaker's difficulty in reconciling his affect and gender script with his original socioeconomic status. Formally, 'Locksley Hall' lends itself to itself to working through this tension by presenting the reader with a range of ambiguities, particularly in terms of masculinity. As a dramatic monologue, it allows Tennyson to present the poem within the frame of a problematic epistemology. The form of the dramatic monologue lends itself to what Isobel Armstrong calls the 'double poem'.[21] At once aesthetic and political, the double poem expresses the sentiment of the single self while contemplating how this self relates to others and their milieu. Though it appears to be an unmediated direct encounter between speaker and reader, the dramatic monologue positions the individual speaker within a specific social context: a time, place, situation and auditor.[22] The dramatic monologue's very attempt at immediacy – the rendering of the medium as invisible, as if it is directly addressing the reader – reveals that it is, in fact, constructed to appear as such. To this effect, the poem's form lends itself to investigating the historical circumstances of the fictional speaker. 'Locksley Hall', on the one hand, presents the voice of the speaker-soldier, with his own subjectivity, thoughts, feelings and ideologies; an individual, who commands what discourse is available to his internal audience and the external reader. On the other hand, by the end of the poem, the speaker negates his individual desires for the promise of a larger force at work – 'the big picture', in William Turner's estimation; ironically, his masculine strength is tied to this very 'withering' into the greater military, national and imperial narrative.

The poem's opening lines alert the reader to a sense of separation from the social by way of the speaker's declarative isolation, intimating how, in many ways, the enlisted man existed on the margins of society, separated by his barracks and his occupation.[23] We see the speaker beginning his monologue in a marginal position, on the edge of the shore, on the edge of his own tight-knit social circle. Singling out his fellow men in arms, he impetrates, 'Comrades, leave me here a little, while as yet 't is early morn: / Leave me here, and when you want me, sound upon the bugle-horn.'[24] Here, the speaker is not only separated from society at large by virtue of his profession; he also excludes himself from his only place of belonging to reflect on the conditions that shaped his present circumstances. This isolation from his comrades, as we will see, is only temporary and imaginary. The poem, while at times seeming to fracture the immediacy of the dramatic monologue by not signalling his comrades as he ventures into the past and future, is uttered in a single temporal moment and physical locale. By the end of the poem, the speaker again addresses his fellow soldiers, returning to the greater whole into which he ultimately dissolves, and, in fact, never left.

The speaker looks on his childhood home in a displaced temporality; 'Locksley Hall' was the manor where he resided, but he clearly did not belong to the house as such. He likely was part of the labour power that sustained it, suggested by the fact that he called it his 'home', yet he compares himself to a boy when he first leaves his father's field.[25] This is compounded by the central conflict: he cannot marry his true love because of his inferior social position. These elements taken together intimate his working-class status. As the speaker recalls his youth, he looks to the past for the sublimity of its present, which had seemed secure in the promise of a domestic future: 'Here about the beach I wander'd, nourishing a youth sublime / With the fairy tales of science, and the long result of Time. When the centuries behind me like a fruitful land reposed; / When I clung to all the present for the promise that it closed.'[26] The speaker links the sublimity of his youth with the Victorian zeitgeist of progress and possibility: 'When I dipt into the future far as human eye could see; Saw the Vision of the world and all the wonder that would be.'[27] In this vision, not only the world but perhaps his social mobility would move forward. In this individual frame, the vision of the world and all its wonder centres on his desired union with his beloved. These hopes are not so much economic but affective and sexual. In the stanzas that follow, Tennyson invokes the vernal and sensual promise of requited love, a place and time where 'in the Spring a young man's fancy lightly turns to thoughts of love'.[28] In the speaker's memory, following a stanza that foreshadows the maritime and spiritual connection tropes of Tennyson's *In Memoriam*, the lovers unite spiritually through embodied contact. 'Many an evening by the waters did we watch the stately ships', the speaker continues connecting his past with the present through the shared proximity of maritime encounters, 'And our spirits rush'd together at the touching of the lips.'[29] The series of references to his loving cousin Amy, coupled with vernal vitality and fertility, however, rapidly decay into 'shallow-hearted[ness]' and 'the barren, barren shore!'[30] In the past, the future held the promise of a domestically fruitful and fertile life – the connotations of fertility signal the reproductivity of the domestic as a social structure by means of children. However, at the time of this utterance, this promise is indeed empty and barren. Yet, as I will show, the speaker ultimately is able to repurpose affect and energy of courtship to a loftier aim beyond the individual, the pair or even the family.

In terms of plot, rejection is the primary narrative conflict. Although Amy professes her love, she leaves the speaker for his social superior, presumably the lord of Locksley Hall, one who outranks him in the classed, patriarchal order of precedence. The speaker denounces his cousin and the social constraints that made their union impossible:

> Falser than all fancy fathoms, falser than all songs have sung,
> Puppet to a father's threat, and servile to a shrewish tongue!
> Is it well to wish thee happy? – having known me – to decline
> On a range of lower feelings and a narrower heart than mine!
> [...]
> Cursed be the social wants that sin against the strength of youth!
> Cursed be the social lies that warp us from the living truth!
> Cursed be the sickly forms that err from honest Nature's rule!
> Cursed be the gold that gilds the straiten'd forehead of the fool![31]

Seeing this as a constructed and enforced class system, the speaker foresees Amy reproducing the same social constraints that her father placed on her: 'O, I see thee old and formal, fitted to thy petty part, / With a little hoard of maxims preaching down a daughter's heart.'[32] Amy's father's 'threats' become her 'hoard of maxims', in essence literalising her comparison to 'a puppet'. The speaker rejects the desires, lies, forms and barriers of the materialist age that determined this outcome, as his position left him ill-equipped for the marriage market.[33] Amy's father makes her marry a social better – one who is, according to the speaker, romantically and affectively inferior to himself. The speaker's reference to the naturalisation of his relationship with Amy speaks to his awareness that the domestic union and paradigm that Amy's father, and Victorian society at large, follow is unnatural and pathological. While his union with Amy would have been 'the living truth' and followed 'nature's rule', the class division has 'warped' this potential relation into the 'sickly form' of Amy's arranged marriage and the ideology it propagates.

The failure to achieve an idealised romantic, domestic marriage, coupled with his low socioeconomic state, prime the speaker for masculinisation through the military order. While we tend to associate the domestic ideal with middle-class ideology, the political system at work that would have shaped the speaker's ideological and material conditions would have created a desire for marriage while restricting, or at least encumbering, its possibilities. The 1834 Poor Law played a significant part in the precarious position of the enlisted man. The ideal unit of the family prompted the state into an ordering of marital and family relations. In practice, the ordering of the Poor Law attempted to foster the idea of family structure or punish those who refused or, more precisely, were not able to institute it, by splitting up the family or making it difficult to marry once one entered the workhouse.[34] The codification of the domestic left soldiers in a difficult position with respect to marriage. Their overcrowded and unhygienic housing, their mobility and reputation for drink and promiscuity, were symptoms of their perceived failure to adopt the domestic ideology. But this was a systemic problem. There existed a certain incompatibility between the Victorian army and the institution of marriage, where the opportunities for marriage were restricted in a number of ways. The military code governing enlisted marriage for the first half of the century was harsh. Enlisted men were not allowed to marry without official permission. Only around 7 per cent of enlisted men were allowed to marry 'on the strength', a condition that allowed women to share quarters with the men. Those who did marry without permission could be punished, whereas married men's wives were not given quarters, allowances or transportation to follow their husbands.[35] While there were exceptions to these restraints, the structure of the military in general made it difficult for enlisted men to pursue the pleasures of the domestic ideal. For those that did marry, the Poor Law constructed the class of men who filled the rank and file as failures for not achieving this marital working-class form of masculinity – a basic provider who kept his family out of the workhouse. Married enlisted men often had trouble providing basic sustenance, leaving their wives and children contested dependents between Poor Law guardians and the War Office.[36] And this is to say nothing of the common stereotype of the enlisted man who intentionally left his family behind with little consequence, fostering a culture of womanising and misogyny.[37] Consequently, the social disruption or difficulty of achieving an approximation of the middle-class domestic ideal in the form of a proper working-class marriage reinforced the diversion of enlisted men's masculinity, strength and drive to the army, nation and empire. He could be a man elsewhere and, in fact, still operate under relations that drew on recognisable family structures.

The military substituted the familial structure with one of horizontal and hierarchical paternal male-male bonding. As Herbert Sussman contends, the speaker in 'Locksley Hall' escapes the terror of his hysterical, failed individual male ego 'by dissolving the self within the mass, by moving in step with other men'.[38] The speaker's dissolution becomes an affirmation of war, as he recommits to the enlisted life. Beyond the mass of his comrades in arms, the enlisted speaker substitutes the familial structure through the replication of the division of labour in the military. Commanding officers played a part in this substitution, serving in a paternal role for the rank and file. Despite this class stratification, the homosocial bonding, as one sergeant's account suggests, attended a kind of developmental masculinity that could continue beyond military service: 'The fondness of the officer continues with the man who fought under his command, to the remotest period of declining years, and the old soldier venerates his aged officer far more than perhaps he did in his youthful days.'[39] While many military historians have suggested that the enlisted man was regarded by his officers as a 'mechanical device, capable of valiant service under the stern guidance of his master',[40] more recent work complicates this relationship. Mathew McCormack contends that by the mid-1700s officers, while seeking to discipline the soldier's body through drill, also aimed to cultivate it. Though still connoting the mechanistic model, contemporary writers wrote about this instruction in terms of beauty, harmony and organicism.[41] Conducive to the logic of 'Lockley Hall''s loss of the individual to the greater whole, McCormack writes that conceptualising drill as a cultivation of a larger body was a more 'tactful simile for the process of subjecting freeborn Englishmen to military discipline'.[42] Tennyson's poem performs similar work, while at the same time drawing attention to the problems and ideologies behind such military subjection.

The social relations between officer and enlisted play an important part in understanding the classed context of the enlisted man. In large part, the relationship between officers and other ranks reflected the class system in civilian life, which was itself a class system that operated on the paternalistic relationship of the aristocracy and landed gentry with the labouring classes, especially in the years before large-scale immigration to urban environments due to rapid industrialisation. The belief that officers – by birth and economic standing – could lead men was due to their civilian status as stewards of the labouring classes. This was based on the model of the country estate: the 'landlord-tenant', or the feudal model.[43] While the problems associated with this model became apparent in the blunders of the Crimean War, during the period in which 'Locksley Hall' was written, it still operated as the paradigm. Often the courageousness displayed by officers – men with everything to lose – reaffirmed the paternalistic system, motivating the men to drive into the breech.

The replacement of the paternal role of the father with military hierarchy and subsequent intractable socioeconomic conditions is linked to the martial work of empire in the poem: the military had a hand in determining the speaker's place in the social hierarchy before he even thought of becoming a soldier. The speaker reveals that his socioeconomic condition was prefigured by the military-imperial system, when his father was killed on a foreign battle field: 'Deep in yonder shining Orient, where my life began to beat; / Where in wild Mahratta-battle fell my father evil-starr'd, – / I was left a trampled orphan, and a selfish uncle's ward.'[44] The speaker refers to the Battle of Assaye, where in 1803, the British fought against a confederacy of native warriors that controlled much of central India. These lines are particularly emblematic of the sets of conditions that drove the speaker to a position wherein he lacked both the opportunity to enter the marriage market as he would have hoped, and a proper model for masculinity. The speaker's heart 'began to beat' in war-torn circumstances, leading to a situation wherein all opportunity was 'barr'd with gold, and open[ed] but to golden keys'.[45] In being left 'a trampled orphan', the speaker suggests that his condition arose from the military marching – literally, insofar as the Indian army overran his father's corpse, which the speaker was figuratively 'under' (in the patriarchal and protective sense), but also in terms of the British imperial imperative that had brought his father there in the first place. Due to his poor circumstances and lack of a proper male role model and guardian, the speaker was easily shaped into the ideal candidate for enlistment, whereupon he was given basic subsistence, a paternal figure and guardian in the form of an officer and a channel to funnel his libidinal energy and the grief from his traumatic wounding as a child and rejection as a younger man.

As an enlisted man, the protagonist consequently finds himself between Scylla and Charybdis in terms of any kind of masculinised fulfilment. On the one hand, the class stratification foreclosed the possibility of him clinging to 'the present for the promise that it closed'. On the other, turning to a military life to displace the desire to achieve any kind of ideal domestic normalcy leaves him in a position to escape the resentment of the past by investing hope in a future he could not enjoy the fruits of: 'What is that which I should turn to, lighting upon days like these? / Every gate is throng'd with suitors, all the markets overflow. / I have but an angry fancy; what is that which I should do?'[46] The speaker acts as a seemingly misbehaving subject, one who does not want to accept the social order that excludes him from the marital economy. In terms of this misconduct, we might recall that a fellow poet and friend of Tennyson, Richard Dixon, discounted the poem as an 'ungentlemanly row'.[47] While Dixon's criticism speaks to Tennyson's poem itself rather than the speaker's rants and ravings, the waywardness of the speaker actually reinscribes him into the very system he wants to resist. The speaker recognises his 'unmanly' row. He comes to terms with the useless harpings of the past when he asks, 'what is that to him that reaps not harvest of his youthful joys, / Tho' the deep heart of existence beat forever like a boy's? Knowledge comes, but wisdom lingers, and I linger on the shore, / And the individual withers, and the world is more and more'.[48] Here, he equates wisdom with developed human knowledge of past experience that abstractly looks forward, as part of the bigger picture of 'mankind'; he comes to terms with his shameful lingering, which brings only transitory knowledge. In response, he allows himself to 'wither' into the force that moves the world 'more and more'. Not two lines later, this plays out in a moment of interruption to his existential ramblings: 'Hark, my merry comrades call me, sounding on the bugle-horn, / They to whom my foolish passion were a target for their scorn.'[49] In this moment, the direct address to the speaker's audience, his fellow soldiers, breaks the immediacy of the dramatic monologue. The poem moves from a hysterical man working through his emotions to one reasserting what little authority he has. It is not coincidental that, in an overcompensation intended to reassert his masculinity, he must affirm the gender hierarchy, suggesting that 'nature made [women] blinder motions bounded / in a shallower brain. / Woman is the lesser man'.[50] By the end of the poem, his commitment to the processual masculinity – one that perpetually feeds on and perpetuates the cultural myth of progress – attached to the nation and empire conscribes him, continually reenlists him, for military duty.

The enlisted man's precarious socioeconomic and sexual subjectivity created the conditions for him to become cannon fodder for nation and empire under this aegis of progress. Military masculinity foregrounds the speaker's entry into this vision of the future. This flash-forward reveals the potentialities of his return to the homosocial bonds of his fellow men, who, as a whole, will move the nation, synecdochally representing 'mankind', forward. He recounts his vision of the future in the period after his failed domestic union in the form a simile of a young boy who gazes into a mass of men:

> Yearning for the large excitement that the coming years would yield,
> Eager-hearted as a boy when first he leaves his father's field,
>
> And at night along the dusky highway near and nearer drawn,
> Sees in heaven the light of London flaring like a dreary dawn;
>
> And his spirit leaps within him to be gone before him then,
> Underneath the light he looks at, in among the throngs of men.[51]

The simile is a continuation of his earlier conceit – when he 'clung to the present for all the promise it closed', and narrates his exodus from civilian working-class life. The simile suggests that the speaker left the landed labour of the Locksley estate, in search of something greater – a kind of 'North Star', which follows his earlier musing on gazing into the sky, where he 'look[ed] on great Orion sloping slowly to the West', and 'Many a night ... saw the Pleiads, rising thro' the mellow shade.'[52] He, like, the boy in the simile, left the lowly condition of a labourer tied to Locksley Hall, following the northern star of the developed world. His vision begins once he looks underneath the glowing light of London, 'among the throngs of men', where he finds 'Men, [his] brothers, men the workers, ever reaping something new: / That which they have done but earnest of the things that they shall do.'[53] In contrast to the broken promises of the present in his younger years with Amy, the future holds the possibility of a purpose, ultimately finding place with his brothers and workers in arms.

'Locksley Hall' oscillates as the speaker works through a Hamlet-like predicament: whether it is more masculine to suffer the slings and arrows of the rejection, waning in affective meditation and intractable despair, or to take up arms against effeminate stagnation and the obstacles to imperial expansion. This tension is reflected in the prosody itself. On the one hand, the trochaic beats sound not unlike the marching forward of soldiers in step, aided by the recurring alliterative fricative: 'Falser than all fancy fathoms',[54] 'foremost files of time',[55] 'forward, forward'.[56] On the other hand, the abrupt caesura after the three or four trochees in every line forces a halt to the forward metrical marching. This tension between movement and halting in poetic form reflects the thematic waxing and waning in the speaker's narrative: Tennyson vacillates between war and peace, where, as Patrick Brantlinger suggests, the former illustrates the highest of virtues, while the latter is indicative of cowardice and greed.[57] This opposition plays out in the speaker's oscillation between peace and war. On the one hand, he considers retreating to the lotus-like tropical paradise along with his entrenchment in emotional despair, speaking to the docile resignation of his masculinity – a peaceful repose, where his labour power drains into the lull of inaction and affect. On the other hand, like a recommitted Hamlet, the speaker ultimately decides to 'mix with action, lest [he] wither by despair'.[58] In action, the speaker diverts his masculine force into the greater good of the military. Ironically, this inevitably leads him to suffer another form of 'withering'.

As he reflects on this process of masculinisation, it becomes clear that this course never did run smooth. He still maintains resentment for his past rejection and is dubious about his desire to soldier for queen and country; he considers turning back within himself and enjoying the fruits of colonialism as an individual. The vacillating desire takes this later colonial iteration toward the end of the poem. Continuing his recollection of his father's death in the Battle of Assaye, the colonial land where the speaker's 'heart began to beat', the protagonist displaces his feelings of grief and sorrow for unrequited love onto an individual imperial conquest of a lesser race:

> Or to burst all links of habit – there to wander far away,
> On from island unto island at the gateways of the day.

> Larger constellations burning, mellow moons and happy skies,
> Breadths of tropic shade and palms in cluster, knots of Paradise.

Never comes the trader, never floats an European flag,
Slides the bird o'er lustrous woodland, swings the trailer from the crag;

Droops the heavy-blossom'd bower, hangs the heavy-fruited tree –
Summer isles of Eden lying in dark-purple spheres of sea.

There methinks would be enjoyment more than in this march of mind,
In the steamship, in the railway, in the thoughts that shake mankind.

There the passions cramp'd no longer shall have scope and breathing
    space;
I will take some savage woman, she shall rear my dusky race.

Iron-jointed, supple-sinew'd, they shall dive, and they shall run,
Catch the wild goat by the hair, and hurl their lances in the sun.[59]

Here, the speaker envisions a certain kind of masculinity that opposes or, rather, displaces his shattered self and energy onto the female, othered body in a colonial fantasy. While this is certainly a narrative of conquest and colonisation, it would fall into Brantlinger's reading of 'peace' in Tennyson's poems, an indication of greed and cowardice. We need not look much further than the closing parallel of infinitives in Tennyson's 'Ulysses' – 'To strive, to seek, to find, and not to yield' – to see its opposite. Said differently, if the speaker were to take this course of individual conquest for personal pleasure, he would be surrendering to a baser nature and masculinity, wherein the brute forces of desire supersede 'the higher virtue' of war – namely, giving oneself to the military scaffolding of the nation at large. In this brief respite from decrying the British social order, he returns to his own colonial connections, but rather than divesting his masculine energy into the bonds of military and nation, he indulges in the tropical repose characteristic of Tennyson's 'Lotos Eaters' – those failed military men who escape the kind of progress, masculinity and energetic drive espoused by Tennyson's 'Ulysses'. This tropical paradise, highly inflected with the tone of the backward and the primitive, ultimately proves unappealing. This would be an 'uncivilised' divestment of his masculine energy, a purely libidinal one that does not serve a higher purpose but, rather, feeds an egocentric, individual one. Very consciously and explicitly, echoing his earlier sentiments of accepting individual withering and being 'content with falling on a foeman's ground',[60] he invests in sacrificing the self for the great movement of the world, a decision contingent on European supremacy:

> Fool, again the dream, the fancy! but I know my words are wild,
> But I count the gray barbarian lower than the Christian child.
>
> I, to herd with narrow foreheads, vacant of our glorious gains,
> Like a beast with lower pleasures, like a beast with lower pains!
>
> Mated with a squalid savage – what to me were sun or clime?
> I the heir of all the ages, in the foremost files of time –
>
> I that rather held it better men should perish one by one,
> Than that earth should stand at gaze like Joshua's moon in Ajalon!
>
> Not in vain the distance beacons. Forward, forward let us range,
> Let the great world spin for ever down the ringing grooves of change.
>
> Thro' the shadow of the globe we sweep into the younger day;
> Better fifty years of Europe than a cycle of Cathay.[61]

The progressive world he espouses is a strikingly Anglo-centric one, subtended by a collective masculinisation – he would rather all men die 'one by one' than live the life of a Lotos-eater. Operating on the auspices of choice, reasoning, faith and masculinity, ultimately the speaker recommits to withering into the military mass, making Britain's progress – aptly represented as the world becoming 'more and more'. The speaker is, like the enlisted man would have been, in for life.

The speaker's investment in the future is based on an assumption of progress. When the speaker 'Dips into the future', in his utopian vision, his first encounters are imperial commerce and technologically enhanced war. He tells how he 'Saw the heavens fill with commerce, argosies of magic sails, Pilots of the purple twilight dropping down with costly bales; / Heard the heavens fill with shouting, and there rain'd a ghastly dew / From the nations' airy navies grappling in the central blue.'[62] While it is clear that he sees what some have characterised as a world union not unlike the United Nations, it appears that the soldier prophesises the end of war and the beginning of a universal common community of the world: 'Till the war-drum throbb'd no longer, and the battle-flags were furl'd in the Parliament of man, the Federation of the world. / There the common sense of most shall hold a fretful realm in awe, / And the kindly earth shall slumber, lapt in universal law.'[63] Yet by the end of the poem, any utopian dream for social equality and erasure of national difference and hierarchy is undercut by the soldier's patriarchal, colonial and bellicose desires: the displacement of masculine drive from the domestic ideal, war and progress onto the racialised female other; the desire for conquest of the exotic; and the curse that Locksley Hall should be destroyed in a violent natural tumult. There is no place for a 'parliament of man', no 'federation of the world', when he 'counts the gray barbarian lower than the Christian child' or when he desires 'fifty years of Europe [more] than a cycle of Cathay'. Moreover, his violent curses on Locksley Hall are framed in terms of a military attack where 'comes a vapour from the margin, blackening over heath and holt, / Cramming all the blast before it, in its breast a thunderbolt. / Let it fall on Locksley Hall, with rain or hail, or fire or snow'.[64] The violent thunderbolt reads like cannon fire, while the 'vapour from the margin' recalls the smoke and artillery when he remembers the degree of his martial commitment: 'I had been content to perish, falling on the foeman's ground, / When the ranks are roll'd in vapour, and the winds are laid with sound.'[65] This connection speaks to the belief that artillery stifled wind,[66] signalling an anthropocentric, technical but, more significantly, martial conquest of nature in the service of progress and the nation. Consequently, the poem's ending casts the speaker's past and present in the same kind of martial discourse that envelops him in the mass of the army.

It is difficult to read these final stanzas of 'Locksley Hall' and not think of Tennyson's 'The Charge of the Light Brigade'. As the speaker throws himself into the large social body of military masculinity, he is not unlike the six hundred men who charged forward into the 'Jaws of Death':

> Forward, the Light Brigade!
> Was there a man dismay'd?
> Not tho' the soldier knew
>   Someone had blunder'd:
> Theirs not to make reply,
> Theirs not to reason why,
> Theirs but to do and die.[67]

Unlike the anonymous men in Tennyson's 'Charge', the speaker in 'Locksley Hall' spends 194 lines trying to 'reason why' before he throws himself into the imperial march. Ultimately, however, it is clear from the material conditions of his existence, coupled with the ideological reinforcement the poem drew from and propagated, that his final function – his 'choice' to 'go' – is in fact simply an affirmation of 'to do and die'.

Catherine Robson notes in her study of the ideological and material effects of the recitation of poetry in England and the United States that poetry likely encouraged young boys to sacrifice themselves in times of war: 'children in British mass education were far more likely to find themselves reciting poems about bravery in the face of defeat than verses celebrating victory.'[68] 'Locksley Hall' served as an ideological enlistment into this kind of narrative – if not for Victorian enlisted men themselves, then for the culture that shaped the possibility of their enlistment. While we might look to Tennyson's 'The Charge of the Light Brigade', as we have seen, 'Locksley Hall' would do the same kind of work, albeit less overtly. It therefore becomes clear why someone like Charles Kingsley praised the poem. The cleric, author and social critic is himself perhaps best known for his own investment in masculinity, in particular, his espousal of 'muscular Christianity' and of martial enterprise. He asserted that the poem's 'spirit' is that of 'a man rising out of sickness into health ... conquering his selfish sorrow, and the moral and intellectual paralysis it produces ... by faith in the progress of science and civilisation, hope in the final triumph of good'.[69] While military men like William Turner, or their political handlers like Winston Churchill and Harry Truman, espoused 'Locksley Hall' for its 'forward-looking' and bravery-inspiring qualities, a historical contextualisation of the poem – putting it back into 'the whole' from which it emerged rather than reading it as a trans-historical, individual abstraction – problematises any such ideological and martial deployment of the poem for 'the triumph of good'.

Notes

1 See, for instance, Mary Poovey, *Making a Social Body: British Cultural Formation, 1830–1864* (Chicago, IL: University of Chicago Press, 1995) and Joseph W. Childers, *Novel Possibilities: Fiction and the Formation of Early Victorian Culture* (Philadelphia, PA: University of Pennsylvania Press, 1995).

2   Lord Tennyson Alfred, 'Locksley Hall', in George B. Woods (ed.), *Poetry of the Victorian Period* (New York: Longman, 1965), pp. 45–8, l. 182.

3   Richard Crowder, *Aftermath: The Makers of the Post-War World* (London: I. B. Tauris, 2015), p. 84.

4   John Peck's *War, The Army and Victorian Literature* (New York: St Martins, 1998), for instance, does not mention 'Locksley Hall' in his discussion of 'Tennyson and War Poetry'. While 'Locksley Hall' is not framed around bellicose conflict in the same way as 'The Charge of the Light Brigade', the soldier and the military are central to its thematics and cultural work.

5   Tennyson, 'Locksley Hall', l. 142.

6   Jac Weller, *Wellington at Waterloo* (New York: Crowell, 1967), p. 186.

7   See Neil Ramsey, '"A Real English Soldier": Suffering, Manliness and Class in the Mid-Nineteenth Century Soldier's Tale', in Catriona Kennedy and Mathew McCormack (eds), *Soldiering in Britain and Ireland, 1750–1850: Men of Arms* (Basingstoke: Palgrave, 2013).

8   Tennyson, 'Locksley Hall', l. 151.

9   Most notably, see Herbert L. Sussman, *Victorian Masculinities: Manhood and Masculine Poetics in Early Victorian Literature and Art* (Cambridge: Cambridge University Press, 1995); see also James Eli Adams, *Dandies and Desert Saints: Styles of Victorian Masculinity* (Ithaca, NY: Cornell University Press, 1995); Thaise E. Morgan, 'The Poetry of Victorian Masculinities', in Joseph Bristow (ed.), *The Cambridge Companion to Victorian Poetry* (Cambridge: Cambridge University Press, 2000).

10   Peter Burroughs, 'The Human Cost of Imperial Defence in the Early Victorian Age', *Victorian Studies* 24:1 (1980), p. 11. It is important to note that the expansion of empire was done not only by the infantry but also the cavalry, the artillery, the navy and, up until 1858, the East India Company. I am grateful to Michael Brown and Joanne Begiato for pointing out this division of military labour.

11   Susan Walton, *Imagining Soldiers and Fathers in the Mid-Victorian Era: Charlotte Yonge's Models of Manliness* (Farnham: Ashgate, 2010), p. 33.

12   Begiato (Bailey), 'Tears and the Manly Sailor', p. 117. For the various representations and public perceptions of military men from the early eighteenth to the nineteenth century see Kennedy and McCormack (eds), *Soldiering in Britain and Ireland, 1750–1850.*

13   Carolyn Steedman quoted in Ramsey, 'A Real English Soldier', p. 136.

14   *Ibid.*; J. E. Cookson, 'War', in Iain McCalman, *et al.* (ed.), *An Oxford Companion to the Romantic Age* (Oxford: Oxford University Press, 1999), p. 30.

15   Ramsey, 'A Real English Soldier', p. 136. For the specific wording quoted by Ramsey, see Cookson, 'War', p. 30.

16   Burroughs, 'The Human Cost of Imperial Defence in the Early Victorian Age', p. 14.

17 John R. Reed, 'Military', in Herbert F. Tucker (ed.), *A New Companion to Victorian Literature and Culture* (West Sussex: John Wiley & Sons, 2014), p. 194. There were periodic instances of shorter terms of enlistment offered during the eighteenth century; Hurl-Eamon, *Marriage and the British Army*, p. 6. See also Harold E. Raugh, *The Victorians at War, 1815–1914: An Encyclopedia of British Military History* (Santa Barbara, CA: ABCCLIO, 2004), pp. 297–8.

18 Joanne Begiato, in the print culture of 1760–1850, finds evidence to suggest that the cult of domesticity was a desirable image for the working-class sailor. Begiato (Bailey), 'Tears and the Manly Sailor', pp. 122–3. Tennyson's poem speaks to the marital challenges that were specific to the army, and uses the rejection from this domestic pleasure as driving force for the speaker's refashioning of himself for larger aims. In this sense, he displaces the tears of rejection into imperial and military ethos, and yet, the memory of that traumatic masculine refashioning remains a core facet of his person.

19 While the cult of domesticity was modelled after the middle class, by the 1840s it had become the cultural norm, and those within the working class and even the upper classes that resisted it were 'deemed to be at odds with the national character'. John Tosh, *A Man's Place*, p. 30.

20 Reed, 'Military', p. 194.

21 Isobel Armstrong, *Victorian Poetry: Poetry, Poetics, and Politics* (London: Routledge, 1993), p. 13.

22 *Ibid.*

23 Myna Trustram, *Women of the Regiment: Marriage and the Victorian Army* (Cambridge: Cambridge University Press, 1984), p. 2.

24 Tennyson, 'Locksley Hall', l. 1–2.

25 *Ibid.*, l. 112.

26 *Ibid.*, l. 10–14.

27 *Ibid.*, l. 15–16.

28 *Ibid.*, l. 20.

29 *Ibid.*, l. 37–8.

30 *Ibid.*, l. 40.

31 *Ibid.*, l. 41–4, 59–62.

32 *Ibid.*, l. 92–3.

33 Roger Ebbatson, 'Tennyson's Locksley Hall: Progress and Destitution', in Valerie Purton (ed.), *Darwin, Tennyson and Their Readers: Explorations in Victorian Literature and Science* (London: Anthem, 2014), p. 2.

34 Trustram, *Women of the Regiment: Marriage and the Victorian Army*, p. 9.

35 *Ibid.*

36 *Ibid.*, p. 144.

37 Hurl-Eamon, *Marriage and the British Army*, p. 9.

38 Sussman, *Victorian Masculinities*, p. 49.

39 Quoted in Richard Holmes, *Redcoat: The British Soldier in the Age of Horse and Musket* (New York: Norton, 2002), p. 179.

40 Richard L. Blanco, 'Reform and Wellington's Post Waterloo Army, 1815–1854', *Military Affairs* 29:3 (1965), pp. 128–9.

41 McCormack, *Embodying the Militia in Georgian England*, p. 100.

42 *Ibid.*, p. 102.

43 Gwyn Harries-Jenkins, *The Army in Victorian Society* (Buffalo, NY: University of Toronto Press, 1977), pp. 52–3.

44 Tennyson, 'Locksley Hall', l. 154–6.

45 *Ibid.*, l. 100.

46 *Ibid.*, l. 99–100.

47 John D. Jump (ed.), *Lord Alfred Tennyson: The Critical Heritage* (London: Routledge, 2013), p. 334.

48 Tennyson, 'Locksley Hall', l. 139–42.

49 *Ibid.*, l. 145.

50 *Ibid.*, l. 149–51.

51 *Ibid.*, l. 111–16.

52 *Ibid.*, l. 9.

53 *Ibid.*, l. 117–18.

54 *Ibid.*, l. 41.

55 *Ibid.*, l. 178.

56 *Ibid.*, l. 181.

57 Patrick Brantlinger, *Rule of Darkness: British Literature and Imperialism, 1830–1914* (Ithaca, NY: Cornell University Press, 1988), p. 9.

58 Tennyson, 'Locksley Hall', l. 98.

59 *Ibid.*, l. 157–70.

60 *Ibid.*, l. 103.

61 *Ibid.*, l. 173–84. Cathay is an alternative name for China.

62 *Ibid.*, l. 122–4.

63 *Ibid.*, l. 127–30. Vapour, here, signifies the smoke from artillery fire.

64 *Ibid.*, l. 191–4.

65 *Ibid.*, l. 103–4, emphasis added.

66 Stephen Greenblatt and M. H. Abrams, *The Norton Anthology of English Literature* (London: W.W. Norton, 2012), p. 2039, n. 8.

67 Lord Tennyson Alfred, 'The Charge of the Light Brigade', in George B. Woods (ed.), *Poetry of the Victorian Period* (New York: Longman, 1965), vol. II, pp. 9–15.

68 Catherine Robson, *Heart Beats: Everyday Life and the Memorized Poem* (Princeton, NJ: Princeton University Press, 2012), p. 89.

69 Charles Kingsley, 'Tennyson', *Fraiser's Magazine* 42:249 (1850), p. 249.

~9~

Charlotte Brontë's 'warrior priest': St John Rivers and the language of war

Karen Turner

In July 1855, the Reverend Patrick Brontë wrote to Elizabeth Gaskell about his children's early fascination with all things military. He particularly noted his daughter Charlotte's fascination with her 'hero', the Duke of Wellington, recalling that the children would engage in heated arguments about the relative merits of Wellington, Bonaparte, Hannibal and Caesar and that he would frequently be called in to arbitrate.[1] Charlotte Brontë's interest in the 'Iron Duke' was to last throughout her life, and the biographical fragments she found in various contemporary sources were to inform the construction of many of the male characters in her mature writing.[2] It is not just the biography of heroic figures that informs her fiction, however: an impressive understanding of military strategy and complex military theory are also demonstrably present in her development of character and plot. I propose in this chapter to explore Brontë's construction and portrayal of St John Rivers, the 'warrior priest' of her 1847 novel *Jane Eyre*, and to examine the ways in which she uses the character to explore a militarised expression of love and masculinity. In her portrayal of Jane and Rochester, and Jane and Rivers, Brontë comments on the potentially combative nature of courtship, at the same time revealing her detailed understanding of historical military campaigns. The Brontës' childhood stories were fuelled by the accounts of military activities in Europe that they read in *Fraser's* and *Blackwood's* magazines in the 1830s, and the insights that Brontë acquired into the very masculine world of war are also clear in *Jane Eyre*. Brontë reveals her understanding of military theory and strategy through her portrayal of Rivers's pursuit of Jane, which is effectively, as I hope later to demonstrate, a war.[3]

Recent scholarship on nineteenth-century masculinities has focused on the tensions between public and domestic expressions of heroic virility, morality and martial adventure, and on discussion of a national identity that became increasingly militarised throughout the century.[4] Some alternative readings explore the value of morality, sacrifice and gentleness in masculine heroic figures and comment on an emerging body of knowledge about 'other' Victorian masculinities.[5] Many nineteenth-century sources themselves promote the value of gentleness and courage over militaristic aggression: for example, Samuel Smiles, in *Self-Help*, describes an idealised form of heroism that values selflessness and kindness over aggression and violence. Neil Ramsey has shown that the growth of nineteenth-century periodicals enabled the general (educated) reader to access material that had previously been exclusive to military publications. He notes that the rate of publication of military books picked up markedly from the second half of the eighteenth century, thus enabling a growing readership to gain some insight into war and military strategy.[6]

One of these publications was Carl von Clausewitz's *On War*. First published posthumously in Germany in 1832, this practical philosophy of military theory gave military analysts a clear conceptual framework for understanding the politics of war. While Clausewitz was not the first to outline the purpose and methodology of war, he remains perhaps the best-known nineteenth-century military philosopher.[7] His work combines historical analysis with practical observation of late eighteenth- and early nineteenth-century campaigns. Until comparatively recently, historical consensus has been that *On War* was not widely read in Britain much before the Franco-Prussian conflict in the 1870s. However, an English review of *On War* was printed in the *Metropolitan Magazine* in 1835, and Colonel John Mitchell's *Thoughts on Tactics and Military Organisation* (1838) refers to Clausewitz's study.[8] The Brontës would almost certainly not have been familiar with Clausewitz's text, though historians now concede that military leaders would have been aware of some of his ideas, as well as those of some of his contemporaries. The Duke of Wellington certainly was aware of Clausewitz, and not only read his work in translation in 1842 but also wrote an informed response to it.[9]

While Brontë may not have had first-hand knowledge of military life, she did know about the daily routines of clergymen in and around Haworth. In her mature writing, she combines her direct knowledge of the clergy with her more indirect knowledge of Wellington and Napoleon, gleaned from contemporary news reports and magazines, to create male characters that are hybrids of warrior and priest. St John

Rivers is constructed not merely as a clergyman, but also as an aspiring missionary whose ambition is to travel overseas and engage in the glory and valour of a Christian battle for souls. Bertrand Taithe has commented on the militaristic language of Christian missionaries in the nineteenth century, pointing out that a combative register enhanced the development of an effective strategy for conversion.[10] Whereas a soldier is one member of a regiment and by necessity a team player, Rivers as missionary is a solitary practitioner and subject, ultimately, to an intangible commander. Although he describes himself as 'the servant of an infallible Master' and cites 'the All-perfect' God as his captain, he strives to set his own agenda to fulfil his ambitions.[11] Rivers's military language throughout the novel reveals the extent of his ambitious quest for personal and professional victory, and this is particularly clear in his negotiation of emotional relationships.

In *Shirley* (published two years after *Jane Eyre* but set in the early nineteenth century), Brontë makes a narratorial comment about the Reverend Helstone:

> I am aware, reader, and you need not remind me, that it is a dreadful thing for a parson to be warlike: I am aware that he should be a man of peace. I have some faint outline of an idea of what a clergyman's mission is amongst mankind, and I remember distinctly whose servant he is.[12]

She then qualifies this comment with a fuller explanation: Helstone 'was not diabolical at all. The evil simply was – he had missed his vocation: he should have been a soldier, and circumstances made him a priest'. She refers to Helstone as a 'clerical Cossack' and continues, 'It seems to me, reader, that you cannot always cut out men to fit their profession, and that you ought not to curse them because that profession sometimes hangs on them ungracefully.'[13] Brontë uses the word 'warlike' in a slightly problematic sense here: the purpose of an army is primarily that of defence, not attack. She appears to intend warlike to signify the opposite of peace, emphasising the domestic, non-aggressive, noncombative qualities generally expected of clergymen, and, indeed, of Christians in general. She also intentionally creates Helstone as a clergyman and not as a soldier, and thereby shows herself to be well aware of the inner conflicts that affected men in both professions.

In *Jane Eyre*, St John Rivers is an earlier model for Helstone. As a clergyman who should have been a soldier, he is ill-suited to domestic peace: 'gloomy and out of place' at the fireside, his faculties stagnate; his frequent stases and silences in the novel are often at odds with his self-declared propensity for war. Jane recognises that he would only emerge as a leader and superior 'in scenes of strife and danger – where courage is proved, and energy exercised, and fortitude tasked'.[14]

The origin of Rivers's professional strife lies in his aspiration to become something more than a clergyman, and Jane soon learns of his self-confessed ambitions and his dissatisfaction with the wearisome routines of the domestic clergy. His bellicose language, however, distinguishes him as a frustrated soldier rather than as a missionary: he declares that, at heart, his is the nature 'of a politician, of a soldier, a votary of glory, a lover of renown, a luster after power'.[15] It is Rivers's yearning for glory, for honour and renown, which helps to identify him as a warrior in disguise. His first words in the novel – '"All men must die"' – are commensurate with both occupations.[16] Priest and soldier are both on intimate terms with death, one knowing its physical form, and the other its spiritual dimension.

As an aspiring missionary, Rivers is more than a country parson from the outset, and for an arduous life overseas he will need determination and courage. Determination, as an expression of courage, is what Clausewitz calls 'the soldier's first requirement'; other qualities needed for the endurance of the hardships of war include staunchness, strength of mind and 'the ability to keep one's head at times of exceptional stress and violent emotion'.[17] Within the necessary strength of character, a soldier can have powerful feelings but must maintain emotional balance and physical restraint in spite of them.[18]

Brontë endows Rivers with an emotional intensity that is stifled at almost every turn. In part, she intends Rivers as a foil to Rochester, of course, whose passions and ardour are fervently and freely expressed; but in creating Rivers as a cold, ambitious strategist, Brontë is able to explore an alternative masculinity that is qualitatively different from that of Rochester. Rivers remains icily calm despite his initial attachment to Rosamond Oliver, who has described the officers with whom she has been dancing as '"the most agreeable men in the world"'.[19] This distinction between 'real' soldiers and Rivers's pseudo-military bearing significantly claims agreeableness in the former which is notably absent in the latter. Rivers at last confesses that he loves Rosamond '"wildly"', but cannot contemplate a quiet life of domestic bliss: 'He could not – he would not – renounce his wild field of mission warfare for the parlours and peace of Vale Hall.'[20] Here, the adverbial 'wildly' and adjectival 'wild' signify something dangerous and uncontainable, identifying

Rivers as berserker-style warrior rather than domestic priest. The wildness of combat seems directly to oppose the rigour and moral discipline demanded by scripture, particularly in clergymen, and, indeed, the more general moral discipline increasingly prescribed for nineteenth-century society.

When Rivers is made to confront his feelings for Rosamond, Brontë allows him temporarily to indulge his wildest emotional 'delirium and delusion': the tumult and confusion of battle are concentrated not on winning Rosamond but rather on suppressing the more internal conflict between his feelings and his knowledge that she would not be a suitable wife. As a result of the effort of surrendering what he feels to the command of what he knows, Brontë has him 'suffer[s] in the conflict'.[21] When it becomes clear that Rosamond will marry someone else, Rivers reverts to the language with which he is most comfortable: "'You see, Jane, the battle is fought, and the victory won ... The event of the conflict is decisive: my way is now clear."'[22] Defeat in one battle allows for potential success in another: in his later manoeuvres against Jane, he employs military precision to impose limits on her emotional freedom.

Besides Rivers' propensity to articulate his experience and ambition through military language, Brontë also depicts the proposal scene, where Rivers urges Jane to marry him and accompany him on his mission to India, as nothing short of a battle, complete with strategic use of landscape and resources. Jane and Rochester have also engaged in a battle of wills earlier in the novel, after their planned wedding is abandoned as a result of the revelation that Rochester's first wife is still living. During the complex moral argument that follows, their language is that of civic law and principle rather than that of combat. Rochester sees the possibility of conquering, but rejects it because he wants a comforter and rescuer, not a defeated opponent. Whereas Rivers is later to insist, "'You shall be mine,'" Rochester prefers Jane to promise "'I will be yours.'"[23] Rochester realises that he may seize and possess Jane's physical body, that he may be the "'conqueror'" of her "'brittle frame'", but it is equal communion with her soul that he most desires.[24]

It is, however, only mismatched love that Brontë portrays as the cause of strife, and she has already made it clear that Rochester and Jane are perfectly suited because they are made of the same stuff: they share a passionate nature that has its foundations in fire. Rochester tells Jane, "'a fervent, solemn passion ... kindling in pure, powerful flame, fuses you and me in one'".[25] Rivers, of course, is the opposite: no fervour infects him; he is a cold, hard man, inexorable as death; his very name suggests water; his nature, ice. He and Jane are natural antagonists. Brontë anticipates Clausewitz almost word for word in this analogy: 'like two incompatible elements, armies must continually destroy one another. Like fire and water they never find themselves in a state of equilibrium, but must keep on interacting until one of them has completely disappeared'.[26] In this battle between fire and ice, that is exactly what happens.

Brontë constructs the final confrontation between Jane and Rivers as a textbook battle scene between two opposing armies. Although she could not have been directly familiar with Clausewitz's work, she anticipates almost exactly the theory that he had set out. When Rivers takes Jane outside, intending to propose marriage, he insists on there being no-one else present. Jane's desire to invite Diana or Mary recalls the practice of calling on seconds, or supporters, to act for each party in a duel. Although Clausewitz suggests that war is essentially a duel on a larger scale, there is a primary cultural difference between the two concepts: a duel is fought as a matter of honour and is usually in response to some personal slight or moral offence; it is to do with satisfaction rather than conquest. A war is fought, as Clausewitz says, either to overthrow the enemy (to render him politically helpless) or for possession of his land. Rivers intends both these aims: he seeks to overthrow Jane's resistance to becoming a missionary's wife, and to take possession of her body and soul. When he tells her, '"You shall be mine,"' he means, as Jane realises, that he prizes her 'as a soldier would a good weapon'.[27]

The tranquil landscape itself gradually becomes a battleground, the imagery changing it from a place of sweetness, pure colour and precious gems to one of hostility and savagery as Jane and Rivers move through the terrain. The breeze from the west coming over the hill is sweet, the sky is stainless blue, there are golden gleams from the sun – until they leave the path and move into more open territory. By the time they reach somewhere to sit, the hills have quite shut them in.

'Let us rest here', said St John, as we reached the first stragglers of a battalion of rocks, guarding a sort of pass, beyond which the beck rushed down a waterfall; and where, still a little further, the mountain shook off turf and flower, had only heath for raiment, and crag for gem – where it exaggerated the wild to the savage, and exchanged the fresh for the frowning – where it guarded the forlorn hope of solitude, and a last refuge for silence.[28]

After a full half hour of silence among this battalion of rocks, there is intense talk of military activity. Rivers talks of his *captain*, and *enlisting* under a *banner*; he talks of the *ranks* of the Chosen; Jane briefly adopts a similar register and speaks of *marching*. Once the 'fatal word' is spoken and Rivers insists that she 'must' be his wife, their purposes diverge as the landscape has done. His use of the imperative 'must' makes clear his initial aim of compelling another to do his will, and Jane initially recoils.[29]

Brontë has Rivers employ a strategy similar to that described by Clausewitz, who writes, 'an aggressor often decides on a war before the innocent defender does, and if he continues to keep his preparations sufficiently secret, he may well take his victim unawares'.[30] Rivers has clearly prepared well, ensuring that he has Jane's full attention and no witnesses; he parries her initial surprise with resounding endorsements of her suitability for the role he proposes to award her. Jane realises that 'he had calculated on these first objections: he was not irritated by them. Indeed, as he leaned back on the crag behind him, folded his arms on his chest, and fixed his countenance, I saw he was prepared for a long and trying opposition'.[31] Clausewitz points out that 'the aggressor is always peace-loving (as Buonaparte always claimed to be); he would prefer to take over our country unopposed'.[32] Rivers, similarly, would prefer Jane's capitulation to occur without strife, but he is pragmatic enough to realise that there must be some inevitable struggle. He has the patience, determination and strength of mind to wait for the desired 'conquest'.[33]

Brontë here is as much a general overseeing military action as a writer of fiction in the way she orchestrates and directs these characters: their movements, parries and ripostes are almost pure theory in action. From that point onward, Brontë portrays the relationship between Jane and Rivers as nothing short of outright psychological combat. She seems intuitively to know that, as Clausewitz states, defence is primarily passive and exists to preserve the status quo; attack is active and exists to achieve the positive end of conquest.[34] Defensive warfare is intrinsically stronger than offensive, since defence exists in protecting what is already in one's own possession. It is rather easier to hold ground than to take it. However, Brontë is aware that war 'does not consist merely in enduring'.[35] Jane's sustained attempts to repel Rivers's advances draw on her own strength of character to resist the 'iron shroud' that contracts around her. She is aware that her very survival depends upon her ability to defend herself, and that capitulation would make her an 'entire victim'.[36]

Rivers's next tactical strategy involves the manipulation of Jane's time and space. He allows her a quarter of an hour to think about his proposal – the same amount of time that he allowed himself to quell his passion for Rosamond Oliver – before clarifying his vision of jointly enlisting under God's banner. Jane concedes a little ground, admitting that she is capable of maintaining 'a comrade's constancy; a fellow-soldier's frankness, fidelity, fraternity' towards Rivers.[37] This is not enough of a victory, and Rivers again demands full possession through marriage. He then allows her a fortnight to reconsider, while he is absent in Cambridge, thus creating a 'space' in which she may reflect.[38] Jane's defensive position is to seek to establish a professional relationship with Rivers to preserve her own emotional freedom: 'There would be recesses in my mind which would only be mine, to which he never came; and sentiments growing there fresh and sheltered, which his austerity could never blight, nor his measured warrior-march trample down.'[39]

Rivers can only contemplate his work in India with Jane as his wife, systematically rejecting her pleas to allow her to go with him as his nominal sister. Again, his demand is for absolute possession, which would be denied if Jane were his 'sister' – as he points out, '"a sister might any day be taken from me"'.[40] It is primarily his strength of character that allows him to be so single-minded on this point, but this is also the source of a strategic error. Rivers's refusal to acknowledge or accept Jane's alternative suggestions reveals his inability to accept anything less than absolute conquest on his part, and absolute capitulation on Jane's.

When Rivers meets 'resistance where [he] expected submission', he experiences an intensified inner conflict between himself as a man and himself as a clergyman.[41] He is not just fighting an external battle to accomplish his 'long-cherished scheme', but he is also aware of the inner clash between his Christianity and his masculinity: 'as a man, he would have wished to coerce me into obedience: it was only as a sincere Christian he bore so patiently with my perversity'.[42] Jane, too, must learn to 'discriminate the Christian from the man'.[43] Over the following weeks, Rivers's strategy corresponds with Clausewitz's observations on how best to secure victory: 'If the enemy is to be coerced you must put him in a situation that is even more unpleasant than the sacrifice you call on him to make.'[44] By behaving coolly towards Jane after his initial proposal of marriage, Rivers perpetrates 'refined, lingering torture' that Jane claims is 'killing' her. Jane's 'violent' accusation almost succeeds in making 'an eternal enemy' of Rivers.[45]

In addition to making life unpleasant for the enemy, Clausewitz remarks that it is 'generally better to go on striking in the same direction than to move one's forces this way and that'.[46] Brontë accordingly has Rivers make a final, third, assault the day before his departure for Cambridge. Interestingly, this is perhaps the closest he comes to achieving victory: he stops behaving like a soldier and is simply a man, capable of a goodness and gentleness 'more potent' than force.[47]

At this point, Rivers intends temporarily to retreat to allow Jane time and space to think about his proposal during his absence, while he attends to other matters beyond his domestic sphere. Here, Brontë appears to be using her knowledge of historical military campaigns to describe the battle between Jane and Rivers. During the attacks on Montereau and Mormant in February 1814, Napoleon turned from Blücher to instead launch an attack on Schwarzenberg. In so doing, he gave Blücher sufficient time and opportunity to recover.[48] Rivers's retreat, and the cessation of his emotional and psychological onslaught, would similarly allow Jane sufficient time and space to re-arm herself and rebuild her defences. At the moment when Jane is almost ready to capitulate, Brontë reintroduces Rochester in the form of a spiritual manifestation. When his voice reminds Jane that the moral force of love is more powerful than the combative force of war, she becomes in that instant more powerful than Rivers. Once Jane has the 'positive object' of Rochester to pursue, she is able to break from Rivers and finds sufficient strength to order him to leave her alone. Like a subordinate soldier, he immediately obeys, and permanently retreats: Jane has sufficient experience to know that 'where there is energy to command well enough, obedience never fails'.[49]

In her portrayal of the battle, Brontë has deployed various elements of strategic effectiveness: the advantage of terrain; the element of surprise; concentric attack while strengthening the theatre of operations; winning popular support; and the exploitation of moral factors.[50] Rivers's first serious attack is made in a terrain that favours his purpose; he succeeds in surprising Jane by his proposal; he strengthens his case by reiterating his ambitious vision in a sustained attack over the following days and weeks; he has the popular support of his sisters, who are initially delighted when they have confirmation of their brother's interest in Jane. It is the discrepancy between Jane's and Rivers's perception of morality, however, that signals his failure. Whereas Rivers deems it ethically and morally right to go to India with Jane only if she becomes his wife, Jane, Diana and Mary agree that to marry for the sake of being only "'a useful tool'" would be "'insupportable – unnatural – out of the question'".[51]

If, in terms of military strategy, Brontë seems to be comparing Rivers with the defeated Napoleon, then little effort is required to stretch the equal and opposite analogy that compares Rochester with Wellington. Several writers have noticed lines of similarity between Wellington, Zamorna and Rochester, but here I suggest not so much a similarity in character, but rather that a similar historic military strategy is instrumental in resolving the tensions in the novel.[52] Rochester has Jane as his 'good angel', his Blücher: together they face and fight the world and its conventions, defeating the despair of solitude. Rochester hopes, more than he expects, that Jane will join him, just as Wellington hoped for, rather than expected, Blücher to arrive with his Prussian troops, Blücher's forces having been defeated just a few days earlier. Again, the pattern is enticingly similar: Jane and Blücher both come from the jaws of defeat towards certain victory.

In her exploration of love and war, and her faith in the triumph of the former over the latter, Brontë anticipates some of the later movements that allowed for the combination of faith and combat, particularly for Christians. The muscular Christianity of Charles Kingsley and Thomas Hughes throughout the 1840s and 1850s allowed for a gradual merging of Christian and martial virtues. In *Tom Brown's Schooldays* (1857), Hughes describes enemies as physical or psychological foes, both of which must be confronted and defeated: 'Every one who is worth his salt has his enemies who must be beaten, be they evil thoughts and habits in himself or spiritual wickedness in high places ... Every soul of them is doing his own piece of fighting, somehow and somewhere.'[53] The process of Christianising the army and militarising English culture and society was well under way by the late 1850s; Olive Anderson suggests that 'there were many claims in religious circles that Christians ... not only made good soldiers, but the best ones'.[54] This is markedly different from the sense of ideological conflict experienced only a generation earlier by Thomas Thrush, who, after his retirement as a navy commander, completed his *Last Thoughts on War* in 1841. He recalls that in January 1825, he had written to George IV to resign his commission, explaining, 'while I have been serving my king and my country, ... I have been acting in open disobedience to the plain and positive commands of another and a superior Master'. He adds, 'it is impossible for a man to be at the same time a faithful follower of Christ, and a warrior by profession'.[55]

By the time William Booth had founded the Christian Mission in 1865, Christian virtues were being securely merged with military ones.[56] Its first annual conference in 1870 saw Booth establish himself as 'general superintendent' of a movement that increasingly combined militaristic terminology and organisation with rigorous Christian practice, adopting the name Salvation Army in 1878. In his history of the movement, Glenn Horridge identifies at least twenty facets of militarism that may have served to attract new members and increase the sense of pride and comradeship that the Salvation Army sought to encourage.[57]

This same bloodless alternative to war and military service was apparent in movements like the Boys' Brigade from 1883 and also features in later Victorian fiction. In Mary Ward's *Robert Elsmere* (1888), the ritualist priest Newcome says of clergymen, "'We are but soldiers under orders,'" and speaks of the "'battle'" for souls.[58] In Margaret Harkness's *In Darkest London* (1889), Captain Lobe has 'no great affection for the Salvation Army. But he did not know any other organisation that worked so hard, that fought so manfully against the world, the flesh, and the devil'.[59] The doctor, with whom Lobe conducts some of his rounds visiting the poor and sick, similarly complains, "'here I fight, day after day, against an overwhelming mass of misery'".[60] Non-military warriors fight sin, injustice and poverty on the streets rather than on the battlefields, their military handbooks replaced by the Bible and church teachings.

In fighting the world, the flesh and himself, Brontë casts St John Rivers as a literal clergyman and a metaphorical soldier; the phrase 'taking orders' at once clerical and military. His fighting spirit is one that strives for possession and conquest while fighting off the temptations of worldliness. Like Helstone, he is also a 'clerical Cossack'. Cossacks were accused by the French of burning parts of towns and villages to render them useless to invaders. In his 1814 memoir *Through Fire and Ice with Napoleon*, Eugène Labaume describes a chateau 'which the Cossacks had pillaged, to deprive us of every comfort which these places could afford'.[61] By destroying the object of desire, the Cossacks confounded the aggressor, but at the same time left themselves with nothing. They signify something bold, fearless and defiant, but equally something self-destructive and self-negating.

Clausewitz writes, 'A soldier is just as proud of the hardships he has overcome as of the dangers he has faced. In short, the seed will grow only in the soil of constant activity and exertion, warmed by the sun of victory.'[62] Jane Rochester, in the closing paragraph of *Jane Eyre*, describes Rivers as 'the warrior Greatheart', hewing down prejudices, his glorious sun hastening to its setting – and it is under the burning sun of victory in India that Rivers is finally able to prove himself worthy of his ambition, ultimately meeting his death as a soldier in the heat of the battle for souls.

Notes

1   Juliet Barker, *The Brontës* (London: Phoenix, 1994), p. 109.

2   See Christine Alexander, 'Charlotte Brontë, Autobiography, and the Image of the Hero', *Brontë Studies* 36:1 (2011), pp. 1–19 and 'Charlotte Brontë's "Anecdotes of the Duke of Wellington"', *Brontë Studies* 35:3 (2010), pp. 208–14 for accounts of Brontë's 'Anecdotes of the Duke of Wellington', compiled between 1829 and 1831.

3   Strictly speaking, it is, as Johann Jacob Otto August Rühle von Lilienstern had described in 1818, a 'small war', or 'battle', where war is 'a battle writ large, and battle a war on a smaller scale' (Johann Jacob Otto August Ruhle von Lilienstern, *Handbuch fur den Offizier zur Belehrung im Frieden und zum Gebrauch im Felde Vol. 2* [Berlin: G. Reimer, 1818], p. 1.)

4   See, for example, Catriona Kennedy's discussion of the tensions between military masculinity and prevailing national culture: 'John Bull into Battle', p. 128ff., and Neil Ramsey's exploration of military discipline, literacy and culture in 'Wartime Reading: Romantic Era Military Periodicals and the Edinburgh Review', *Australian Literary Studies* 29:3 (2014), p. 33ff.

5   See Furneaux, *Military Men of Feeling*, pp. 14–15 and ff., and Ingrid Hanson, *William Morris and the Uses of Violence* (London: Anthem Press Ltd., 2013), p. xiii, both of whom seek to uncover a more nuanced way of understanding the prevailing Victorian tendency to glorify war.

6   Ramsey, 'Wartime Reading', p. 29.

7   Gerhard von Scharnhorst published his *Handbook for Officers for Use in the Field* in 1793. Clausewitz's fellow student, Johann Jakob Otto August Rühle von Lilienstern, revised Scharnhorst's work and made a clear connection between politics and war. In 1829, while Clausewitz was still working on his text, fellow Prussian general Johann Gottfried von Hoyer anticipated Clausewitz's thoughts when he attempted his own definition of the purpose and function of war: 'War is the action of a State to obtain by force what it cannot obtain through negotiations.' Quoted in Beatrice Heuser, *The Strategy Makers: Thoughts on War and Society from Machiavelli to Clausewitz* (Oxford: Praeger, 2010), p. 3.

8   Christopher Bassford, *Clausewitz in English: The Reception of Clausewitz in Britain and America 1815–1945* (Oxford: Oxford University Press, 1994), pp. 37–40ff.

9   *Ibid.*: 'Significant commentaries on Clausewitz were made in the 1840s by members of the duke of Wellington's circle (including the duke himself)'; 'important elements of [Clausewitz's] theoretical argument became available in the English language within a few years of their publication in Germany. At least two of his historical works were read, in English, within the highest circles of the small British military academy in the 1840s' (Bassford, *Clausewitz in English*, pp. 4, 35).

10 Bertrand Taithe, 'Missionary Militarism? The Armed Brother of the Sahara and Léopold Joubert in the Congo', in Owen White and J. P. Daughton (eds), *In God's Empire: French Missionaries and the Modern World* (Oxford: Oxford University Press, 2012), p. 131. See also Judith Rowbotham's discussion of missionaries, heroism and martyrdom in '"Soldiers of Christ"? Images of Female Missionaries in Late Nineteenth-Century Britain: Issues of Heroism and Martyrdom', in *Gender and History* 12:1 (April 2000), pp. 82–106.

11 Charlotte Brontë, *Jane Eyre* (1847) (London & New York: W. W. Norton & Co. Inc., 2001), p. 342.

12 Charlotte Brontë, *Shirley* (1849) (London: Penguin Classics, 2006), p. 35.

13 *Ibid.*

14 Brontë, *Jane Eyre*, p. 335.

15 *Ibid.*, p. 308.

16 *Ibid.*, p. 286.

17 Carl von Clausewitz, *On War* (1832) (Oxford: Oxford's World Classics, 2007), pp. 45; 51.

18 For a fuller discussion of unregulated manly emotions in early Victorian England, see Joanne Begiato, 'Punishing the Unregulated Male Body and Emotions in Early Victorian England', in Joanne Ella Parsons and Ruth Heholt (eds), *The Victorian Male Body* (Edinburgh: Edinburgh University Press, 2018), pp. 46–64.

19 Brontë, *Jane Eyre*, p. 310.

20 *Ibid.*, pp. 318, 313.

21 *Ibid.*, pp. 318–19.

22 *Ibid.*, p. 337.

23 *Ibid.*, p. 269.

24 *Ibid.*, p. 271.

25 *Ibid.*, p. 269.

26 Clausewitz, *On War*, p. 152.

27 Brontë, *Jane Eyre*, p. 345.

28 *Ibid.*, p. 341.

29 *Ibid.*, p. 342.

30 Clausewitz, *On War*, p. 147.

31 Brontë, *Jane Eyre*, p. 343.

32 Clausewitz, *On War*, p. 167.

33 Brontë, *Jane Eyre*, p. 343.
34 Clausewitz, *On War*, p. 160.
35 *Ibid.*, p. 166.
36 Brontë, *Jane Eyre*, pp. 344–5.
37 *Ibid.*, p. 348.
38 *Ibid.*, p. 356.
39 *Ibid.*, p. 347.
40 *Ibid.*, p. 346.
41 *Ibid.*, p. 349.
42 *Ibid.*
43 *Ibid.*, p. 347.
44 Clausewitz, *On War*, p. 15.
45 Brontë, *Jane Eyre*, pp. 350–1.
46 Clausewitz, *On War*, p. 120.
47 Brontë, *Jane Eyre*, p. 357.
48 Clausewitz, *On War*, p. 115.
49 Brontë, *Jane Eyre*, p. 358.
50 Clausewitz, *On War*, pp. 162–3.
51 Brontë, *Jane Eyre*, p. 354.
52 Valerie Sanders and Emma Butcher note that the 'Glass Town' and 'Angria' juvenilia feature characters constructed from composite overlapping models 'from the historical military figure of the Duke of Wellington, through the caricatured Napoleonic despot Northangerland, to the volatile Romantic father Zamorna' in '"Mortal Hostility": Masculinity and Fatherly Conflict in the Glass Town and Angrian sagas', in Judith E. Pike and Lucy Morrison (eds), *Charlotte Brontë from the Beginning: New Essays from the Juvenilia to the Major Works* (Oxon and New York: Routledge, 2017), p. 61. See also, for further commentary on Zamorna and Brontë's early writing: Frederick R. Karl, 'The Brontës: The Outsider and Protagonist', in Harold Bloom (ed.), *The Victorian Novel* (New York: Chelsea House, 2004), p. 162; John Seelye, *Jane Eyre's American Daughters: From the Wide, Wide World to Anne of Green Gables* (Cranbury, NJ: Associated University Presses, 2005), p. 31ff.; and Kathleen Constable, *A Stranger within the Gates: Charlotte Brontë and Victorian Irishness* (Oxford and Lanham, MD: University Presses of America Inc., 2000), p. 136.
53 Thomas Hughes, *Tom Brown's Schooldays* (1857) (Oxford: Oxford University Press, 2008), p. 283.
54 Olive Anderson, 'The Growth of Christian Militarism in mid-Victorian Britain', *The English Historical Review* 86:338 (January 1971), p. 51.
55 Thomas Thrush, 'Thomas Thrush: The Warrior Turned Christian', *The Advocate of Peace* 5:14 (February 1844), p. 158.
56 The year 1865 is also when Father Sabine Baring-Gould wrote the processional hymn, 'Onward, Christian Soldiers'.

57 Horridge identifies the following militaristic elements of the Salvation Army: 'uniforms, flags, bands, songs, mass-rallies, the novelty of being an identifiable religious Army, simple and broad-based theological message, use of working-class rhetoric, names of people (nicknames), being identified as working-class, names of buildings, corps (having a distinct local headquarters), style of meetings, posters, clear way to gain more converts (person to person), young people's work, no Sunday work, women's equality, organisation and discipline'. See Glen Horridge, *The Salvation Army: Origins and Early Days 1865–1900* (Godalming, Surrey: Ammonite Books, 1993), p. 45.

58 Mary Ward, *Robert Elsmere* (1888) (Oxford: Oxford University Press, 1987), p. 164.

59 Margaret Harkness, *In Darkest London* (1889) (Cambridge: Black Apollo Press, 2003), p. 162.

60 *Ibid.*, p. 65. For a discussion of heroic masculinity in the medical profession, see Michael Brown, '"Like a Devoted Army": Medicine, Heroic Masculinity, and the Military Paradigm of Victorian Britain', *Journal of British Studies* 49 (July 2010), pp. 592–4ff.

61 Eugène Labaume, *Through Fire and Ice with Napoleon: A French Officer's Memoir of the Campaign in Russia* (Solihull: Helion & Co. Ltd., 2002), p. 79.

62 Clausewitz, *On War*, p. 147.

~10~

'Something which every boy can learn': accessible knightly masculinities in children's Arthuriana, 1903–11

Elly McCausland

In 1909, London literary journal *The Academy* published an article simply entitled 'Adventure'. 'It is a large thing to write of adventure,' the author acknowledged:

> So much glamour and romance, such blare of trumpets summoning to arms, such drums throbbing and calling to great deeds are in the wind that a man's heart must quiver to be up and away upon the road to fortune, leading the regiment of his ambitions and in front of the standard of chivalry. I have no patience with those who cry that Adventure is dead and lies among the limbo of forgotten years. The trumpets, perhaps, are somewhat rusty and the drums are not so insistent in their call, but the regiment of ambition is ever upon the march and the standards honourably stained with the red tokens of war are yet to the front.[1]

The article assumes that men are naturally drawn to excitement, compelled to place themselves in fortune's hands and to emulate the standards of medieval chivalry. It depicts an idealised masculinity characterised by a penchant for adventurous exploits and couched in specifically military terms, glamorising 'great deeds' of arms. Should the reader wish to encounter more of this 'Joyful Adventure', the writer notes, they should turn to 'Sir Thomas Malory's great book'. Responding to an apparent feeling that adventure was dead, the writer invokes Malory's *Morte Darthur*, the fifteenth-century prose tale of King Arthur and his knights, as a source of inspiration to revive flagging masculine ambitions.[2] The nineteenth-century medieval revival in Britain and America had frequently exalted the knights of the Arthurian legend as paragons of idealised manhood, in line with what Graham Dawson has perceived as a tendency for the 'soldier hero' to shape the narrative imagining of masculinity during this period.[3] Arthur's knights were often presented to young boys as part of inspirational anthologies of heroic adventures. Yet there was also a growing sense that such exhortations, with their overtones of military prowess, were patently anachronistic. In 1913, a writer in the *New York Tribune* declared, 'if an adventure has to possess shining armour and clashing steel and beautiful, useless Burne-Jones ladies in order to be an adventure, then we have not the material at hand'.[4] During the early twentieth century, the relevance of a medieval value system rooted in skill with sword and shield came under particular scrutiny within the burgeoning industry of children's literature, which often presented heroic stories as exemplary for young readers. Concurrently, scouting movements in Britain and America sought to translate military heroism into qualities that could be honed within the more prosaic reality of the modern child, deploying 'adventure' as an elastic term that encompassed both the escapades of famous soldiers and the activities of young scouts in their woodland camps. Richard Phillips has argued that 'masculinities mapped in the geography of adventure reflect the characteristics of that geography', and we can read in the 'joyful adventure' of children's culture during this period an idealised hybrid masculinity comprising both soldierly and civilian virtues.[5] This reflected what John Price and Michael Brown have identified as an 'everyday heroism' arising in the later nineteenth century, combining, albeit with tensions, civil and military elements.[6] If, as Joseph Kestner contends, the 'primary if narrow agenda of many adventure texts [is] to model masculinity and interrogate it', then British and American adaptations of Arthurian adventure for boy readers during the early 1900s sought to simultaneously promote and subtly redefine chivalric masculinity for a modern age.[7] In doing so, they retained the imaginative framework of the 'soldier hero', but focused on the moral rather than physical virtues of such a figure, lauding a romanticised 'gentleman' whose courtesy, duty and dedication were drawn from the chivalric model but whose resilience and courage were not confined to the battlefield.

It has been pointed out that the *Morte Darthur* is not an obvious choice for child readers. 'Malory did not write for children,' Andrew Lynch argues. 'His book makes no concessions to a young audience and he never interpellates its audience as young'.[8] There are few child characters in the *Morte*, and when they do appear, they make a swift and unacknowledged transition to knightly adulthood. However, in 1862, James Knowles, literary editor and friend of Alfred Tennyson, produced the first version of the text for children, clearly perceiving some quality in it that he connected with a young audience.[9] Tapping into a Victorian fascination with the medieval, and the popularity of Tennyson's *Idylls of the King* (1859–85), the book was a success, reaching its eighth edition by 1895 and initiating a trend for children's Arthuriana that continues to the present day.[10] The adaptations that followed Knowles during the nineteenth century were straightforward, abridged versions of Malory's tale, with illustrations to attract child readers but little original content. However, as the title of Sidney Lanier's *The Boy's King Arthur* (1880) demonstrates, there was perceived to be some fundamental affiliation between Malory's *Morte* and the state of boyhood, requiring the intervention of adapters to bring it to the fore.[11] It was not until the Edwardian period that authors began to develop Malory to produce the *real* 'boy's King Arthur': texts that directly co-opted the Arthurian story for the socialisation of their readers and explicitly considered the relevance of chivalric military masculinity to a generation centuries removed from its heyday.

American author and artist Howard Pyle and British children's writer Henry Gilbert were the first authors to re-write – rather than merely abridge or simplify – Malory for a child readership. Pyle, nicknamed 'The Bloody Quaker' in childhood for his love of pirate and highway-man adventure stories, worked as an art teacher in Philadelphia before beginning to write original and adapted books for children in the 1880s.[12] His four-book Arthuriad, published between 1903 and 1910, is predominantly based on Malory's *Morte* and adorned with his own woodcut illustrations.[13] Like Pyle, popular children's author Henry Gilbert also turned his hand to pirate stories and children's adaptations during the early 1900s. His *King Arthur's Knights* (1911), illustrated by Walter Crane, is based primarily on the *Morte*, but also features material from French poet Chrétien de Troyes's *Yvain, the Knight of the Lion*.[14] In his preface, Gilbert claims that these tales offer 'something which every boy can learn', while Pyle notes that Arthur's knights 'have afforded such a perfect example of courage and humility that anyone might do exceedingly well to follow after their manner of behaviour in such measure as he is able to do'.[15] This third-person address to the implied reader, always a 'he', is characteristic of these texts, which declare themselves to be educative for a specifically male audience.

Debra Mancoff, tracing the Arthurian revival during the nineteenth century, notes that hero worship was a 'potent constructive force', teaching virtue through example and inspiring 'the desire to strive for heroic belief and action, wedding practical energy to romantic association'.[16]

This filtered into the burgeoning industry of children's literature, evident in the large number of hero-focused collections for (predominantly) boys that encouraged identification with great men. The author of *Heroes Every Child Should Know* (1906), which included King Arthur and Sir Galahad, explained that children 'see in their heroes the kind of men they would like to be; for the possibilities of the heroic are in almost all men'.[17] These works strove to present the lessons offered by heroic figures in accessible form to young readers, responding to what Price perceives as a growing respect during the early twentieth century for 'everyday heroism': acts of self-sacrifice and bravery that could be carried out by children as well as adults in a non-military context.[18] However, as Brown has identified, heroism was intricately bound up with the language of combat during this period, revealing the difficulties of entirely 'transposing such models into the civil sphere'.[19] Boys' Arthuriana during this period reveals similar tensions between idealised military role models and more accessible civilian virtues, which moreover were extant in its very source material: as Tison Pugh and Angela Weisl point out, part of the 'mythical allure' of figures like King Arthur 'lies in the possibility – slight though it may be – that they were real men'.[20] For this reason, 'Arthur's actions cast a matrix for British manhood,' because he offered, importantly, both 'a point of recognition and a force of inspiration'.[21] The resonance of Arthur and his knights within the artistic and literary discourse of the Victorian medieval revival required holding both these aspects in balance, presenting what Tennyson termed 'ideal manhood closed in real man'.[22] These children's texts do not entirely relinquish the militaristic roots of the heroism they promote, lauding knighthood as a dynamic, vital 'force of inspiration', but attempt to temper and mediate such discourse through a focus on the 'gentlemanly' values of courtesy, respect and courage that were also an important facet of medieval chivalry.

Both Pyle and Gilbert address the problem that Lynch would identify nearly a century later: 'Malory did not write for children.'[23] By focusing on – and often inventing – the childhoods of Arthur's renowned knights, Pyle and Gilbert offer youthful role models for their readers while simultaneously emphasising the 'soldier hero' as the ultimate goal. Rather than moving straight from Arthur's birth to his pulling of the sword from the stone and subsequent kingship, as happens in Malory's *Morte* over the space of a few pages, Pyle devotes a substantial part of his first book to Arthur's boyhood, divided into three sections: 'the Winning of Knighthood', 'the Winning of a Sword' and 'the Winning of a Queen'. The change offers the boy reader a character with whom he can identify, as the young Arthur faces the trials of adolescence and strives for what is implied to be the essential triumvirate of masculinity. Indeed, the narrator explicitly articulates the connection between the reader and Arthur: 'any man may be a king in that life in which he is placed if so be he may draw forth the sword of success from out of the iron of circumstance. Wherefore when your time of assay cometh, I do hope it may be with you as it was with Arthur that day.'[24] Rather than depicting Arthur's status as inherited, Pyle teaches that chivalric masculinity must be 'won', and is not an innate prerogative. Consequently, his Arthurian world is populated by young men eager to earn their knightly status, implicitly mirroring the condition of Pyle's boy readers as they too work their way towards manhood.

Gilbert's *King Arthur's Knights* incorporates Chrétien de Troyes's *Yvain* but, importantly, invents a childhood for him. He is introduced as a 'little page-boy, fair of face', fleeing from the tyrannous Sir Turquine.[25] Rescued by Arthur, 'Owen' becomes a devoted servant, saving the king's life and nearly dying in the process. Merlin predicts that 'this brave lad here [...] shall be a passing good man when he shall have attained his full strength'.[26] Owen does indeed grow up to be a valiant knight, but, as with Arthur in Pyle's text, he must win his accomplishments: his story is entitled 'How Sir Owen Won the Earldom of the Fountain', and relates how Owen 'in prowess and knightly achievements was among the most famous of the knights of the Round Table'.[27] Gilbert also narrates the childhood of Perceval, who grows up with an overprotective mother, 'never suffering him to see a weapon, nor to hear a tale of war or knightly prowess'.[28] Yet, inspired by a chance meeting with Sir Owen (now a knight), he decides, 'I will be a knight also.'[29] Perceval proves himself by overthrowing several wicked knights; on his return to Camelot, he is greeted by Arthur as 'fair young warrior' and knighted, later achieving the Holy Grail.[30] Gilbert's Launcelot begins his eponymous tale not as a knight, as in the *Morte*, but as a boy sent to Arthur's court 'to learn knightly deeds and noble prowess'.[31] He volunteers to fight the cruel Sir Caradoc when none of Arthur's knights dares, and only following this test of courage and skill is he knighted by Arthur - a confirmation that he has indeed 'learned' knighthood. Gilbert consistently portrays knighthood as something that must be acquired gradually through learning, practice and experience; his story of Perceval is entitled

'How Sir Perceval was Taught Chivalry'.[32] His Gareth, battling with the Red Knight on a quest, 'learned much from him, though it was at the cost of many a gaping wound'.[33] Gareth's injuries are justified by the knightly lessons he has acquired, suggesting that masculinity is not constituted by physical skill alone, but must be cultivated through training. Moreover, the comment implies the instability of knightly masculinity, positing it as a fragile set of attributes that must be constantly tested and re-validated.

Kelly Boyd notes a trend in Edwardian boys' tales to portray heroes with 'a less assured hold on masculinity': it 'was no longer seen as something that resided naturally in only one segment of the population, the aristocracy; instead, its acquisition was the result of hard work and the acceptance of society's rules'.[34] In his preface, Gilbert claims that 'the great and simple lesson of chivalry which the tales of King Arthur teach is, in a few words, to merit "the fine old name of gentleman"'.[35] Gilbert's deployment of the term 'gentleman', in moral rather than class-based terms, refigures an elitist, 'innate' masculinity as a meritocracy, requiring a series of emotional and ethical qualities that are always being honed and developed. His novel reimagines heroism in line with what Brown identifies as 'a middle-class vision of professional society defined by expertise and meritocratic reward'.[36] However, although ostensibly offering a modern, moral interpretation of gentlemanliness, it is telling that Gilbert still couches his vision in terms of the 'fine old name of gentleman', signalling uncertainty regarding how one might separate the integral qualities of knighthood from their medieval trappings. This juxtaposition also reflected a common tendency in the nineteenth and early twentieth centuries to depict the medieval period, and medieval literature, as representing both the 'childhood' of Anglophone literature - an infantilised repository of values that subsequent generations would develop and refine - and a 'timeless' stronghold of universal truths that transcended history and offered fundamental insight into human nature.[37] Gilbert's vision similarly attempts to imply the timelessness of a legend that is, in fact, deeply rooted in a very specific sociopolitical context; to evoke the romance of the 'fine old name of gentleman', a relic of a past age, while lauding the supposedly universal values signified by such a name. Pyle also suggests that the moral qualities of 'gentleman' equal the physical prowess of 'knight', but it is telling that he still deploys chivalric militaristic language to promote them: Tristram, having fought against Launcelot, declares, 'Messire, I yield myself unto thee, being overcome not more by thy prowess than by thy courtesy.'[38] 'Courtesy' is envisaged as a weapon, potent as Launcelot's actual sword. Although these texts present a more egalitarian version of chivalry that can be learned and acquired through hard work, humility and dedication, regardless of birth or class, they still draw on militaristic language and offer a nostalgic vision of past days in their valorisation of the knightly 'gentleman'.

In many ways, these novels are the textual equivalents of the boys' groups that became popular in Britain and America around the turn of the twentieth century. Influenced by developments in child psychology and an increasing awareness of the concept of adolescence, these groups targeted what American minister William Byron Forbush identified as 'the boy problem': the 'barbarous behaviour' of the male adolescent, 'endowed with the passions and independence of manhood while still a child in foresight and judgement', and the issue of how to socialise these boys into desirable masculine roles.[39] Forbush's group, the Knights of King Arthur, was established in 1893 in America, and planned to 'fulfil the prophecy of King Arthur that he would return to re-establish a kingdom of righteousness, honor and service'.[40] Boys adopted the name of an Arthurian hero, and attempted to emulate his defining traits. They were encouraged to perform 'tournaments' (athletic competitions) and 'quests' (deeds of kindness or charity). Pyle and Gilbert's texts reflect this 'remaking of chivalry into a bourgeois male ideal, comprising values of self-reliance, duty, and industry', and there is some evidence that Pyle was inspired to produce his Arthuriad by Forbush's Knights of King Arthur.[41] Robert Baden-Powell's British Boy Scouts, founded in 1908, also drew inspiration from the Arthurian legend: Baden-Powell named Arthur as the 'real' founder of the movement and compared scouts to questers for the Grail.[42] Like Pyle and Gilbert, Baden-Powell argued that 'a knight (or scout) is at all times a gentleman', but divested the term of its class connotations: 'many people seem to think that a gentleman must have lots of money. That does not make a gentleman. A gentleman is anyone who carries out the rules of chivalry of the knights.'[43] Again, we witness a curious juxtaposition between a modern vision of 'gentleman', divested of its class connotations, and adherence to a medieval value system far removed from contemporary British and American society. Although many of these groups were rooted in chivalric practice – Baden-Powell identified St George as the patron saint of scouting – they were primarily concerned with transforming military masculinity into a versatile civilian masculinity that would enable boys to contend with the vicissitudes of modern life, as exemplified by the famous scout slogan, 'Be

Prepared'.[44] Such a vision hinged on preparedness for unexpected testing scenarios: in other words, adventures.

At the beginning of Pyle's 'Story of Sir Gawaine', Gawaine accidentally beheads a damsel in his rashness, as in the *Morte Darthur*. Guinevere is furious, and Pyle's reader is encouraged to empathise: 'ye [...] may feel as Queen Guinevere did, that Sir Gawaine was not rightwise courteous as a belted knight should have been in that adventure'.[45] Although Gawaine has also shown martial prowess during the adventure by defeating a series of knights in battle, this is insufficient to redeem him in the eyes of the court and guarantee him respectable knighthood. A second adventure occurs – loosely based on John Gower's fourteenth-century *Tale of Florent* – during which Gawaine must display the moral, 'gentlemanly' qualities that Pyle implies are also essential for knighthood.[46] He marries a hideous old crone out of duty to King Arthur, who had promised the woman he would fulfil her wish after she saved his life. Although Gawaine initially feels shame and humiliation, shutting himself away from the world and his hideous new bride, he is eventually overcome with 'a certain strength', and apologises to his wife for his neglect, vowing to 'do all that is in my power to recompense thee'.[47] She transforms into a beautiful young woman, offering Gawaine the choice to have her beautiful either during the day or during the night. Gawaine allows the lady to choose. Having passed this final trial by allowing her sovereignty in all things, the spell is broken, and he is rewarded with a wife who is always beautiful. She tells Gawaine that she came to Camelot 'so that I might test the entire nobility of thy knighthood', and Gawaine, this time, is not found wanting.[48] The tale concludes with a joyous wedding feast, and Pyle's customary moral interpretation for the reader:

> As that poor ugly beldame appeared unto the eyes of Sir Gawaine, so doth a man's duty sometimes appear to him to be ugly and exceedingly ill-favored unto his desires. But when he shall have wedded himself unto that duty so that he hath made it one with him as a bridegroom maketh himself one with his bride, then doth that duty become of a sudden very beautiful unto him and unto others.[49]

The loathly lady is a test for Gawaine's knighthood, initiating an adventure that requires no skill with weapons. Instead, he is tested for a different kind of 'strength': kindness, magnanimity and duty. Pyle's concluding maxim implies that the reader can become Gawaine's equal:

When you shall have become entirely wedded unto your duty, then shall you become equally worthy with that good knight and gentleman Sir Gawaine; for it needs not that a man shall wear armor for to be a true knight, but only that he shall do his best endeavor with all patience and humility as it hath been ordained for him to do. Wherefore, when your time cometh unto you to display your knightness by assuming your duty, I do pray that you also may approve yourself as worthy as Sir Gawaine approved himself in this story.[50]

Gawaine's goodness inheres in two distinct, but interlinked, attributes: his martial skill ('knight') but also his moral fibre ('gentleman'). The soldier hero is thus redrawn as a composite being whose martial prowess is only validated through the possession of complementary moral qualities. 'When your time cometh unto you to display your knightness', as with his earlier 'when your time of assay cometh', epitomises Pyle's model of chivalry as a series of attributes that are displayed in response to testing situations.

Phillips claims that 'masculinities and imperialisms [...] are not simply reproduced; they are actively constructed and reconstructed, in the geography of adventure'.[51] According to these texts, masculinity is acquired through 'approving' oneself. Adventures are the means whereby Arthur's knights construct and reconstruct their manhood by proving able to cope with the unknown. 'Adventure' in Middle English was a capacious term that encompassed quests, daring deeds, risk, danger, fortune and the miraculous or marvellous.[52] However, Dawson has identified the 'deepening association of adventure with enterprise' since the Middle Ages, marking 'the developing confidence of attempts to control and shape the world according to human desire and design'.[53] Pyle and Gilbert invoke this more active meaning: for their knights, adventure offers 'a challenge to assert human will and test human capabilities against the vicissitudes of a world that remains deeply uncertain'.[54] As a writer in American magazine *Outlook* summarised in 1912, 'whatever calls forth one's powers to meet unexpected and hazardous exigencies with skill and success may properly be called an adventure'.[55] Sir Myles of the White Fountain is assured by a damsel that he will find 'adventure enough for to satisfy any man' if he takes a certain forest path.[56] Pyle posits a direct correlation between chivalric masculinity and readiness for adventure: Myles 'had a mind to seek adventure in such manner as beseemed a good knight who would be errant'.[57] Gawaine is given Arthur's leave to complete a quest and asks the king if he can take his younger brother, Gaheris, as his squire, 'for he groweth apace unto manhood, and yet he hath never beheld any considerable adventure at arms'.[58] What David Gilmore describes as the 'recurrent notion that manhood is problematic, a critical threshold that boys must pass through testing' is evident in these Arthurian representations of masculinity.[59] Adventure dramatises these critical thresholds by rendering them spatial and literal: it involves transitioning into an unknown and often dangerous space (frequently signified by a mysterious forest or castle) to prove oneself in response to unforeseen trials. However, the mindset behind this transition is implicitly more important than the transition itself: these texts emphasise mental acuity as an essential component of military action, suggesting that physical skill is meaningless, even dangerous, without a solid foundation of preparedness and consideration.

Arthur is described by Merlin as 'a very brave man to have so much appetite for battle' when he announces his intention to undertake a second combat with King Pellinore. Yet Merlin also asks him, incredulously, 'how mayst thou hope to undertake this adventure without due preparation? For, lo! thou hast no sword, nor hast thou a spear, nor hast thou even thy misericordia for to do battle withal'. Arthur responds, 'I will presently seek for some weapon as soon as may be. For, even an I have no better weapon than an oaken cudgel, yet would I assay this battle again with so poor a tool as that'.[60] Although this exchange implies that Arthur's military skill is so great that it does not require advanced weapons, it also indicates that Merlin is misguided regarding what constitutes 'preparation' for an adventure. Military masculinity is a state of mind rather than the condition of being armed and armoured. It is more about bravery and courage, and the willingness to undertake risky adventures, than the martial aptitude that may be displayed during such adventures. When Arthur succeeds in defeating Pellinore, he achieves the magical sword Excalibur. A token of military prowess, the sword metaphorically represents Arthur's martial skill but also alludes to his earlier readiness to commit to dangerous adventure *without* a weapon, symbolising masculine heroism as an essential combination of physical capability and mental preparedness. However, it also indicates the continued reliance of these texts on military metaphors to delineate their supposedly democratic, civilian model of masculinity.

In their emphasis on testing adventures as the means whereby masculinity is defined and maintained, these texts evince a fraught relationship with domesticity, particularly its feminine associations. On the one hand, a domestic feminine presence contributes to the refashioning of knighthood as a series of moral qualities replicable by an Edwardian boy. Pyle's loathly lady is a metaphor for Gawaine's knightly obligations: he becomes literally 'wedded to his duty'. In Gilbert's text, Perceval's overprotective mother has a similar function. When Perceval convinces her that he must ride into the world and become a knight, she bids him farewell with an emotional speech:

> Make all the haste ye may to the court of King Arthur at Caerleon-upon-Usk, for there are the best and the boldest and the most worshipful of knights. And the king will give thee knighthood. And wherever thou seest a church, go kneel and repeat thy prayers therein; and if thou hearest an outcry, go quickly and defend the weak, the poor and the unprotected. And be ever tender towards women, my son, and remember that thy mother loves thee and prays for thy stay in health and life.[61]

This advice has several parallels with Malory's 'Pentecostal Oath', his most explicit codification of the knightly value system, within which knights are charged 'never to do outrage nor murder, and alway to flee treason […] to give mercy unto him that asked mercy […] and alway to doo ladies, damosels, and gentlewomen succour upon paine of death. Also that no man take no battailes in a wrong quarrel'.[62] It is significant that Gilbert dispenses with this speech from Malory, instead offering a simplified explication of the knightly creed that is closely linked to the domestic. Perceval's mother's assertion, 'the king will give thee knighthood', implies that the qualities she lists – religious devotion, defence of the weak, gentility towards women, filial affection – are constitutive of true knightliness. Although some of these are still vague, the speech presents more practical ways of demonstrating chivalry than refraining from murder or giving mercy: church attendance; prayer; respect for women and the family.

Yet, as Dawson has identified, on the other hand, the very concept of adventurous masculinity necessitates the evasion of domesticity. The *Oxford English Dictionary* usage of 'abroad' as a generalised location for adventure originally meant 'out of one's house', before its extension, around 1450, to 'out of one's home country'.[63] Dawson notes that 'this shift catches perfectly the widening thresholds of the unknown beyond which increasingly perilous adventures may occur, their engulfing conflicts taking place in locations safely distant from "home" and family'.[64] Domesticity precludes adventure, the nature of which requires a leap into the unknown and the abandonment of the familiar and even familial. Gilbert's Perceval must escape the constraints of his mother before he can achieve chivalric glory. Although she teaches him 'all manner of nobleness in thought and action and in learning', she never permits him to see a weapon.[65] Perceval, having spied a group of knights on the road back to Camelot, is 'torn between his love for his mother, and the strange restlessness which the sight of the three warriors had caused in him', but the latter prevails.[66] His internal conflict perfectly captures wider tensions in the representation of heroic masculinity within these texts: a series of 'timeless' moral virtues replicable by the child, such as parental love and duty, but extolled and delineated using specifically military metaphors and language. Although knightliness requires 'gentlemanly' moral qualities, Gilbert implies, without physical adventure boys cannot hope to achieve it. The virtues Perceval's mother teaches him are insufficient: he must 'go into the world to become a knight'.[67]

Gilbert's Tristram also 'cared not overmuch to be with ladies, but was more joyful to be in hall, talking of hunting, jousting and hawking', yet when he is injured in battle and healed by La Belle Isoude, she 'forbade him gently to take violent exercise'.[68] As Gilbert notes, 'Sir Tristram was impatient to be in the saddle again, with lance in rest and his great charger leaping beneath him'.[69] It is implied that women threaten active masculinities, their 'gentleness' hindering the expression of supposedly natural manly propensities for violence. Eugène Vinaver argues that that 'love is not allowed to interfere with the customs of knighthood' in the *Morte Darthur*, and Malory's text is deeply concerned with the detrimental effects that romantic love might have on knightly prowess, particularly in relation to Launcelot, whose adulterous love for Guinevere ultimately prevents him from achieving the Holy Grail.[70] Gilbert's Tristram story presents a particularly interesting revision of Malory's original. In the *Morte*, Tristram refuses to fight at a tournament because Isoude, his lover, will not be present. She is outraged: 'What shall be said among the knights? Se how sir Tristram hunteth and hawketh, and courteth within the castle with his lady, and forsaketh his worship. Alas! shall some say, it is pittie that ever he was made a knight, or that ever he should have the love of a lady'. Isoude is also concerned for her own reputation: 'What shall queenes and ladies say of me? It is pitie that I have my life, that I wil hold so noble a knight as yee are from your worship'.[71] Malory's Isoude is aware of the risks posed by romantic love to knighthood, fearing lest she confirm courtly suspicions that female paramours cause men to forsake their 'worship' (a complex term used in the *Morte* to signify a combination

of physical and moral prowess). She in fact maintains Tristram's worship by demanding that he fulfil his knightly obligations. However, in
Gilbert's rewriting, Tristram would never consider abandoning his
chivalric pursuits for the sake of a lady, despite Isoude's entreaty, and
his masculinity is thus linked to his ability to resist the pressures of the
domestic feminine. Gilbert presents a simplified version of the gender
dynamic articulated by Isoude in the *Morte*: women are always a barrier
to knightly achievements, keeping men engaged in domestic pursuits
when they should be adventuring in the unknown.

Gilbert intimates that a healthy, enthusiastic attitude towards physical adventure is a necessary component of idealised manhood. 'I crave
not to be married', Tristram declares. 'I would be free and go forth
into strange lands to seek adventures'.[72] As Kestner has pointed out,
'adventure fiction enables the investigation of masculinities because its
premise is wandering, encountering all sorts and conditions of men';
moreover, these excursions do not 'only map the exterior geography
but also map the internal responses of the protagonists'.[73] The impa-
tience and restlessness of Gilbert's Tristram, whose desire to 'wander'
is implied to be intrinsic to his very manhood, exemplifies what John
Tosh has identified as a 'flight from domesticity' in his study of late
nineteenth- and early twentieth-century masculinity. From the 1870s,
Tosh notes, 'the view was increasingly heard that domesticity was
unglamorous, unfulfilling and – ultimately – unmasculine'.[74] A boom in
adventure fiction in the 1880s, combined with the trend for biographies
of imperial heroes such as Gordon, Kitchener and Baden-Powell, 'gave
credence to the belief that the empire, in which Britain's destiny seemed
to lie at that time, was quintessentially a masculine arena, where men
worked better without the company of women'.[75] Pyle and Gilbert
implicitly posit the domestic and the feminine as a barrier to manly
chivalry, reflecting a late nineteenth-century trend for boys' adventure
novels that focused on homosocial relationships in imperial locations,
such as the works of H. Rider Haggard (whose preface to his 1885 *King
Solomon's Mines* famously declared, 'there is not a *petticoat* in the whole
history').[76] Service of the feminine is an important motivating factor
within their reimagining of chivalry, but ultimately domesticity inhib-
its the achievement of full manhood because it hinders the undertaking
of adventures.

Although these authors are keen to prove that adventure does not
'lie among the limbo of forgotten years', their reimagining of Malorian
adventure for the early twentieth century has much in common with

the escapist fantasies of *fin de siècle* adventure fiction and their 'flight from domesticity', suggesting that Malory as a model for masculinity sat in uneasy relation to modern reconfigurations of gender relations and identities. These texts themselves exist in a 'limbo' period, announcing their intention to offer 'something every boy can learn' while simultaneously couching such lessons in the language of medieval militarism and romance. Replicating Malory's model of masculine adventure – as fundamentally incompatible with women and the domestic – these texts evaded the significant question of masculine identity in a world where women were being assigned increasing legal, economic and social power. Furthermore, in gendering their readers as male, they also avoided the more difficult task of rendering the Arthurian legend accessible to girl readers. It would take another three decades and two world wars for a writer to offer a truly 'modern' take on Malory's classic text, one that interpreted and interrogated Arthurian adventure in line with altered twentieth-century attitudes towards sexuality, child-rearing, psychology and warfare: T. H. White's *Once and Future King* tetralogy, perhaps the most popular and best-known Arthurian adaptation today.[77]

In 1888, Frederick Ryland declared in the *English Illustrated Magazine* that Malory's *Morte Darthur* 'is not a book with a large audience of young people'. They would 'never think of turning for instruction and amusement to a fifteenth century recension of a set of twelfth century romances'.[78] By the beginning of the twentieth century, this situation had changed. Capitalising on the success of J. T. Knowles's adaptation, Pyle and Gilbert produced versions of Malory's tale that addressed the problem Ryland had identified a decade beforehand. Influenced by the medieval revival of the nineteenth century, the popularity of hero fiction for young boys and the success of scouting movements that translated chivalric virtues into practical goals, these texts adapted Malory to offer both instruction and amusement to their boy readers. They reformulated a specifically military model of masculinity by emphasising the moral side of knighthood, positing character virtues such as duty and courtesy as equally constitutive of idealised manliness. However, they also retained the 'soldier hero' as a framework for this moral interpretation, reflecting trends in children's literature for exciting tales of 'red-blooded' adventure but also hinting at the impossibility of clearly differentiating civil and military heroism during this period. Furthermore, their dependence on the language of chivalric militarism and their adherence to a Malorian model of gender relations hinted at a fundamental incompatibility between an idealised 'timeless' medievalism and the increasing complexities of modern sexuality and gender identity. These texts aimed to prove that the 'joyful adventure' of Malory's *Morte Darthur* could, in fact, translate into adventures in modernity. Yet although they may have dispensed with 'useless Burne-Jones ladies', this updated model of masculine heroism never quite managed to escape its longstanding associations with 'shining armour and clashing steel'.[79]

Notes

1 'Adventure', *The Academy*, 1935 (1909), pp. 181–2.

2 For an edition of Malory popular in the nineteenth and early twentieth centuries, see Thomas Wright (ed.), *The History of King Arthur and of the Knights of the Round Table, Compiled by Sir Thomas Malory* (London: John Russell Smith, 1858).

3 Graham Dawson, *Soldier Heroes: British Adventure, Empire and the Imagining of Masculinities* (London: Routledge, 1994), p. 22.

4 'The Great Adventure', *New York Tribune* (30 July 1913), p. 6.

5 Richard Phillips, *Mapping Men & Empire: A Geography of Adventure* (London: Routledge, 1997), p. 18.

6 See John Price, *Everyday Heroism: Victorian Constructions of the Heroic Civilian* (London: Bloomsbury, 2014) and Michael Brown, '"Like a Devoted Army': Medicine, Heroic Masculinity, and the Military Paradigm in Victorian Britain", *Journal of British Studies* 49.3 (2010): 592–622.

7 Joseph A. Kestner, *Masculinities in British Adventure Fiction, 1880–1915* (Surrey: Ashgate, 2010), p. 7.

8 Andrew Lynch, '*Le Morte Darthur* for Children: Malory's Third Tradition' in Barbara Tepa Lupack (ed.), *Adapting the Arthurian Legends for Children* (New York: Palgrave Macmillan, 2004), p. 4.

9 J. T. Knowles, *The Story of King Arthur and His Knights of the Round Table* (London: Griffith & Farrow, 1862).

10 Alfred Tennyson, *Idylls of the King* (London: Penguin Books, 1983). The twelve narrative poems, inspired by Malory's *Morte*, were published in stages between 1859 and 1885.

11 Sidney Lanier, *The Boy's King Arthur* (London: Sampson Low, Marston, Searle & Rivington, 1880).

12 Lucien Agosta, *Howard Pyle* (Boston, MA: Twayne, 1987), p. 1.

13 Howard Pyle, *The Story of the Champions of the Round Table* (New York: Dover Publications, 1968 [1903]); *The Story of the Grail and the Passing of Arthur* (New York: Dover Publications, 1992 [1905]); *The Story of King Arthur and His Knights* (New York: Dover Publications, 1965 [1907]); *The Story of Sir Launcelot and His Companions* (New York: Dover Publications, 1991 [1910]).

14   Probably written in the 1170s, the poem is an Arthurian romance narrating the brave deeds performed by the knight Yvain to regain the favour of his lady. See Chrétien de Troyes, *Yvain: The Knight of the Lion*, trans. Burton Raffel (New Haven, CT: Yale University Pres, 1987).

15   Henry Gilbert, *King Arthur's Knights* (Edinburgh: T. C. & E. C. Jack, n.d., c. 1911), p. vi; Pyle, *Story of King Arthur*, p.v.

16   Debra Mancoff, 'To Take Excalibur: King Arthur and the Construction of Victorian Manhood', in Edward Donald Kennedy (ed.), *King Arthur: A Casebook* (New York: Routledge, 2002), p. 259.

17   H. W. Mabie, *Heroes Every Child Should Know* (New York: Doubleday, Page & Co., 1906), p. 4.

18   Price suggests that everyday heroism was 'relatively well understood' by the early 1900s, shaped by events such as the introduction of the Albert Medal and memorials to working- or middle-class men, women and children who had risked their lives to save others. The 1900 Memorial to Heroic Self-Sacrifice in London's Postman's Park featured the names of several child heroes. See Price, *Everyday Heroism*, p. 129.

19   Brown, 'Like a Devoted Army', p. 622.

20   Tison Pugh and Angela Jane Weisl, *Medievalisms: Making the Past in the Present* (London: Routledge, 2013), p. 65.

21   Mancoff, 'To Take Excalibur', pp. 258, 262.

22   Tennyson, *Idylls*, p. 302, l. 38.

23   Lynch, '*Le Morte Darthur* for Children', p. 4.

24   Pyle, *Story of King Arthur*, p. 35.

25   Gilbert, *King Arthur's Knights*, p. 16.

26   *Ibid.*, p. 21.

27   *Ibid.*, p. 194.

28   *Ibid.*, p. 165.

29   *Ibid.*, p. 169.

30   *Ibid.*, p. 252.

31   *Ibid.*, p. 53.

32   *Ibid.*, p. 164.

33   *Ibid.*, p. 96.

34   Kelly Boyd, *Manliness and the Boys' Story Paper in Britain: A Cultural History, 1855–1940* (New York: Palgrave Macmillan, 2003), p. 71.

35   Gilbert, *King Arthur's Knights*, p. vii.

36   Brown, 'Like a Devoted Army', p. 595.

37   See Elly McCausland, 'King Arthur in the Classroom: Teaching Malory in the Early Twentieth Century', *Review of English Studies* 68:283 (February 2017), pp. 23–43.

38   Pyle, *Champions of the Round Table*, p. 166.

39   Alan Lupack, 'Arthurian Youth Groups in America', in Barbara Tepa Lupack (ed.), *Adapting the Arthurian Legends for Children* (New York: Palgrave Macmillan, 2004), p. 199.

40 *Ibid.*, p. 200.
41 Julie Nelson Couch, 'Howard Pyle's *The Story of King Arthur and his Knights* and the Bourgeois Boy Reader', *Arthuriana* 13:2 (2003), p. 208. Lucien Agosta suggests that Pyle was aware of the 'apparently unappeasable late nineteenth-century appetite for Arthurian works' following Forbush's creation of the Knights of King Arthur, and therefore suggested to publisher Scribner's in 1902 that he write a book telling the story of Arthur. See Agosta, *Howard Pyle*, p. 43.
42 Robert Baden-Powell, *Yarns for Boy Scouts Told Round the Camp Fire* (London: C. Arthur Pearson, 1910), p. 117.
43 See Robert Baden-Powell (ed. Elleke Boehmer), *Scouting for Boys: A Handbook for Instruction in Good Citizenship* (Oxford: Oxford University Press, 2004), p. 214.
44 *Ibid.*
45 Pyle, *King Arthur*, p. 292.
46 John Gower, 'The Tale of Florent', in G. C. Macaulay (ed.), *The Complete Works of John Gower* (Oxford: Clarendon Press, 1901), vol. 2, pp. 75–86. The tale dates from the late 1380s.
47 Pyle, *King Arthur*, p. 308.
48 *Ibid.*, p. 310.
49 *Ibid.*, p. 311.
50 *Ibid.*, p. 312.
51 Phillips, *Mapping Men*, p. 89.
52 *Middle English Dictionary Online*, University of Michigan, *n.* adventure. Available at: http://quod.lib.umich.edu/cgi/m/mec/med-idx?type=id&id=MED3150 (accessed 11 May 2018).
53 Dawson, *Soldier Heroes*, p. 53.
54 *Ibid.*
55 'The Adventure of Homemaking', *Outlook* 101:4 (1912), p. 158.
56 Pyle, *King Arthur*, p. 43.
57 *Ibid.*
58 *Ibid.*, p. 283.
59 David D. Gilmore, *Manhood in the Making: Cultural Concepts of Masculinity* (New Haven, CT: Yale University Press, 1990), p. 11.
60 Pyle, *King Arthur*, pp. 65–6.
61 Gilbert, *King Arthur's Knights*, p. 171.
62 Wright, *Malory*, vol. 1, p. 115.
63 Cited in Dawson, *Soldier Heroes*, p. 58.
64 *Ibid.*
65 Gilbert, *King Arthur's Knights*, p. 165.
66 *Ibid.*, p. 170.
67 *Ibid.*, pp. 171–2.
68 *Ibid.*, p. 110.

69   *Ibid.*

70   Cited in Richard W. Kaeuper, *Chivalry and Violence in Medieval Europe* (New York: Oxford University Press, 2001), p. 149.

71   Wright, *Malory*, vol. 3, p. 44.

72   Gilbert, *King Arthur's Knights*, p. 114.

73   Kestner, *Masculinities*, pp. 10, 63.

74   John Tosh, *A Man's Place: Masculinity and the Middle-Class Home in Victorian England* (New Haven, CT: Yale University Press, 1999), pp. 6–7.

75   *Ibid.*, p. 174.

76   H. Rider Haggard, *King Solomon's Mines* (Oxford: Oxford University Press, 2016 [1885]), p. 10 (italics in original).

77   T. H. White, *The Once & Future King: The Complete Edition* (London: Harper Collins, 1996). The first three books were published between 1939 and 1941; the final book was added when they were published collectively in 1958.

78   Frederick Ryland, 'The *Morte d'Arthur*', *English Illustrated Magazine* 6 (1888–89), p. 55.

79   'The Great Adventure', p. 6.

11

'A story of treasure, war and wild adventure': hero-worship, imperial masculinities and inter-generational ideologies in H. Rider Haggard's 1880s fiction

Helen Goodman

As the Christmas holidays of 1885–86 drew to a close, George Salmon wrote a piece for the *Fortnightly Review*, pondering the selection of fiction on the market for boys' presents that year.[1] Bound in bright red cloth, emblazoned with gold lettering on the spine and an enticing collection of weaponry on its cover, 2,000 copies of an attractive new book of this kind had appeared on booksellers' shelves that very autumn. The novel bore all the hallmarks that would characterise the most popular adventure fiction of its time: extreme temperatures, hostile landscapes, hidden treasure, heroic acts and three pale-skinned musketeers. *King Solomon's Mines* would become a bestseller and treasured favourite for generations to come. According to the *Saturday Review*, this was the most 'healthily exciting volume' for boys since *Treasure Island*, and it 'would be hard to say whether the piratical John Silver or the mysteriously aged witch Gagool (of *King Solomon's Mines*) strikes to the youthful heart with more delightful terror and apprehension'.[2]

The 1861 census recorded more than one million male youths aged between ten and fourteen, and almost as many aged fifteen to nineteen, in England and Wales alone. Kelly Boyd calculates that the audience for the 'new story paper' was between 5 per cent and 10 per cent of the population.[3] A burgeoning market for adventure stories popularised novels and short stories in new juvenile periodicals such as *The Boy's Own Paper* (1879–1967).[4] This magazine interspersed first-person accounts of imperial battles with short fiction.[5] Militaristic hero-worship stories were by no means a new phenomenon in the mid-1880s when H. Rider Haggard's book became a bestseller. However, a timely combination of factors enabled the 'hero industry' to expand and thrive: the emergence of a larger market for toys and books for children, a rise in the disposable income of many middle-class families, the popular perception of imperial peace and success, the technology required for cheap mass production and a pervasive national mood of excitement and optimism.[6] These favourable conditions continued into the 1890s, as renewed public support for Queen Victoria (and Empress of India) around the time of the 1897 Diamond Jubilee contributed to a spike in the popularity of imperial adventure fiction as it 'swept the people into a highly enjoyable craze of Empire ... a pageant'.[7] In 1902, following the death of G. A. Henty (the bestselling writer in the 'adventure', 'quest' or 'Lost World' genre), *The Times* remarked that 'For many Christmas seasons, no books have been so eagerly expected and so gladly welcomed by boys as his.'[8] Nonetheless, his rival, Haggard, is more well known today. He adopted a range of narrative techniques and plural models of martial masculinity to maximise the appeal of a literary genre which is, and was, derided by some as simplistic and formulaic.[9]

The timing of the publication of *King Solomon's Mines* was fundamental to its success, enabling Haggard to combine political shifts and emerging technologies with innovative characterisation. Appearing in print just months after the conclusion of the Berlin Conference (November 1845–February 1885), the fictional hunter Allan Quatermain's accounts depicted the landscape of the recent past, shortly after the Anglo-Zulu War (1879) and just before the majority of the region he traverses came under British rule. The year 1885 also saw the development of Linotype and Monotype, implemented by Cassells to print 8,000 copies of *King Solomon's Mines* within three months.[10] Haggard chose a 'mature man' for central characters, for the most part, rather than versions of R. M. Ballantyne's 'adolescents performing adolescent feats for adolescent readers'.[11] Stephen Gray considers Quatermain an entirely different narrator from those who came before, and Haggard's 'one stroke of genius'.[12]

This chapter will investigate various ways in which *King Solomon's Mines* (1885), *Allan Quatermain* (1887) and *She* (1887) didactically encouraged the veneration of military masculinities in the form of a comprehensive system of hero-worship. However, these novels were not a straightforward call to arms. Haggard renegotiated earlier models of hero-worship to create fictional reports of pseudo-military African adventures which contributed to the cultural longevity of support for the British Empire and glamorised imperial careers. Sport has long been acknowledged as a valuable tool in constructing and sustaining martial masculine identity by encouraging comradeship in combat and the pursuit of a shared purpose, building physical strength and skill in competitive or combative situations. Similarly, a direct relationship may be drawn between adventure fiction and martial aspirations and skills. Bestselling novels by authors such as Haggard and Henty not only instilled imperial ideologies in new generations but blurred the lines between military and leisure pursuits. *King Solomon's Mines*, Haggard's first major commercial success, published when he was twenty-nine, is often seen as 'the quintessential example of the genre, at its very best and at its very worst'.[13]

Haggard is best remembered for two particularly enigmatic leaders: the adventurous Allan Quatermain and the haunting Ayesha - 'She who must be obeyed'.[14] Quatermain is more than what Wendy Katz calls 'Haggard's version of Everyman'.[15] His blurring of military and civilian roles is a particularly potent recipe for hero-worship. As a retired elephant hunter with a detailed knowledge of local terrain and experience with weapons, Quatermain has appealing military skills, with independence and freedom instead of discipline and restraint. He meets Sir Henry Curtis and Captain John Good on a ship to Natal and agrees to help them find George (known as Neville). Curtis's younger brother had gone to Africa to seek his fortune after a quarrel about inheriting the family estate. After a series of Homeric near-death adventures across mountains and deserts, the three men find Neville too ill to be moved and return home with pockets filled with diamonds, to retire as wealthy men. The search for a missing compatriot provides the moral impetus for a journey in which the men strive to locate, penetrate and take ownership of a legendary mine filled with gold, diamonds and ivory. At least for adult readers, it seems plausible that Gerald Monsmon is correct in surmising, 'Everyone knows that the trio in *King Solomon's Mines* went to Kukanaland for its diamonds; the rescue ... served only as a convenient pretext for recovering Solomon's treasures.'[16] The male characters - pale-skinned former hunters and members of the armed forces - embody an intrinsically British colonial identity, becoming role models for new generations of middle- and upper-class boys, at whom Haggard's fiction was aimed in a project of Carlylean 'hero-worship'.

Haggard allowed his readership to assume that he was himself a heroic military man - despite being solely employed in administration during his six years in South Africa. His influential father secured him an unpaid post as secretary to the Governor of Natal from the age of nineteen.[17] A succession of administrative roles meant that the realities of armed combat were at a distance, leaving his appetite for adventure unassuaged. His career in 'military-adjacent' rather than direct military action functioned as an impetus that not only spurred his idealisation of martial men, free from disillusionment, but also led him to embellish his plots and characterisation in innovative ways. His brand of military masculinity adapted in response to the defeats, as well as the victories, of imperial conflicts, and Haggard was actively engaged in inculcating an appealing form of military masculinity in his young readers, whom he considered 'sons'.[18] The following sections reveal how Haggard's fiction combined with other militaristic and imperialist cultural phenomena in the 1880s and capitalised on print technology and conditions in the literary marketplace. Combined, they demonstrate how the author drew on the successes of the past, adjusted to present conditions and negotiated an enduring legacy for his adventure fiction by engaging with ideological structures, military triumphs and narrative techniques.

Identity and ideological apparatus

Didactic prefaces were widespread in children's novels during this period, and Haggard used them to target an explicitly inter-generational and exclusively male readership, boasting that there was 'not a *petticoat* in the whole history' of Quatermain.[19] Major publishing houses such as Nelson, Macmillan and Blackie began to specialise in 'simple, direct adventure fiction' for boys, and neither supply nor demand for this central component of the hero 'industry' showed signs of slowing.[20] The apparent martyrdom of General Gordon at Khartoum in 1885 (several months before the publication of *King Solomon's Mines*) made him a hero in the media.[21] In 1884, *The Illustrated London News* explicitly connected Gordon to literary heroes, claiming that 'his achievements as Governor of the Equatorial Provinces from 1874 to 1879 were more wonderful than are to be found in the wildest Oriental romance'.[22] Accounts of the lives and deaths of prominent military men in newspapers, magazines and books sold in vast numbers and were imitated in fiction for boys. Haggard's fiction both capitalised on this public appetite and ensured its appeal long after his death with various surprisingly shrewd strategies. Often dismissed as simple jingoistic bellicosity, Haggard's 1880s novels combine innovations in plot, characterisation, frontmatter and illustration, forging a unique strategy for the inculcation of inter-generational martial masculinities during the rise of New Imperialism.

As James Gibson has observed, when tied to nationhood, 'being a warrior is not an occupation but a male identity'.[23] Similarly, Haggard did more than glorify and promote military careers in the expansion of the imperial project by offering a lens through which young boys could imagine themselves becoming soldiers. He constructed and perpetuated a compelling ideal: a fully formed identity beyond the merely military, comprised of an endless thirst for wild adventure; manly qualities of courage, bravery and endurance, rooted in 'muscular Christianity' (in the tradition of Thomas Hughes's *Tom Brown's School Days* (1857) and Charles Kingsley's fiction) and heroic distinction in the service of queen and country. Haggard's 1880s novels reify the alleged virtues of the military in relation to empire and masculinity, depicting male identities that both constitute and are constituted by imperial instincts to control and subdue hostile, feminised African landscapes.[24] Unexpectedly, they also convey an acceptance, and even a celebration, of imperfect masculinities, which make their heroes more comic and more human.

Haggard's adventure fiction functioned as a highly effective example of what Louis Althusser (1970) terms 'Ideological State Apparatus', constructed through schools, the media and sports (as opposed to 'Repressive State Apparatus', including the army and the courts).[25] In this context, fiction aimed at males across different generations can be seen as part of an attempt by the pro-empire establishment to stabilise and reinforce concepts of ideal masculinity in the face of perceived national degeneration and weakness in the wake of revolts in India and Ireland. Accounts of real or fictitious war had to be tempered by moral justifications to gain widespread approval back home. The Zulu War raised questions about whether the 'civilising' project of imperial expansion justified mass bloodshed on both sides. One writer in the *Illustrated London News* demanded to know, 'Can we hammer civilisation into savage minds by sheer force? Have we any proof that such policy has been largely successful?'[26] While Henty's brand of hero-worship was limited to the explicitly military, Haggard's version made broader civilian, domestic and homosocial connections to win hearts and minds. Furthermore, Haggard's readers witness relatively little bloodshed first hand. Silvestra's original map to King Solomon's Mines is written in blood, and Ayesha tells us that 'once in a generation' she 'slay[s] a score by torture' to maintain her rule of 'terror'.[27] Nonetheless, for Haggard's heroes the battle for survival is at least as much against heat and hostile landscapes as against armies of 'savages', broadening the scope of the forms that duty and self-sacrifice might take.

Contemporary pro-empire publications presented colonial expansion as a duty to the nation, to the queen and to God. J. E. C. Welldon (headmaster of Harrow, 1885–98 – the peak of Haggard's writing career) defined the spirit of empire as 'a strong and solemn consciousness that the British Empire had been divinely ordered as an instrument of freedom, justice and righteousness'.[28] This central tenet of British imperial masculinity had been gaining ground over the previous two to three decades. In 1861, a senior official in the Colonial Office had argued that the success of the empire was grounded in an explicitly militaristic 'sense of national honour', resulting from closely knit constituent parts of the collective British (male) consciousness: 'pride of blood, tenacious spirit of self-defence, the sympathies of kindred communities, the instincts of a dominant race' and the 'generous desire to spread our civilisation and our religion over the world'.[29] However, evidence of some detractors in the press reveals a degree of ambivalence across the nation as a whole. In the pro-empire *Fortnightly Review*, William Watson observed an 'erroneous conception of the nature of true gentility' in the 'unseemly' violence of *Allan Quatermain*, and 'sighed' that Haggard's novels were 'the pabulum that is to go to the making of our future Sidneys and Falklands'.[30]

Schools, didactic novels and the promotion of the imperial hero

In 1888, a survey of schoolboys (attending various different kinds of schools) noted that *Robinson Crusoe* (1719) was the title most often listed as their favourite novel.[31] Adventure novels by Haggard and Henty were compared to this text more than any other, with many readers and critics tracing a direct lineage from *Crusoe* to *King Solomon* which centred on the heroic British male subduing exotic lands and their inhabitants. Masculine ideals of stoicism, physical and moral strength, rational thought and pragmatism were major strands of this literary heritage. The narrative lent itself perfectly to the government's demand for healthy, dedicated soldiers to defend and expand the British Empire.[32] In boys' fiction through the late Victorian period (and into the Edwardian era), the most popular role model was undoubtedly the military hero. The courage and intrepid spirit embodied by Haggard's heroes appealed to boys brought up at the height of empire, while their sense of duty and honour appealed to the parents, relatives and teachers who held the lion's share of their purchasing power in the literary marketplace. The benefits of hero-worship to facilitate transitions from boyhood to manhood had been outlined a generation earlier in Carlyle's lectures *On Heroes* (1841) and consolidated in bestselling advice manuals.[33] Haggard shared the Carlylean conception of manliness which demanded mental as well as physical resilience: 'sheer obstinate toughness of muscles; but much more, what we call toughness of heart ... persistence hopeful and even desperate, unsubduable patience ... candid openness, clearness of mind: all this shall be "strength"'.[34] This focus on 'character' above and beyond the muscular body reinforced an ideology of hero-worship which was more accessible than that of his literary rivals, and all the more powerful for moving beyond the sports field and the battlefield.

The system of public schools was in many ways a juvenile replication of military order and played a key role in promoting imperial military masculinities in the form of muscular Christianity.[35] Noting Edmund Burke's famous dictum that 'example is the school of mankind', Salmon argued compellingly in the *Fortnightly Review* that

> To the young, the *dramatis personae* of a story become living entities ... What the hero may do the reader considers himself justified in attempting to do ... [arousing] in the boyish breast a desire to emulate, not less strong than that infused into the heart of a soldier by the daring of his officer.[36]

Salmon suggested that much could be gained by the strategic cultural placement of positive role models. The burgeoning market for manifestly gendered literature, clothing, activities and toys for boys reinforced connections with martial life.[37] From the Boys' Brigade to sailor suits, and wooden swords to adventure stories, military masculinities featured prominently in the late Victorian cultural imagination.[38] In his opening sentence, Salmon assumes that 'among the questions which have agitated the parental mind during the holidays ... doubtless that of the literary influences at work on the minds of the boys has occupied a prominent place'.[39] Parents, teachers, religious groups and other interested members of society expressed considerable anxiety over what Joseph Bristow has referred to as the 'moral prescriptions about the rights and wrongs of books to give to children'.[40]

Educators such as Thomas Arnold and Samuel Smiles had largely eschewed the idea of boys reading fiction purely for pleasure earlier in the nineteenth century, promoting the moral influence of worthy, edifying novels. In 1839, Arnold blamed 'exciting books of amusement like Pickwick and Nickleby, Bentley's Magazine. & c.' for the 'growing fault' of 'childishness' in boys, who were 'totally palled [for] regular work'.[41] By the mid-1880s, the quantity of entertaining magazines and novels for boys had multiplied exponentially, and many of these texts extolled the virtues of martial masculinities. The cult of hero-worship concentrated on a handful of military leaders, but used language stressing the bonds of nationhood to reify vast swathes of ordinary soldiers and civil servants by association. Haggard's main narrators, such as Allan Quatermain and Horace Holly, directly address a young, male readership on numerous occasions. *She* addresses 'my boy' eight times, and 'dear boy' once. Such phrases support Andrea White's claim that adventure fiction 'bore the same relationship to its readers as parents to children'.[42] Haggard's preface to the 1898 edition of *King Solomon's Mines* expresses his hope that the novel 'may in years to come continue to afford amusement to those who are still young enough at heart to love a story of treasure, war, and wild adventure'.[43] The attached note dedicates the story 'to all the big and little boys who read it', highlighting the deliberate inter-generational transfer of British imperial ideology and its concurrent ideals of masculinity.[44]

Quatermain and his companions frequently discuss their plans and strategies in ways that seem to be deliberately clarified for young readers. This tendency, together with a self-consciously educational tone and extensive militaristic parallels, builds a structured framework of implicitly martial hero-worship. Haggard's models of masculinity, too, seem deliberately shaped by a desire to inspire young readers' awe and respect for an earlier generation of military heroes. Quatermain and Good are tempted back from retirement for what they anticipate will be their final adventure, and their most dangerous yet. Haggard's heroes also stand apart from some others in adventure fiction in possessing distinctly loquacious tendencies, reinforcing a sense of their daring prowess by regaling their companions with tales of their glory days. In contrast, Kipling's brand of hero was 'the strong, silent man of action for whom words are deeds, not aesthetic toys'.[45]

The very nature of the African expeditions depicted by Haggard ensures that his audience cannot possibly know for certain whether his plots are based on real events. Though vivid, Haggard's prose is not heavily embroidered, creating the illusion of genuine biographical accounts pieced together from travel journals. First-person narration and the inclusion of prefaces 'in character' reinforce this impression. Quatermain expresses his regrets about not providing more details about local fauna and explicitly military matters. Nonetheless, even his narrative style is framed in terms of weaponry: 'I am more accustomed to handle a rifle than a pen ... [but] "A sharp spear", runs the Kukuana saying, "needs no polish"; and on the same principle I venture to hope that a true story, however strange it may be, does not require to be decked out in fine words.'[46] An imperative for the suspension of disbelief enabled Haggard to appeal to young boys, their elder brothers and their fathers and grandfathers, who would share in domestic storytelling.

Post-truth heroism: fact, fiction and fantasy

King Solomon's Mines (and its most successful sequels), set in southern and eastern Africa, and *She* (and its sequels), set in northern Africa, were published at the height of British colonisation of the continent.[47] Haggard was extraordinarily prolific through these years, and extraordinarily popular. When the serialisation of *She* began in *The Graphic* in October 1886, Haggard still had his novel *Jess* (set in South Africa) running in the *Cornhill*, and *Allan Quatermain* had just finished in *Longman's Magazine*. *King Solomon's Mines* had sold 25,000 copies in 1886 – 'a huge sale at that time'.[48] Military successes, described in indulgent detail to newspaper readers, drove the demand for yet more adventure stories, but fortunately, Haggard's strategy did not rely on perpetual victories on the battlefields of empire. Fiction allowed artistic license to distract readers from the humiliation of the Battle of Isandlwana (January 1879), the death of General Gordon at Khartoum (January 1885, while Haggard was writing *King Solomon's Mines*) and other events which threatened to disrupt the dominant triumphalist narrative of New Imperialism.[49]

Haggard modified his style through the 1880s and 1890s to reframe military disasters as heroic successes. As Neil Hultgren observes, *Jess* (1886) adopts melodrama 'to imagine a British victory in the failed Transvaal War'.[50] Rapid responses, adapting to imperial events, singled Haggard out in the competitive 'survival of the fittest' literary market of the last years of the nineteenth century. Being professionally separated from the realities of army life, he could easily gloss over its less heroic, less glorious, more disturbing or even more mundane elements. His depictions of danger and combat may seem far-fetched, but this was unlikely to trouble a juvenile audience; in fact, the more fantastic elements made the novels more attractive and ensured the longevity of their appeal. Haggard featured prominently on Longman's popular

Empire Readers series in 1905, and epitomised associations between 'manly virtue', 'patriotic ardour' and the 'golden age' of war disseminated by 'the pre-1914 generation of schoolteachers, army officers and Scoutmasters' who held pivotal roles in the Repressive *and* Ideological State Apparatus of the British Empire.[51]

Haggard also capitalised on the excitement caused by recent discoveries of diamonds in southern Africa, and the subsequent competition to annex potentially valuable land in the 'scramble for Africa'. The famous 'Star of Africa' diamond was found in Griequaland West in 1869, and in 1871 many more of the gems were found where the Orange and Vaal Rivers meet, leading to the British annexation of the Transvaal.[52] Wilkie Collins's *The Moonstone* (1868) had popularised the literary plot of the search for a diamond from colonial India, and Haggard's *King Solomon's Mines* combined mystery with heroic adventure, blending military nostalgia with the topical subject matter of real-life treasure hunts.

Haggard's first-person narrator introduces the novel as an authentic account of an expedition around southeastern Africa, from Durban in what was then the British colony of Natal to King Solomon's legendary mines, which he believes are located in the Congo Free State.[53] This and other framing devices found in *King Solomon's Mines* and its sequels position the stories as true accounts, and its characters as examples of the 'living entities' or role models described by Salmon.[54] The inclusion of one or more maps at the beginning or the end was common practice in the journals and letters of Henry Morton Stanley, David Livingstone and other explorers published in this period.[55] Haggard's novel included a map purportedly drawn by José da Silvestra, a Portuguese explorer, on a scrap of linen, using his own blood, as he lay in a cave 'dying of hunger' in 1590.[56] The original (see figure 11.1), is a prized artefact, kept safely at Quatermain's home in Durban, but he carries an English translation and facsimile with him (see figure 11.2). By using specific geographical markers and basing key characters on real explorers, Haggard bridged what would otherwise be an obvious gap between imagined and real places, people and events.

Additional frontmatter such as dedications and prefaces appeared in his later novels, and in later editions of *King Solomon's Mines*, demonstrating that Haggard (or at any rate his publisher, Longman) extended this strategy of presenting fiction as fact. The frontispiece for *Allan Quatermain* (1887) draws on conventions of autobiography by including a sketch of Quatermain (see figure 11.3) turning from his desk as

Figure 11.1 'Map of route to King Solomon's Mines, now in the possession of Allan Quatermain, Esq.' 067307.

though he has just completed the manuscript of this new memoir, with a signature in apparent testament to the authenticity of the document. In *Longman's Magazine*, each instalment promised not only 'further adventures' but also further 'discoveries in company with Sir Henry Curtis, Bart., Commander John Good, R. N., and one Umslopogaas'. The use of rank further rooted the text in contemporary Victorian taxonomies of manliness. On recent maps, 'UNEXPLORED REGION' was printed across the bulk of the continent, stretching from the Sahara to the Kalahari Desert, and accounts claiming to describe 'discoveries' in these places, whether real or imaginary, continued to create considerable excitement.[57]

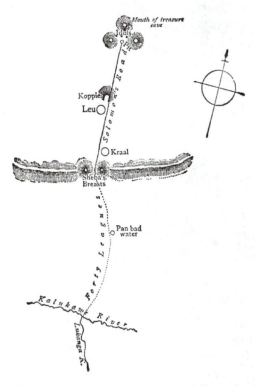

Figure 11.2 'The Way to Kukuanaland (facsimile of the map, if it can be called a map)', *King Solomon's Mines* (London: Cassell and Co., 1885).

The vast differences between the adventures depicted in fiction and the likely realities of a young reader's future career in the colonies do not seem to have produced much comment. Imagination and practicality are intermingled to give an illusion of realism through Haggard's details about domestic innovations, such as hippopotamus fat lamps, appealing to creative boy-scout types.[58] In spite of, or perhaps precisely *because* of, the limits of Haggard's civilian role in colonial administration (to say nothing of his failed attempt at ostrich farming), his early non-fiction romanticised African 'Nature as she was on the morrow of the Creation'.[59] A few years later, however, Haggard's fictional depictions of regions he had never visited were sufficient to convince many reviewers of authenticity. The *Saturday Review* confidently reported that Haggard was not 'one of the hack book-makers for boys who

Figure 11.3 Frontispiece for the first illustrated edition of *Allan Quatermain* (London: Longmans, Green and Co., 1888) by Charles H. M. Kerr. Wood engraving executed by J. Cooper. 067312.

describe adventures they never tasted in lands which they only know from geography books'.[60]

Muscular Christianity

Following the 'racial science' of Knox and others, Christian European 'glorified specimen[s] of humanity' were presented in fiction as hereditarily destined to rule.[61] Sir Henry Curtis is 'about thirty' (about the author's own age), and impressive for his muscular physique: 'one of the biggest-chested and longest-armed men I ever saw ... I never saw a finer looking man'. Being 'of Danish blood', he strikes Quatermain as a fair-haired 'kind of white Zulu'.[62] Similarly, in *She*, Leo Vincey is introduced as a 'very tall, very broad ... statue of Apollo come to life', nicknamed '"the Greek god"'.[63] Both Haggard's description and E. K. Johnson's illustration (see figure 11.4) emphasise Vincey's physical superiority and neat, groomed appearance as intrinsic parts of his identity, in contrast to his guardian, 'Charon', an 'ugly', 'bow-legged' man with dark hair which 'grew right down on his forehead'.[64]

The novelist Charles Kingsley was an important influence on Haggard's depiction of military masculinities. He had used Greek gods

Figure 11.4 'A tall man of about thirty, with the remains of great personal beauty, came hurrying in, staggering beneath the weight of a massive iron box.' Illustration by E. K. Johnson for Part I of *She* in *The Graphic*, vol. 34, no. 879 (2 October 1886).

to promote muscular Christianity some years earlier in *The Heroes* (1856), presenting them as flawed but heroic men who could teach important lessons through 'fairy tales for children'.[65] Like Carlyle, Kingsley identified moral courage as a prerequisite for true heroism, and extended this by attaching it to self-sacrifice for a nationalist agenda which he admired in Greek heroes:

> men who were brave and skilful, and dare do more than other men …
> [but] it came to mean something more … men who helped their coun-
> try … who killed fierce beasts and evil men, and drained swamps, and
> founded towns, and therefore after they were dead, were honoured …
> And we call such a man a hero in English to this day.[66]

Haggard drew on this definition by implying that his imperial heroes, including the naval officer Leo Vincey, not only helped their own coun- try but left 'half-wild' African regions 'better than they found' them.[67] Kingsley's elevation of roles which might include engineering, build- ing and colonial administration to 'heroic' status was especially useful for Haggard, providing a platform for him to extend heroism further beyond strictly martial or muscular masculinities.

The courage of Haggard's protagonists in the face of physical dan- gers sensationalised colonial life in the military (and by association, the civil service) to all back home who had a stake in nation-building. Haggard positions his heroes in *She* and elsewhere as engaged in battles for the triumph of masculine Christian reason over effeminate super- stition in unexplored territories, adding mischievousness to avoid the trap of dry didacticism. The three white heroes in *King Solomon's Mines* undertake their risky mission entirely voluntarily, without being sub- ject to martial orders. They formally agree, first, that the mission is to find Neville (with ivory, diamonds and any other loot merely a wel- come by-product); second, that Neville is almost certainly dead; and third, that they are almost equally certain to die during their journey.[68] At times, their supposed bravery and stoicism barely veneers the dis- tinctly unheroic weaknesses of unreason and greed, and the promised diamonds outshine even the riches described in *Treasure Island* three years earlier.[69] There is also a moral discrepancy between muscular Christianity (based on precepts such as honesty and fair play), and the artifice employed by Quatermain and his comrades to trick the local Kukuana army, implying that Captain Good's false teeth and glass eye were artefacts of witchcraft:

'How is it, O strangers', asked the old man solemnly, 'that this fat man (pointing to Good, who was clad in nothing but a flannel shirt, and had only half finished his shaving), whose body is clothed, and whose legs are bare, who grows hair on one side of his sickly face and not on the other, and who wears one shining and transparent eye … has teeth which move of themselves, coming away from the jaws and returning of their own will?'[70]

Earlier in the century Dickens had remarked that the most effective melodramatic techniques juxtaposed comedy and tragedy, like 'the layers of red and white in a side of streaky, well-cured bacon'.[71] Haggard creates a similarly 'streaky' effect here to keep his readers hooked, with the tension of imminent death quickly relieved by the comedic subject with the broadest appeal: the physical body.

Good's military background connotes a different form of heroism from Quatermain's, who had chosen not to 'serve the Queen', preferring to 'earn [his] bread as a hunter'.[72] Good's pale skin is emphasised in frequent references to the 'snowy loveliness' of his 'beautiful', 'exceedingly white' legs, and Quatermain instantly identifies him as a naval officer by his neat appearance and meticulous toilette, which he is determined to maintain in Kukuanaland.[73] Haggard frames Good's false teeth and glass eye as fortuitous props to establish supernatural myths, rather than medical corrections for practical bodily defects. This reconstitutes disability from injuries sustained in conflict in heroic terms and adds comedic novelty to a man with seventeen years' naval experience.[74] The comforts of domestic martial masculinities are united with the excitement of wild adventure and imperial violence, thus establishing an emotional, familial attachment to the heroes of empire.[75]

Haggard's later novels were less commercially successful. The image of clean-cut, morally virtuous British military heroism was severely damaged by the Second Boer War (1899–1902) in particular, with its lengthy battles, military disasters and mechanised weaponry. Over the last twenty years, historians have explored the ways in which different elements of conflicts including the Second Boer War and the First World War interrogated and reshaped notions of martial masculinity.[76] Most recently, Michael Brown has demonstrated that new technologies of warfare led to revisions of earlier notions of martial heroism grounded in close combat.[77] The sheer scale of loss of life, much of it closer to home, meant that adventure fiction rapidly declined during and after the First World War, in which Haggard's own son died.[78] Between the

Crimean and Boer Wars, however, the genre flourished, building selectively on elements of martial masculinity developed much earlier, following the Napoleonic Wars.

Much as Haggard, other colonial administrators and bored soldiers sought excitement by imagining risky adventures and encounters with unknown tribes, boys in Britain looked to fiction in recompense for the relative mundanity of school and home life.[79] This alignment meant that both Haggard and his readers shared a hunger for excitement that could only be fed by the imagination. For Salmon, it was 'impossible to overrate the importance of the influence of [the supply of adventure fiction] on the national character and culture. Mind, equally with body, will develop according to what it feeds on'.[80] The vastness and complexity of the British imperial network meant that each of Haggard's young readers could envisage a position in which he could excel, even if his school reports revealed an ineptitude for sport or an insurmountable resistance to the discipline required for military life. Martial metaphors of masculine glory were reflected in civil life. The structural layering of storytelling itself in Haggard's narratives even provided boys with models of heroism to emulate when writing their own diaries, memoirs and letters home as adults, propagating the myth of the imperial hero for future generations. Variations on this myth had been in circulation in British fiction and the media for many years by the time *King Solomon's Mines* reached booksellers' shelves, and it was ripe for exploitation in the burgeoning print culture of the 1880s. A tightly bound network of associations between the military, colonial administration, patriotism, muscular Christianity, the man of letters and other nineteenth-century masculinities had been systematically built and reinforced in spite of the decidedly chequered history of British imperial victories and failures during that period.

By including hunters and explorers as well as military men in his groups of adventuring protagonists, Haggard elided national martial and personal civilian endeavours. This blending technique spread the cultural currency of war heroes whilst avoiding the strict codes of self-sacrifice and honour to which an entirely military imperial mission would be held accountable. Some young readers would indeed grow up to join the armed forces, and even be killed in action. As Salmon argued as early as 1886, it seemed 'impossible to overrate' the role of reading adventure fiction in shaping 'national character and culture'.[81] The representation of stoicism, honour and other manly virtues as physically embodied, as established by Carlyle and both developed and interrogated in Haggard's fiction, meant that sporting prowess was only one of many characteristics which boys sought to emulate, and could be set aside by those whose strengths lay elsewhere. However, the most effective element of Haggard's narrative apparatus is his compelling construction of sincerity and virtually simultaneous comedy. By compressing these components at intervals to rapidly swing from tension to relief and back again, Haggard created an addictively giddy sensation which held the reader's attention so as to effectively imbue imperial ideology and plural heroic martial masculinities. Haggard's skilful juxtaposition of danger and comedy made his early novels particularly appealing (and well-concealed) documents of ideological influence. By celebrating a comprehensive range of heroic and less perfect pseudo-military masculinities and holding fast to a core definition of Englishmen as 'adventurers to the backbone', with a 'magnificent muster-roll of colonies to prove it', all the 'little and big boys' who read Haggard's stories could share in the dreams of empire.[82]

Notes

1 Salmon, 'What Boys Read', *Fortnightly Review* 39:45 (February 1886), pp. 248–59.

2 'King Solomon's Mines', *Saturday Review* (10 October 1885), p. 485.

3 Boyd, *Manliness and the Boys' Story Paper in Britain*, p. 13.

4 This magazine was established by the Religious Tract Society in London 1879 to instil Christian moral values its young readers' formative years.

5 See, for example, C. M. Archibald, 'A Soldier's Story: The Battle of Bithoor', *Boy's Own Paper*, no. 411 (27 November 1886), pp. 134–5.

6 On the 'pleasure culture of war' see Paris, *Warrior Nation*, pp. 13–48.

7 James Morris, *Farewell the Trumpets: An Imperial Retreat* (London: Faber and Faber, 1978), p. 28.

8 Joseph Bristow places the total sales of Henty's books at around 25 million. *Empire Boys: Adventures in a Man's World* (London: Routledge, 1991), pp. 146–7. 'Mr G. A. Henty', *The Times* (17 November 1902), p. 10.

9 See G. A. Henty, *By Sheer Pluck: A Tale of the Ashanti War* (Auckland: The Floating Press, 2014), p. 101; Dennis Butts, 'Exploiting a Formula: The Adventure Stories of G. A. Henty (1832–1902)', in Julia Briggs, Dennis Butts, and M. O. Grenby (eds), *Popular Children's Literature in Britain*, (Aldershot: Ashgate, 2008), p. 160; *The Athenaeum*, no. 2970 (27 September 1884), p. 388.

10 D. S. Higgins, *Rider Haggard: A Biography* (New York: Stein and Day, 1983), p. 85. Also see Kestner, *Masculinities in British Adventure Fiction, 1880–1915*, p. 66; Wendy R. Katz, *Rider Haggard and the Fiction of Empire* (Cambridge: Cambridge University Press, 1987).

11   Stephen Gray, *South African Literature: An Introduction* (Cape Town: David Philip, 1979), p. 120.

12   *Ibid.*

13   *Ibid.*

14   Sequels and prequels include *Allan Quatermain* (1887), *Hunter Quatermain's Story* (1887), *Allan the Hunter: A Tale of Three Lions* (1887), *Allan's Wife* (1889), *She and Allan* (1920), *The Ancient Allan* (1920) (he must have been ancient indeed by this point, having retired in 1885) and *Allan and the Ice-gods* (1927). See *She* (Peterborough, Ontario: Broadview Press, 2006), p. 242.

15   Katz, *Rider Haggard*, p. 33.

16   Conveniently, as 'the wisest and richest of Biblical rulers, Solomon would have provided the strongest moral sanction for … mineral extraction on the dark continent.' Monsmon, 'Of Diamonds and Deities: Social Anthropology in H. Rider Haggard's *King Solomon's Mines*', *English Literature in Transition, 1880–1920* 43:3 (2000), p. 280.

17   See Haggard's correspondence, MC 33 and MC 34, Norfolk Record Office.

18   'Dedication', *King Solomon's Mines* (London: Penguin, 2007), p. 3.

19   'There is no woman in it – except Foulata. Stop, though! There is Gagaoola, if she was a woman and not a fiend. But she was a hundred at least, and therefore not marriageable, so I don't count her.' *King Solomon's Mines*, p. 10.

20   See John Kucich, *Imperial Masochism: British Fiction, Fantasy, and Social Class* (Princeton, NJ: Princeton University Press, 2007).

21   See W. T. Stead's 'Too Late!', *Pall Mall Gazette Extra* (19 February 1885), which sold 50,000 copies. On Gordon as martyr, see Michael Anton Budd, 'C. G. Gordon: Hybrid Heroic Technologist and Anti-modern Other' in Heather Ellis and Jessica Meyer (eds), *Masculinity and the Other: Historical Perspectives*, (Newcastle: Cambridge Scholars, 2009), pp. 200–3; Anti-Gladstone items available on the market included bookmarks and scraps for children's albums.

22   Quoted in Andrew Griffiths, *New Journalism, The New Imperialism and the Fiction of Empire, 1870–1900* (Basingstoke: Palgrave, 2015), p. 1.

23   James William Gibson, *American Paramilitary Culture and the Reconstitution of the Vietnam War*, in Francesca M. Cancian and James William Gibson (eds), *Making War Making Peace: The Social Foundations of Violent Conflict* (Belmont, CA: Wadsworth, 1990), p. 96.

24   See Lindy Stiebel, *Imagining Africa: Landscape in H. Rider Haggard's African Romances* (Westport, CT and London: Greenwood Press, 2001); Helen Goodman, 'Masculinity, Tourism and Adventure in English Nineteenth-Century Travel Fiction', in Thomas Thurnell-Read and Mark Casey (eds), *Men, Masculinities, Travel and Tourism* (Basingstoke: Palgrave, 2014), pp. 13–27.

25 Louis Althusser, 'Ideology and Ideological State Apparatus', in *On Ideology* (London: Verso Books, 2008), pp. 8–9, 17.

26 'The Zulu War', *Illustrated London News*, no. 6702 (15 March 1879).

27 *She* (Oxford: Oxford University Press, 1991), p. 175. The phrase 'of the imagination' in the first edition (on which the OUP is based) replaced 'a moral one', which had appeared in *The Graphic*, on which the Broadview is based.

28 Norman Vance, *Sinews of the Spirit: The Ideal of Christian Manliness in Victorian Literature and Religious Thought* (Cambridge: Cambridge University Press, 1985), pp. 196–7.

29 Herman Merivale, *Lectures on Colonisation and Colonies* (London: n. p., 1861), p. 675.

30 William Watson, 'The Fall of Fiction', *Fortnightly Review* 50 (September 1888), p. 325.

31 A. J. Jenkinson, *What Do Boys and Girls Read?* (London: Methuen and Co., 1940), pp. 36–9, cited in the Jeffrey Richards, *Imperialism and Juvenile Literature*, p. 8. Also see Walton, *Imagining Soldiers and Fathers in the Mid-Victorian Era*, p. 51.

32 See Max Nordau, *Degeneration* (New York: D. Appleton and Co., 1895); Arnold White, *Efficiency and Empire* (London: Methuen, 1901); and Daniel Pick, *Faces of Degeneration: A European Disorder, c. 1848–1918* (Cambridge: Cambridge University Press, 1993). *Queen Sheba's Ring* (1910) reveals Haggard's increasing anxiety about national degeneration. For Paris, the novel is a 'warning bell' about 'the consequences of the loss of the warlike spirit and military unpreparedness … so obviously a portrait of Britain and Germany that even the youngest schoolboy could not fail to learn the lesson'. *Warrior Nation*, pp. 102–3.

33 Carlyle's *On Heroes, Hero-Worship, and the Heroic in History* (London: Chapman and Hall, 1841). Also see Samuel Smiles's *Self-Help* (self-published in 1859 and the second bestseller in Britain that century); Arthur King, *Our Sons* (London: Frederick Warne and Co., 1880).

34 Carlyle, *Past and Present* (London: Ward, Lock and Co., 1910), p. 220.

35 See Geoffrey Best, 'Militarism and the Victorian Public School', in B. Simon and I. Bradley (eds), *The Victorian Public School* (London: Macmillan, 1975), pp. 129–46; J. A. Mangan and Regina Gagnier, *Subjectivities: A History of Self-Representation in Britain, 1832–1920* (Oxford: Oxford University Press, 1991), p. 178.

36 Edmund Burke, 'Letters on a Regicide Peace', in *The Works of the Right Honourable Edmund Burke* (London: F. and C. Rivington, 1801), vol. 8, p. 123.

37 Quatermain remains a popular commodity to this day, incarnate in television and film (played by Sean Connery (2003), Patrick Swayze (2004) and others), computer games, fan fiction and an action-figure doll.

38 Pre-dating the scouting movement, the Boys' Brigade was established in 1883 for 'the promotion of habits of Reverence, Discipline, Self-Respect and all that tends towards a true Christian manliness' ('Obedience' was added in 1893). Also see Paris, *Warrior Nation*, and Olsen, *Juvenile Nation*.

39 Salmon, 'What Boys Read', p. 248.

40 Bristow, *Empire Boys*, p. 14. Also see Jenny Holt, *Public School Literature, Civic Education and the Politics of Male Adolescence* (Abingdon: Routledge, 2016).

41 Arnold, letter to Rev. G. Cornish (6 July 1839) (ed. Arthur Penrhyn Stanley), *The Life and Correspondence of Thomas Arnold*, (London: B. Fellowes, 1845) vol. 2, pp. 161–2. Also see Fabrice Neddam, 'Constructing Masculinities under Thomas Arnold of Rugby', *Gender and Education* 16:3 (2004), pp. 303–26.

42 Andrea White, *Joseph Conrad and the Adventure Tradition* (Cambridge: Cambridge University Press, 1993), p. 56.

43 Haggard, 'Author's Note', *King Solomon's Mines*, p. vii.

44 'Dedication', *King Solomon's Mines*, p. v.

45 David H. Stewart, 'Kipling's Portrait of the Artists', *English Literature in Translation, 1880–1920* 31:3 (1988), p. 275.

46 'Preface', *King Solomon's Mines*, p. xi.

47 'Britain took over Zanzibar in 1888, the East African Protectorate (now Kenya) in 1885, Egypt in 1882 and the Soudan the same year.' Bristow, *Empire Boys*, p. 128.

48 Tom Pocock, *Rider Haggard and the Lost Empire* (London: Wiesenfeld and Nicolson, 1993), p. 68.

49 A total of 1,300 British soldiers were killed in this first major battle of the Anglo-Zulu War, despite superior modern weaponry. Gordon underestimated the Ansar as 'some 500 determined men and some 2000 rag-tag Arabs'. See James Perry, *Arrogant Armies: Great Military Disasters and the Generals Behind Them* (2005), p. 180; *The Times* (21 April 1884), p. 5.

50 Neil Hultgren, *Melodramatic Imperial Writing: From the Sepoy Rebellion to Cecil Rhodes* (Athens: Ohio University Press, 2014), p. 85. Also see R. W. Connell, *Masculinities* (Cambridge: Polity Press, 2005), p. 213.

51 Zara S. Steiner, *Britain and the Origins of the First World War* (London: Macmillan, 1977), p. 157; John O. Springhall, '"Up Guards and at Them!" British Imperialism and Popular Art, 1880–1914' in John M. MacKenzie (ed.), *Imperialism and Popular Culture*, (Manchester: Manchester University Press, 1986), p. 50; Caroline Davis, 'Creating a Book Empire: Longmans in Africa' in Davis and David Johnson (eds), *The Book in Africa*, (Basingstoke: Palgrave, 2015), pp. 128–52.

52 Now a region of central South Africa. Anthony Nutting, *The Scramble for Africa: The Great Trek to the Boer War* (Trowbridge and London: Redwood Press, 1972), p. 80. On subsequent searches and diamond mines

in the Transvaal, see 'Where the Famous Cullinan Diamond Was Found', *Wonders of the World* (London: Hutchinson and Co., 1910), pp. 110–12.

53   The region came under the rule of King Leopold II of Belgium at the Berlin Conference, November 1884–February 1885.

54   Salmon, 'What Boys Read', pp. 248–9.

55   Henry Morton Stanley, *How I Found Livingstone: Travels, Adventures and Discoveries in Central Africa* (New York: Scribner, Armstrong and Co., 1872); J. P. R. Wallis (ed.), *The Zambezi Expedition of David Livingstone, 1858–1863* (London: Chatto and Windus, 1956).

56   *King Solomon's Mines*, p. 25.

57   Francis Galton, *Narratives of an Explorer in Tropical South Africa* (London: John Murray, 1853), p. 5.

58   *King Solomon's Mines*, p. 125. Such tips resonated with earlier field guides about Africa, such as Francis Galton's *Art of Travel* (London: John Murray, 1855).

59   Haggard, 'A Zulu War Dance', *Gentleman's Magazine* no. 241 (July 1877), p. 99; Lilias Haggard, *The Cloak That I Left: A Biography of the Author Henry Rider Haggard* (London: Hodder and Stoughton, 1951), p. 32; Brantlinger, *Rule of Darkness*, pp. 137–8.

60   Anon., 'King Solomon's Mines', *Saturday Review* (10 October 1885), p. 485.

61   *She*, p. 35.

62   *King Solomon's Mines*, p. 12. Also see Streets, *Martial Races*.

63   *She*, p. 35.

64   Charon, the elderly, blind ferryman who rows dead souls across the Styx in Greek mythology, represents death and decay in contrast to Vincey's vitality and vigour. *She*, pp. 35–6. On the contexts of the 'martial moustache' see Christopher Oldstone-Moore, 'The Beard Movement in Britain', *Victorian Studies* 48:1 (Autumn 2005), pp. 7–34.

65   On the assimilation of neoclassical idealised male bodies in the ideal Victorian 'clean-cut Englishman' and 'national character', see George L. Mosse, *The Image of Man: The Creation of Modern Masculinity* (Oxford: Oxford University Press, 1996), p. 109.

66   Kingsley, *The Heroes; or Greek Fairy Tales for My Children* (London: A. C. and Black, 1915), pp. 4–5. Also see *The Heroes with the Story of the Twelve Labours of Hercules* (London: J. M. Dent and Sons, 1906) and *Hypatia; or New Foes with an Old Face* (London: Macmillan, 1894).

67   *Ibid.*, p. 5.

68   *King Solomon's Mines*, p. 33.

69   Lilias Haggard, pp. 121–2. Haggard's novel allegedly resulted from a wager with his older brother, who 'bet a bob' he could not write a novel half as good as Stevenson's. Robert Fraser, *Victorian Quest Romance* (Plymouth: Northcote House, 1998), p. 28.

70   *King Solomon's Mines*, pp. 102–3.
71   Dickens, *Oliver Twist* (London: Penguin, 2003), p. 134.
72   *King Solomon's Mines*, p. 13.
73   *Ibid.*, pp. 12, 97.
74   *Ibid.*, p. 13.
75   Stephanie Olsen analyses informal education and imperial domestic manliness to extend the concept of the British Empire as a 'family' in *Juvenile Nation: Youth, Emotions and the Making of the Modern British Citizen, 1880–1914* (London: Bloomsbury, 2014). On earlier domestic military masculinities see Furneaux, *Military Men of Feeling*.
76   See, for example, Bourke, *Dismembering the Male* and *Wounding the World: How Military Violence and War-Play Invade our Lives* (London: Virago, 2014), pp. 109–11; Meyer, *Men of War*; Roper, *The Secret Battle*.
77   Brown, 'Cold Steel, Weak Flesh', pp. 155–81. Also see John Ellis, *The Social History of the Machine Gun* (Baltimore, MD: Johns Hopkins University Press, 1975); Pick, *War Machine*.
78   Gray, *South African Literature*, p. 124.
79   See Jeffrey A. Auerbach, *Imperial Boredom: Monotony and the British Empire* (Oxford: Oxford University Press, 2018).
80   Salmon, 'What Boys Read', p. 248.
81   *Ibid.*, p. 248.
82   *Allan Quatermain* (London: Penguin, 1995), pp. 93–4.

Epilogue: Gendered virtue, gendered vigour and gendered valour

Isaac Land

Elly McCausland proposes that knighthood – and perhaps by extension, military masculinity more generally – was 'a fragile set of attributes that cannot be secured, but must be constantly tested and re-validated'. What were these recurrent attributes and themes, judging by the chapters in this edited volume? Susan Walton's chapter neatly showcases a set of strictures: cultivate 'coolness of head in the very heat of action'; trust your leader, but also remain capable of initiative on your own; avoid paralysis or stagnation, look for a path forward instead; temper accomplishment with modesty; temper power with kindness and magnanimity; remember that any character trait, carried to excess, can become a fault. For example, as Karen Turner notes in her discussion of military virtues as applied to courtship, even the most aggressive intentions of conquest must be tempered with patience and pragmatic restraint, or the plans might backfire. Helen Goodman refers to the 'inter-generational transfer of masculine ideals', but reading these worthy platitudes, it is less clear what was truly gendered or gender-specific about these putatively 'manly' qualities.

If the definitive attributes of manly conduct (balance, courage, maturity, self-discipline) have close affinities with those promulgated in the ancient texts sometimes referred to as 'wisdom literature' (such as the Bible's Book of Proverbs), or indeed with the sort of slogans that we see today on inspirational posters, this should give us pause. A major challenge for scholars will be to isolate the component of the wisdom literature that is *about* masculinity and not just about wisdom. Some cultures, admittedly, have worked hard to confound the two; readers of Machiavelli learn to distinguish when are we speaking of *virtù*, when of virtue and when just of *vir-*, but it is hard not to sense the resonances and overlap among all of these in his usage.

Epilogue

The colloquial term 'adulting' (conducting oneself as an adult; living up to the adult role) has become familiar in the last ten years. Adulting, as we like to say, is hard. There is some evidence in this volume that the parables and practical advice about 'manhood' fulfilled a function similar to our discourse of adulting. The contrast to 'man' in these pages is more often 'boy' than 'woman'. It is more common to see the (unwise, irresponsible, impulsive) youth contrasted with (wiser, duty-bound, reflective) maturity here, than to see unmanly qualities disparaged as womanish. Masculinity as 'adulting' would be an ideal adhered to throughout life, but one whose meaning was meant to change and mature over time. The impetuous youth might pine for the day when he could 'draw forth the sword of success from out of the iron of circumstance' only to discover that the closest thing to tournaments were sports matches, and his quest might be a job in a charitable organisation. However, the different stages of life each held their own teachable moments and characteristic virtues. Boyhood and manhood were validated in their own way, although the transition to manhood remained a paramount concern. For example, the older man's restraint and capacity for strategic thinking had its place, but so did the boy's spirit of adventure.

Do these codes of conduct appear on the verge of collapsing from their own contradictions? This is a statement that could be made about almost any compilation of wisdom literature. It is not necessarily a sign of fragility or incoherence, however. The focus in wisdom literature tends to be on how to honourably navigate the contradictions, or find the strength to persevere when the codes do not match up to situations that arise in real life. A persistent theme is the search for balance and appropriateness, a recognition that different situations can, and should, call forth different registers of behaviour. In her chapter, Louise Carter deftly explores the paradoxes of military life which required – at times – that a man behave as if he 'knows no country but the camp' and – at other times – that he validate his manhood by fulfilling his duties as a head-of-household. The expectation that fathers and husbands *should* remain in communication with their family members even found expression in legislation: the Postage Act of 1795 lowered the rates for those serving in the armed forces.

A different way to approach balance – as noted by Helen Metcalfe – would be to embrace the idea of multiple military masculinities, rather than demanding that a single individual unite all the necessary qualities. Perhaps the concept of multiple, equally valid, military masculinities is another example of the way that discussions about manhood were interwoven with teachable moments intended to encourage boys and youths (perhaps accustomed to looking for the 'hero') to think about the world in increasingly mature, pragmatic or at least nuanced ways. Readers of Homer encountered sulking Achilles, proud Agamemnon and crafty Odysseus, all quite impressive and successful examples of Greek military masculinity but rarely, if ever, impressive in the same way. In our own era we have had bestselling self-help books with titles like *Leadership Secrets of Attila the Hun*, but also one entitled *Make It So: Leadership Secrets from Star Trek: The Next Generation*. (They happen to be by the same author.) If military masculinity is primarily defined as *being the person who gets the job done*, then we should expect as many variations of military masculinity as there are jobs that need doing, or roles that need inhabiting. Holding up different kinds of role models suggested that part of manhood, at least for the mature man, was knowing what part to play at the appropriate juncture, or perhaps even knowing when to defer to others who had the gifts called for at this particular moment.

We are left with the impression that manhood was aspirational, even for men. Would the individual rise to the occasion and do what was required? If *men* did not know if they would be equal to the demands of military masculinity until they were actually on the spot and faced the challenge, then a woman who really 'walked the walk' might have a credible claim to the masculine virtues, and whatever laurels or accolades might accompany them. If Charlotte Yonge saw the study of military virtue as preparing girls for the 'battlefield of life', surely this was the implied point. It is worth reflecting that many of Yonge's favourite virtues are the sort of thing that we routinely see today on motivational posters illustrated not with any particular sort of human being (old or young, male or female), but rather with soaring eagles, tenacious trees clinging to cliff faces or bright flowers blooming in defiance of towering rainclouds.

Yet, as we have also seen, in the long nineteenth century there was a pervasive cultural pattern of identifying a long list of virtues – courage, self-discipline, duty, 'resilience, resourcefulness and fortitude', preparedness and initiative in meeting the unexpected and hazardous – as masculine, in an explicitly proscriptive or gender-restrictive way.[1] Remarkably, self-sacrifice, including a willingness to risk or lay down one's own life for others, figures as a specifically masculine attribute, most vividly in Lorenzo Servitje's chapter ('do and die') but in several others as well.[2] Perhaps certain forms of sacrifice, such as the loss of a limb, were more likely for men, and the occasional cases where much ado was made about a battlefield amputation (as in the case of Lord Uxbridge's leg, discussed by Julia Banister) may speak to this in an oblique way. Nevertheless, it is worth considering what was at stake here in terms of gendered power. Practical, everyday examples abounded of ways that women could, and did, display every one of these virtues without assuming a male role or doing 'men's work'. Carolyn D. Williams has made the significant point that the woman who rushed into a burning cottage to save her infant did not receive the same accolades as the man who performed an act of valour in a war.[3] Even when women found themselves in war zones, there was a double standard. In the Royal Navy, the wives of warrant officers (such as carpenters and gunners) sailed with the ship. Such women sometimes worked as powder monkeys, helping to service the cannon in battle. The presumption remained that these women were not really combatants. The (male) baby born during the battle of the Glorious First of June, 1794, eventually received a medal for his presence at that great naval victory; the woman who birthed him did not.[4]

Perhaps the ultimate test of how stoutly defended these (putatively) gender-specific virtues and accomplishments were, is to consider what happened when women assumed male garb, 'passed' for long periods and successfully mastered the full spectrum of tasks on a ship or a battlefield. In light of the extensive discussion in this volume of military masculinity's aspirational potential, the experiences of these women deserve a closer look.[5] Relying mostly on short notices in newspapers, Anna Clark found thirty-eight instances of 'women who tried to enlist or actually served as sailors and soldiers' for the period 1780–1845 in Britain; Fraser Easton, looking at a longer period (1660–1832), identified more than sixty cases.[6]

One self-published autobiographical account is noteworthy for its lack of sensationalism and its attentiveness to the inner life and anxieties of the cross-dresser. Mary Lacy assumed the name of William Chandler and became the servant to Richard Baker, the carpenter on board the HMS *Sandwich*, a ninety-gun ship of the line with a complement of 750 men.[7] Suzanne Stark has shown that there is archival evidence to support Lacy's claims of service on this ship in the Seven Years War.[8] Lacy was recognised by Henry Hambrook, a young man from her village, but he chose to remain silent. She continued to worry about exposure; every illness, injury or wet shirt was an occasion for concern.[9]

She would eventually publish *The History of the Female Shipwright*, a lengthy account of her life as a man, on board ship and later in the Royal Dockyards.[10] Yet her autobiography – by its very existence, a form of evidence that cross-dressing was neither unthinkable nor unmentionable – has a surprising amount to say about the persistent, gnawing anxiety and 'dreadful apprehensions' that her cross-dressing brought with it.[11]

How representative was Mary Lacy's experience, and her deep concerns about what fate awaited her if she were discovered? Rudolf Dekker and Lotte van de Pol's widely cited 1989 book *The Tradition of Female Transvestism in Early Modern Europe*, despite its title, was in fact quite cautious on the issue of acceptance. While they noted that 'toleration ... tends to leave fewer traces in the archives than its opposite',[12] they also warned: 'We should not underestimate the pressure that these women in men's clothing permanently experienced,' adding that 'Rejection was the most common reaction [upon discovery].'[13] Dekker and van de Pol stated that the tradition remained 'underground' and never became 'an accepted social practice which women could choose openly'.[14] They also provided an admirably nuanced discussion of the diverse reactions encountered by Dutch women who were ultimately caught. 'Aal the Dragoon' ended up after her death as a stuffed specimen in an anatomical museum, while Trijntje Simons received a hero's burial in the town square.[15] It was hard to predict the reaction, although one constant theme was that discovery meant an end to the masquerade.

More recent scholars have offered a less nuanced verdict, maintaining that gender was understood as the equivalent of a sociological category; cross-dressing women were engaged in 'social climbing'.[16] In a 2004 publication, Alfred Young (citing Dekker and van de Pol as evidence of a 'tradition') stated flatly that a cross-dressed female soldier 'would not have raised many eyebrows' in the era of the American Revolution.[17] Another form of evidence that might seem to confirm the idea of a 'tradition' of cross-dressing would be the ballads heaping praise on *fictional* heroines.[18] These are an intriguing cultural record, but they are not necessarily the best guide to how someone might feel about meeting a real cross-dresser in the flesh.

In Britain, we know that some cross-dressers received severe punishments, while others were praised. In an important article, Fraser Easton has proposed a reconciliation of the evidence, arguing that most cross-dressers assumed only the vigour of the male 'sexed body', but did not make inroads on the virility of the male 'sexual body'.[19] For plebeian women, passing as a man was understood by magistrates as a pragmatic path to superior wages; such women were overachievers rather than failures, having demonstrated 'worthy industry'.[20] Easton stated that cross-dressed women 'routinely worked' in a range of traditionally male occupations (although he does not explain why *routine* behaviour merited inclusion in the newspapers, where he found so many published notices of it).[21] Prosecutors 'carefully distinguished' such women from 'female husbands', who were thought to have sexually penetrated another woman's body. Such women were often accused of fraud or theft.[22] Ann Marrow – convicted of crimes connected to her behaviour as a 'female husband' – was pelted by a frenzied crowd while she stood helpless in the pillory. She lost the sight in both of her eyes.[23]

In the context of military masculinity, I would suggest that in addition to Easton's 'vigour' and 'virility', we need to add a third category: valour. When Mary Anne Talbot boasted how fire from her ship scattered the French sailors 'like mice upon the ocean', or when she claimed to have performed difficult feats of seamanship that were beyond the competency of anyone else on board, she was laying claim to something beyond vigour.[24] It is important to recognise that doing even a day's work as a man – particularly in certain occupations – could carry tremendous weight in the arena of sexual politics. In the 1830s, Anne Jane Thornton found herself first blackmailed by a shipmate, then threatened by the captain and finally 'grossly insulted' by the entire crew with 'gibes, jeers, and curses' and the immediate prospect of serial rape. At sea, there was nowhere for her to go. She fended them off, barely, 'by calling God to witness that she would prosecute every man in the ship'. On arrival in port, the captain insulted her in another way by pocketing her wages. His argument was that 'he had agreed to pay a man and not a woman'.[25]

It was simply not possible to enact female courage in a military context (such as the Royal Navy) without making some form of commentary on the disproportionate value that society placed on male courage. To defend male prerogatives, masculine women were portrayed as 'wonders' or marvels, reinforcing the idea that women, generically, could not compete with men. It is worth remembering that throughout the early modern period and into the long nineteenth century, male exclusivity somehow found a way to persist in many types of labour despite the occasional border raids carried out by intrepid cross-dressers.

The disparagement of the successful cross-dresser could take relatively subtle forms, such as representing each individual case as unique

Epilogue

(which virtually every newspaper account and published first-person narrative did). It could also take an aggressive and direct approach, as when published accounts of female sailors were surrounded with exotic or disgusting medical anecdotes. Accounts of passing women appeared regularly in newspapers and periodicals, alongside the hailstorms mixed with frogs and the two-headed calves. The fact that the publishers continued to consider such women as newsworthy may say more about the morbid entertainment value of this topic than about the degree to which the press, and its readership, accepted cross-dressing as part of an ongoing tradition.

Today, readers of Mary Anne Talbot's autobiography are likely to read it by itself, or alongside other accounts of cross-dressing, but its original place of publication in *Kirby's Wonderful and Eccentric Museum* tells a different story.[26] The female sailor appears a few pages after readers learned of an 'enormous wen' or tumour. This monstrous growth evoked such anatomical interest that it prompted a bidding war between two medical faculties in Vienna while its owner lay on his deathbed. Immediately following Talbot's narrative we find 'A Violent Asthma Cured by a Musket Ball' and an account of a freakish accident, 'A Shepherd's Boy Hanged by his Whip'.[27] Such placement militated against serious reflection on the larger meaning of Talbot's story.

Why did Mary Anne Talbot merit inclusion in such a compilation? It seems that cross-dressers remained something of a wonder. I am reminded here of Nerea Aresti's interpretation of the contemporary praise for an earlier figure, the conquistador Catalina de Erauso, as a positive reception that was underpinned by a misogynist discourse:

> the Lieutenant Nun was judged according to a single code of values that were widely thought to be positive and typically masculine: courage, strength, loyalty and continence ... In a society that was strongly misogynist, but only partially organized along lines of sexual difference, Erauso was universally treated not as a representative of her sex but as an exception to it. And as such, she was granted the privilege of masculinity.[28]

In later periods as well, gender-bending episodes were rarely adduced as evidence for a systematic reappraisal of the prevailing gender regime; instead, they were recorded as 'discovery' stories in which 'the dissolution of disguise is as important as the disguise itself'. It was necessary to conclude with a report stating, in effect, that 'the woman's body is finally relocated in its cultural place'.[29]

It does seem, then, that despite the fondness for platitudes and generic, abstract statements about virtues (courage, calm, resolution), there is a need to reflect further on to what extent military masculinity was constituted by gendered power and, indeed, misogyny. It is interesting to read Anna Maria Barry's chapter in this context. The singer Charles Incledon found himself much in demand for sailor roles on stage, in large part because promoters (and audiences) placed a high value on hearing from the genuine article, instead of a singer who merely put on a sailor's outfit. Ironically, although even Incledon's critics did not question the veracity of his naval service, his later career as an opera singer, coupled with his fashion choices (the lace, the seven gold rings on his fingers) left him vulnerable to charges of effeminacy. The insistence that even someone with a proven service record must come clad head to toe in indisputably masculine accoutrements to be received as wholly authentic is another example of the ways that the borders of gendered virtue and gendered valour were patrolled with attentive zeal, and even a touch of vindictiveness. Barring the way for effeminate men who sought to claim the virtues associated with military masculinity may have been acceptable, to some, as part of the project of excluding women altogether.

Did decrepitude or disability also render the male body effeminate? Here, the verdict was more uncertain. If the masculine military body was celebrated as the body that got things done and performed what was expected of it in the hour of need, then elderly veterans donning their old uniforms and re-enacting a mock battle scene could evoke ambivalent emotions. Joanne Begiato and Michael Brown offer a careful reading of the way that the spectacle of the aged veteran might register, variously, on a scale all the way from the pathos of dependency to the admiring reaction to 'a fine piece of weather-beaten anatomy' which might even merit an adjective such as virile. The contrast with Mary Anne Talbot's appearance alongside accounts of anatomical aberrations and uncanny freaks of nature is significant here. Although these bodies were, by and large, past the point where they might render useful service on a battlefield, the marks of age or the scars of battle were often interpreted not in terms of disability but as testaments of sacrifice, or proofs of an obligation honourably fulfilled. Thus, a 'marked proliferation of veterans in visual and literary culture' might well arise from an anxiety about lost martial virtues and a perceived need for appropriate role models for the younger generation, who might be called on to imitate these examples themselves. In some quarters, the aged veteran was represented as the distilled quintessence of military masculine values.

Of course, some individual veterans rebelled against this, seeking instead to use their role as teachers to the younger generation to undermine facile notions of battlefield glamour.[30] Even literary accounts, which could avail themselves of fantasies and attractive embellishments at will, sometimes struck quite sombre notes, perhaps influenced by encounters with actual veterans. Begiato and Brown draw attention to a story in which a veteran relates the notably unheroic experience of being trampled by a French horse while he lay helpless on the ground, and goes on to remind a listening audience of children about the 'misery that war brings to peoples'. As Barbara Leonardi shows in her chapter, even in the afterglow of Waterloo, James Hogg could resist the widespread notion that warfare was chivalrous, emphasising instead its waste and folly and likening it to cannibalism.

It is probably unfair to expect that a volume on military masculinity should delve extensively into *anti*-military sentiment or outright pacifism. It remains desirable to balance examples of those who held up military virtues as representing human nature at its best – the aspirational reference point for women as well as for men, the best source of role models for children – with an awareness that others found this very attitude disheartening. The words 'militarism' and 'militarist' – both pejorative – entered the English language in the period covered by this volume.[31] Teasing out which elements of anti-military sentiment were merely irreverent, and which represented deeply held convictions, poses a challenge for scholars akin to the difficulty of distinguishing between actual unbelief and rejection of church teachings, and the anti-clerical jokes that circulated widely in early modern Europe. Henry Angelo characterised the colourful uniforms of the Duke of Cumberland's Sharpshooters as 'picturesque', a word with mixed associations in this period, but when he adds that this uniform made Charles Incledon appear 'green as a cabbage', the ridicule becomes clear. Military parades, ideally, permitted a flawless display of discipline, unity and professional skill. Angelo's account, in contrast, features Incledon's staggering, breathless progress across Hampstead Heath, tripping over his own sword and asking the spectators for help in carrying his heavy firearm. The Sharpshooters were a volunteer regiment raised in haste in response to an invasion scare, so perhaps the derision here is aimed at civilians who imagine that they can play at being real soldiers. Incledon's youthful service in the Royal Navy was well behind him at this point in his life. The impression remains, nevertheless, of a military procession greeted not with respect and admiration – but with laughter.

Epilogue

Notes

1   It was women who raised and acculturated the warriors in their earliest youth, a paradox dating back to Rousseau if not earlier.

2   The purest form of military masculinity may be losing yourself in the regiment, which does not sit well with the more individualistic, not to say anarchic, conceptions of masculine identity.

3   Carolyn D. Williams, 'Women Behaving Well: Early Modern Examples of Female Courage', in Chris Mounsey (ed.), *Presenting Gender: Changing Sex in Early-Modern Culture* (London: Associated University Presses, 2001), quoted p. 72.

4   Suzanne J. Stark, *Female Tars: Women aboard Ship in the Age of Sail* (Annapolis, MD: Naval Institute Press, 1996), p. 81.

5   Georgina Lock and David Worrall, 'Cross-Dressed Performance at the Theatrical Margins: Hannah Snell, the Manual Exercise, and the New Wells Spa Theater, 1750', *Huntington Library Quarterly* 77:1 (Spring 2014), pp. 17–36; there is also a very pertinent forthcoming publication: Ellen Malenas Ledoux, 'The Queer Contact Zone: Empire and Military Masculinity in the Memoirs of Hannah Snell and Mary Anne Talbot, 1750–1810', *The Eighteenth Century: Theory and Interpretation* 60:3 (2019). Available at: https://doi.org/doi:10.7282/T3D79F8M (accessed 20 July 2018).

6   Anna Kirsten Clark, 'Womanhood and Manhood in the Transition from Plebeian to Working-Class Culture: London, 1780–1845' (PhD Dissertation, Rutgers, The State University of New Jersey, 1987), p. 205, and see the larger discussion on pp. 196–219; Fraser Easton, 'Gender's Two Bodies: Women Warriors, Female Husbands and Plebeian Life', *Past and Present* 180 (August 2003), pp. 131–74, specifically pp. 142–3. See also Fraser Easton, 'Covering Sexual Disguise: Passing Women and Generic Constraint', in Jeffrey S. Ravel and Linda Zionkowski (ed.), *Studies in Eighteenth-Century Culture* (Baltimore, MD: Johns Hopkins University Press, 2006), vol. 35, pp. 95–125.

7   Mary Lacy (ed. Margarette Lincoln), *The History of the Female Shipwright* (London: National Maritime Museum, 2008).

8   Stark, *Female Tars*, pp. 194–5, notes 7 and 8.

9   Lacy, *History*, pp. 33, 65, 162–3.

10 Stark, *Female Tars*, pp. 123–67; Peter Guillery, 'The Further Adventures of Mary Lacy: "Seaman," Shipwright, Builder', *History Workshop Journal* 49 (2000), pp. 212–20.

11 See for example Lacy, *History*, pp. 9, 35.

12 Rudolf Dekker and Lotte van de Pol, *The Tradition of Female Transvestism in Early Modern Europe* (New York: St Martin's, 1989), p. 82.

13 *Ibid.*, pp. 24, 98.

14 *Ibid.*, p. 40.

15 *Ibid.*, p. 73.

16 Nerea Aresti, 'The Gendered Identities of the "Lieutenant Nun"': Rethinking the Story of a Female Warrior in Early Modern Spain', *Gender and History* 19:3 (November 2007), pp. 401–18, quoted p. 402.

17 Alfred Young, *Masquerade: The Life and Times of Deborah Sampson, Continental Soldier* (New York: Alfred A. Knopf, 2004), p. 8. Nadezhda Durova, *The Cavalry Maiden: Journals of a Russian Officer in the Napoleonic Wars*, trans. Mary Fleming Zirin (Bloomington: Indiana University Press, 1988) is also of interest here.

18 Dianne Dugaw, *Warrior Women and Popular Balladry, 1650–1850* (Cambridge: Cambridge University Press, 1989).

19 *Ibid.*, pp. 133, 168. His thesis is anticipated in a remark of Dekker and van de Pol, *Tradition*, p. 88.

20 Easton, 'Gender's Two Bodies', p. 152.

21 *Ibid.*, p. 136.

22 *Ibid.*, p. 132.

23 *Ibid.*, p. 160.

24 *Kirby's Wonderful and Scientific Museum* (London: R.S. Kirby, 1804), vol. 2, p. 176.

25 Anne Jane Thornton, *Interesting Life and Wonderful Adventures of … Anne Jane Thornton* (London: J. Thompson, 1835), pp. 5–6.

26 The content and target audience of Kirby's volumes continued in the tradition of the popular 'wonder books' described in Lorraine Daston and Katharine Park, 'Unnatural Conceptions: The Study of Monsters in Sixteenth- and Seventeenth-Century France and England', *Past and Present* 92 (August 1981), pp. 20–54. See also the discussion of how women who possessed actual facial hair were characterised in scientific discourse: Ula Lukszo Klein, 'Eighteenth-Century Female Cross-Dressers and their Beards', *Journal for Early Modern Cultural Studies* 16:4 (Fall 2016), pp. 119–43 (specifically pp. 125–6).

27 *Kirby's*, vol. 2, pp. 160–225.

28 Aresti, 'Gendered Identities', p. 408. For a similar interpretation, see Mary Elizabeth Perry, *Gender and Disorder in Early Modern Seville* (Princeton, NJ: Princeton University Press, 1990), pp. 131, 133–5.

29 It is significant that studies of cross-dressed women in periods separated by one thousand years or more have so much common ground: Geertje Mak, 'Sandor/Sarolta Vay: From Passing Woman to Sexual Invert', *Journal of Women's History* 16:1 (2004), pp. 54–77, quoted p. 56, and Valerie R. Hotchkiss, *Clothes Make the Man: Female Cross-Dressing in Medieval Europe* (New York: Garland, 1996), p. 128. Also of interest here: Sally O'Driscoll, 'The Pirate's Breasts: Criminal Women and the Meanings of the Body', *The Eighteenth Century* 53:3 (Fall 2012), pp. 357–79, as well as a more recent publication from Geertje Mak, *Doubting Sex: Inscriptions,*

Bodies, and Selves in Nineteenth-Century Hermaphrodite Case Histories (Manchester: Manchester University Press, 2012).

30 Land, *War, Nationalism, and the British Sailor, 1750–1850*, pp. 123–30, particularly 126–7.

31 *Oxford English Dictionary*, s.v. 'militarism', available at: www.oed.com/view/Entry/118424?redirectedFrom=militarism; 'militarist', available at: www.oed.com/view/Entry/118425?redirectedFrom=militarist (accessed 27 July 2018).

Index